P9-DHQ-751

SCOTT FORESMAN • ADDISON WESLEY

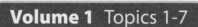
Volume 1 Topics 1-7

Authors

Randall I. Charles
Professor Emeritus
Department of Mathematics
San Jose State University
San Jose, California

Jennifer Bay-Williams
Professor of Mathematics Education
College of Education and Human
Development
University of Louisville
Louisville, Kentucky

Robert Q. Berry, III
Associate Professor of
Mathematics Education
Department of Curriculum,
Instruction and Special Education
University of Virginia
Charlottesville, Virginia

Janet H. Caldwell
Professor of Mathematics
Rowan University
Glassboro, New Jersey

Zachary Champagne
Assistant in Research
Florida Center for Research in Science,
Technology, Engineering, and
Mathematics (FCR-STEM)
Jacksonville, Florida

Juanita Copley
Professor Emerita, College of Education
University of Houston
Houston, Texas

Warren Crown
Professor Emeritus of Mathematics
Education
Graduate School of Education
Rutgers University
New Brunswick, New Jersey

Francis (Skip) Fennell
L. Stanley Bowlsbey Professor
of Education and Graduate and
Professional Studies
McDaniel College
Westminster, Maryland

Karen Karp
Professor of Mathematics Education
Department of Early Childhood and
Elementary Education
University of Louisville
Louisville, Kentucky

Stuart J. Murphy
Visual Learning Specialist
Boston, Massachusetts

Jane F. Schielack
Professor of Mathematics
Associate Dean for Assessment and
Pre K-12 Education, College of Science
Texas A&M University
College Station, Texas

Jennifer M. Suh
Associate Professor for
Mathematics Education
George Mason University
Fairfax, Virginia

Jonathan A. Wray
Mathematics Instructional Facilitator
Howard County Public Schools
Ellicott City, Maryland

PEARSON

Glenview, Illinois   Boston, Massachusetts   Chandler, Arizona   Hoboken, New Jersey

Mathematicians

Roger Howe
Professor of Mathematics
Yale University
New Haven, Connecticut

Gary Lippman
Professor of Mathematics and
Computer Science
California State University, East Bay
Hayward, California

ELL Consultants

Janice R. Corona
Independent Education Consultant
Dallas, Texas

Jim Cummins
Professor
The University of Toronto
Toronto, Canada

Debbie Crisco
Math Coach
Beebe Public Schools
Beebe, Arkansas

Kathleen A. Cuff
Teacher
Kings Park Central School District
Kings Park, New York

Erika Doyle
Math and Science Coordinator
Richland School District
Richland, Washington

Reviewers

Susan Jarvis
Math and Science Curriculum Coordinator
Ocean Springs Schools
Ocean Springs, Mississippi

ISBN-13: 978-0-328-88708-8
ISBN-10: 0-328-88708-0
12 2022

Digital Resources

You'll be using these digital resources throughout the year!

Go to PearsonRealize.com

 MP

Math Practices Animations to play anytime

 Glossary

Animated Glossary in English and Spanish

 Help

Another Look Homework Video for extra help

 ACTIVe-book

Student Edition online for showing your work

 Solve

Solve & Share problems plus math tools

 Tools

Math Tools to help you understand

 Games

Math Games to help you learn

 Learn

Visual Learning Animation Plus with animation, interaction, and math tools

 Assessment

Quick Check for each lesson

eText

Student Edition online

PEARSON realize. Everything you need for math anytime, anywhere

Hi, we're here to help you.
Let's have a great year!
I'm Alex.
I'm Jada.
I'm Daniel.
I'm Jackson.
I'm Marta.
I'm Carlos.
I'm Emily.

Contents

KEY

🔴 Operations and Algebra

🔴 Numbers and Computation

🔴 Measurement and Data

🔴 Geometry

Digital Resources at PearsonRealize.com

TOPICS

And remember your eText is available at PearsonRealize.com!

TOPIC 1
Solve Addition and Subtraction Problems to 10

This shows how you can add the parts to find the sum.

$4 + 2 = \boxed{}$

© Pearson Education, Inc. 1

Contents

TOPIC 2
Fluently Add and Subtract Within 10

You can think addition to subtract.

$$7 - 3 = \boxed{?}$$

$$3 + \boxed{?} = 7$$

TOPIC 3
Addition Facts to 20: Use Strategies

You can use different ways to remember addition facts.

Doubles   Near Doubles

Make 10

© Pearson Education, Inc. 1

TOPIC 4
Subtraction Facts to 20: Use Strategies

You can count back to solve subtraction problems.

$$10 - 3 = 7$$

TOPIC 5
Work with Addition and Subtraction Equations

You can add three numbers in different ways.

© Pearson Education, Inc. 1

Contents

TOPIC 6
Represent and Interpret Data

You can show data in a tally chart.

Black	Red	Blue
T|||	||||	||

TOPIC 7
Extend the Counting Sequence

Counting above 100 is just like counting below 100.

100, 101

Contents

TOPIC 8 in Volume 2
Understand Place Value

TOPIC 9 in Volume 2
Compare Two-Digit Numbers

TOPIC 10 in Volume 2
Use Models and Strategies to Add Tens and Ones

TOPIC 11 in Volume 2
Use Models and Strategies to Subtract Tens

© Pearson Education, Inc. 1

Contents

TOPIC 12 in Volume 2
Measure Lengths

TOPIC 13 in Volume 2
Time

TOPIC 14 in Volume 2
Reason with Shapes and Their Attributes

TOPIC 15 in Volume 2
Equal Shares of Circles and Rectangles

STEP UP to Grade 2 in Volume 2

These lessons help prepare you for Grade 2.

PearsonRealize.com

Problem Solving Handbook

Math practices are ways we think about and do math.

Math practices will help you solve problems.

Math Practices

1. Make sense of problems and persevere in solving them.

2. Reason abstractly and quantitatively.

3. Construct viable arguments and critique the reasoning of others.

4. Model with mathematics.

5. Use appropriate tools strategically.

6. Attend to precision.

7. Look for and make use of structure.

8. Look for and express regularity in repeated reasoning.

There are good Thinking Habits for each of these math practices.

1 Make sense of problems and persevere in solving them.

My plan was to find all the ways 9 counters can be put into 2 groups.

Good math thinkers know what the problem is about. They have a plan to solve it. They keep trying if they get stuck.

What pairs of numbers from 0 to 9 add to 9?

0 + 9 = 9
1 + 8 = 9
2 + 7 = 9

Thinking Habits

What do I need to find?

What do I know?

What's my plan for solving the problem?

What else can I try if I get stuck?

How can I check that my solution makes sense?

2 Reason abstractly and quantitatively.
MP

I thought about what numbers would make 8. I used an equation with those numbers to show the problem.

Good math thinkers know how to think about words and numbers to solve problems.

Alan has 8 blue marbles.
He wants to give them to Tom and Rosi.
How can Alan break apart the
8 blue marbles?

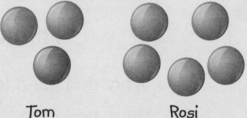

Tom   Rosi

$8 = 3 + 5$

Thinking Habits

What do the numbers stand for?

How are the numbers in the problem related?

How can I show a word problem using pictures or numbers?

How can I use a word problem to show what an equation means?

Problem Solving Handbook

3 Construct viable arguments and critique the reasoning of others.

I used a picture and words to explain my thinking.

Good math thinkers use math to explain why they are right. They talk about math that others do, too.

Joan has 7 pencils. Sam has 9 pencils.
Who has more pencils? Show how you know.

I drew pencils for Joan and for Sam. I matched up the pencils. Sam has more pencils than Joan.

Joan's pencils

Sam's pencils

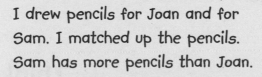

Thinking Habits

How can I use math to explain my work?

Am I using numbers and symbols correctly?

Is my explanation clear?

What questions can I ask to understand other people's thinking?

Are there mistakes in other people's thinking?

Can I improve other people's thinking?

4 Model with mathematics.

MP

I used ten-frames to show the problem.

Good math thinkers use math they know to show and solve problems.

Ali collects rocks. He puts 17 rocks in boxes. Each box holds 10 rocks. He fills 1 box. How many rocks are in the second box?

Thinking Habits

How can I use the math I know to help solve this problem?

Can I use a drawing, diagram, table, graph, or objects to show the problem?

Can I write an equation to show the problem?

Problem Solving Handbook

5 Use appropriate tools strategically.

MP

I chose to use cubes to solve the problem.

Good math thinkers know how to pick the right tools to solve math problems.

Ed finds 5 nuts on a tree. He finds 4 more nuts in the grass. How many nuts does Ed find?

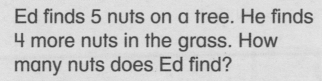

Thinking Habits

Which tools can I use?

Is there a different tool I could use?

Am I using the tool correctly?

6 Attend to precision.

I used math words correctly to write what I noticed.

Good math thinkers are careful about what they write and say, so their ideas about math are clear.

How are these shapes alike?

They have 4 sides.
They have 4 corners.
They have straight sides.

Thinking Habits

Am I using numbers, units, and symbols correctly?

Am I using the correct definitions?

Is my answer clear?

7 Look for and make use of structure.

Good math thinkers look for patterns in math to help solve problems.

I found a pattern.

What are the next two numbers?
Fill in the blanks. Explain and show your thinking.

15, 16, 17, 18, 19, _____, _____

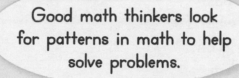

Thinking Habits

Is there a pattern?

How can I describe the pattern?

Can I break the problem into simpler parts?

8 Look for and express regularity in repeated reasoning.

MP

Each new person has 1 more box. I used what I know about counting on to solve this problem.

Good math thinkers look for things that repeat in a problem. They use what they learn from one problem to help them solve other problems.

Jay has 3 boxes.
Nicole has 1 more box than Jay.
Krista has 1 more box than Nicole.
How many boxes does Nicole have?
How many boxes does Krista have? Explain.

1 more than 3 is 4.
Nicole has 4 boxes.
1 more than 4 is 5.
Krista has 5 boxes.

Thinking Habits

Does something repeat in the problem?

How can the solution help me solve another problem?

Problem Solving Guide

These questions can help you solve problems.

Make Sense of the Problem

Reason
- What do I need to find?
- What given information can I use?
- How are the quantities related?

Think About Similar Problems
- Have I solved problems like this before?

Persevere in Solving the Problem

Model with Math
- How can I use the math I know?
- How can I show the problem?
- Is there a pattern I can use?

Use Appropriate Tools
- What math tools could I use?
- How can I use those tools?

Check the Answer

Make Sense of the Answer
- Is my answer reasonable?

Check for Precision
- Did I check my work?
- Is my answer clear?
- Is my explanation clear?

Some Ways to Show Problems

- Draw a Picture
- Draw a Number Line
- Write an Equation

Some Math Tools

- Objects
- Technology
- Paper and Pencil

Problem Solving Recording Sheet

This sheet helps you organize your work.

Name **Ehrin**

Teaching Tool **1**

Problem Solving Recording Sheet

Problem:
Billy has 8 green marbles and 4 blue marbles.
How many marbles does he have in all?

Make 10 to solve.
Show your work.

MAKE SENSE OF THE PROBLEM

Need to Find	**Given**
I need to find how many marbles Billy has in all.	Billy has 8 green marbles and 4 blue marbles.

PERSEVERE IN SOLVING THE PROBLEM

Some Ways to Represent Problems
☑ Draw a Picture
☐ Draw a Number Line
☑ Write an Equation

Some Math Tools
☐ Objects
☐ Technology
☑ Paper and Pencil

Solution and Answer

10   2

$8 + 2 = 10$
$10 + 2 = 12$
Billy has 12 marbles.

CHECK THE ANSWER

I counted the counters I drew.
There are 12.
My answer is correct.

Name _____

Writing Numbers 0 to 4

Practice writing the numbers 0–4.

1. 0 0 0

2. 1 1 1

3. 2 2 2

4. 3 3 3

5. 4 4 4

Writing Numbers 5 to 9

Practice writing the numbers 5–9.

1.

2.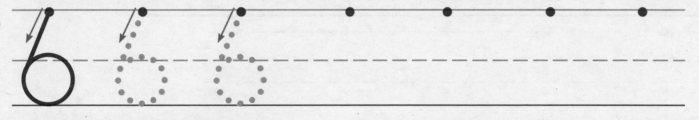

3.

4.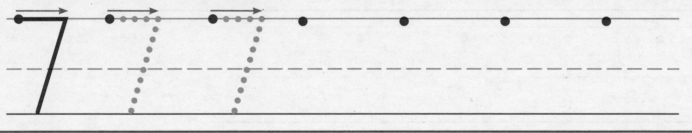

5.

Name ____________________

GRADE 1 Readiness

Counting and Writing to 9

Count and write the number of dots.

1. 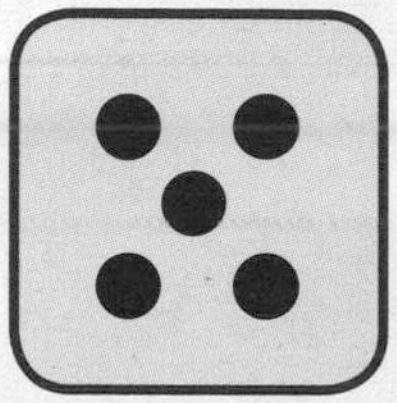 ______

2. 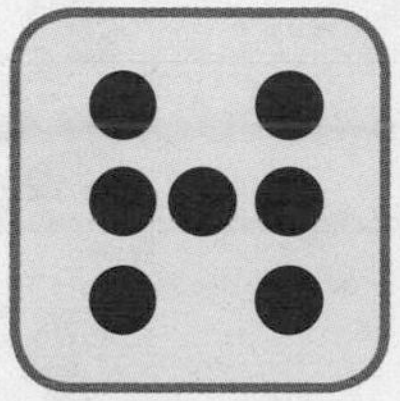 ______

3. 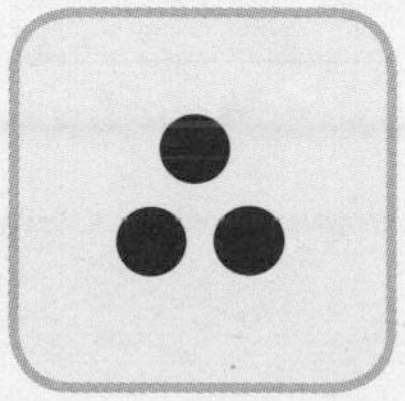 ______

4. 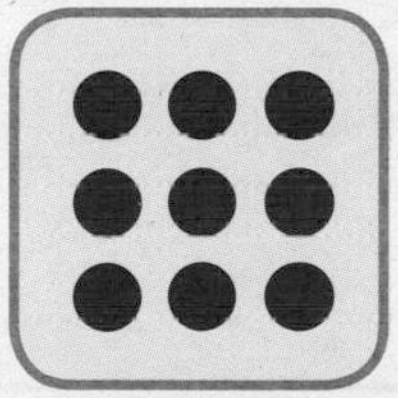 ______

5. 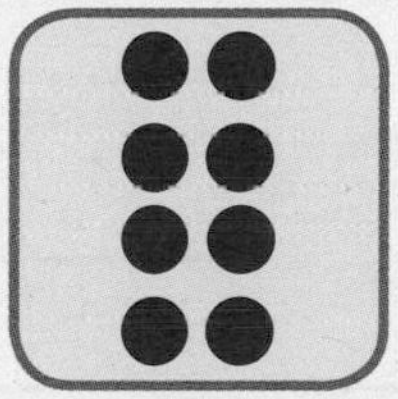 ______

6. 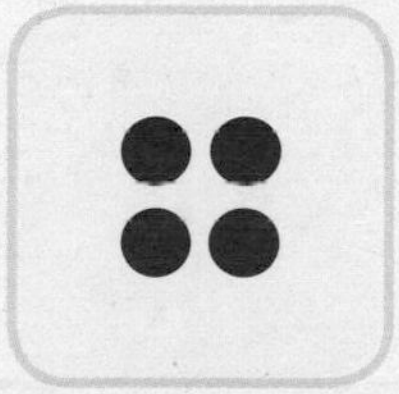 ______

7. 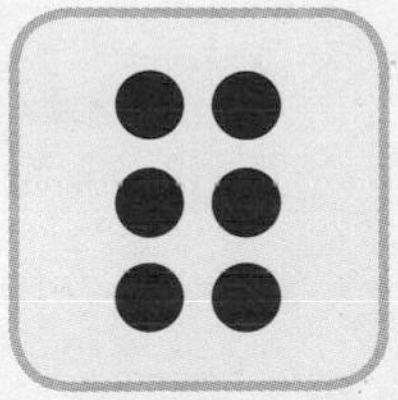 ______

8. 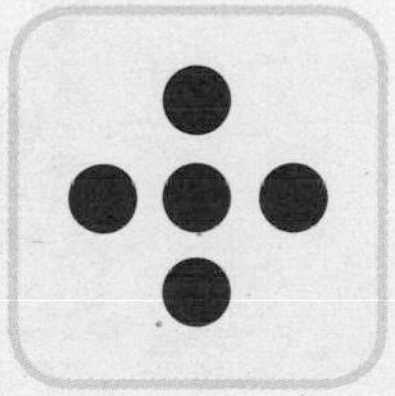 ______

9. 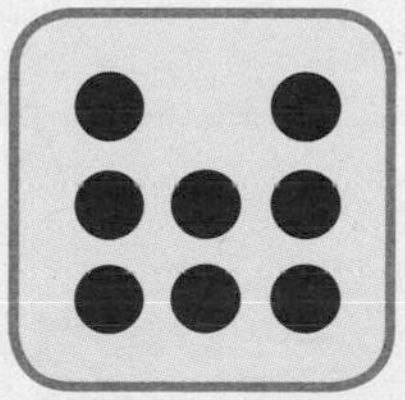 ______

Comparing Numbers Through 5

Write the number that tells how many.
Then circle the number that is less.

1.

2.

3.

4.

Grade 1 | Readiness

Comparing Numbers Through 10

Write the number that tells how many.
Then circle the number that is greater.

1.

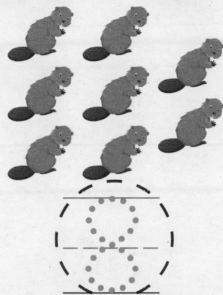

7   (9)

2.

_____   _____

- - - - -   - - - - -

_____   _____

Making Numbers 6 to 9

Write the number inside and outside.
Then write the number in all.

I.

_____ inside   _____ outside   _____ in all

2.

_____ inside   _____ outside   _____ in all

Write the numbers to show the parts.

3.

_____  and _____ 🎈

4.

_____ 🎈 and _____

Grade 1 | Readiness

Finding Missing Parts of Numbers 6 to 9

Find the missing parts. Then write the numbers.

1. 6 bones in all.

 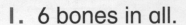

_____   _____
part I know   missing part

2. 6 bones in all.

 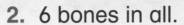 

_____   _____
part I know   missing part

3. 7 bones in all.

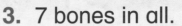 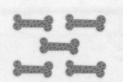 

_____   _____
part I know   missing part

4. ⬛ 8 ⬛

_____   _____
part I know   missing part

5. ⬛ 9 ⬛

_____   _____
part I know   missing part

6. ⬛ 8 ⬛

_____   _____
part I know   missing part

Find the missing part. Then complete the addition equation.

7. Mark has 9 bagels. He cooks 4 of them. How many bagels are **NOT** cooked?

$4 + \underline{\quad} = 9$

8. Hanna has 7 eggs. 5 eggs hatched. How many eggs are **NOT** hatched?

$5 + \underline{\quad} = 7$

Shapes

Color each shape below.

© Pearson Education, Inc. 1

Solve Addition and Subtraction Problems to 10

Essential Question: What are ways to think about addition and subtraction?

Digital Resources

Solve Learn Glossary

Tools Assessment Help Games

> Look at the adult and baby giraffes.

> How are they the same? How are they different?

> Wow! Let's do this project and learn more.

Math and Science Project: Parents and Babies

Find Out Talk to friends and relatives about different animals and their babies. Ask them how the parents and babies are the same and how they are different.

Journal: Make a Book Show what you found. In your book, also:

- Draw some animals, including the parents and babies.

- Create and solve addition and subtraction stories about some animals and their babies.

Name _____

Review What You Know

A-Z Vocabulary

1. Count the fish. Write the number that tells how many.

_____

‾ ‾ ‾ ‾ ‾ ‾

_____

2. Join the two groups and write how many.

_____

‾ ‾ ‾ ‾ ‾ ‾

_____

3. Write how many soccer balls there are **in all**.

_____

‾ ‾ ‾ ‾ ‾ ‾

_____

Counting

4. Tammy has 4 balloons. Draw a picture of her balloons.

5. Write the number that tells how many cats.

_____

   ‾ ‾ ‾ ‾ ‾

_____

Sums

6. Circle the number that shows how many crabs you see.

2   3   4   5

My Word Cards

Study the words on the front of the card. Complete the activity on the back.

A-Z
Glossary

add

$$5 + 3 = 8$$

sum

$$2 + 3 = 5$$

↑

sum

plus

$$5 + 4$$

5 **plus** 4

This means 4 is added to 5.

equation

$$6 + 4 = 10 \quad 6 - 2 = 4$$

$$10 = 6 + 4 \quad 4 = 6 - 2$$

$$6 + 4 = 8 + 2$$

These are **equations.**

equals

$$5 = 4 + 1$$

5 **equals** 4 plus 1.

$$5 + 2 = 7$$

5 plus 2 **equals** 7.

part

2 and 3 are parts of 5.

My Word Cards

Use what you know to complete the sentences.
Extend learning by writing your own sentence using each word.

2 _____

2 equals 4.

The answer to an addition equation is called the

_____.

I use a plus sign to

_____.

A _____

is a piece of a whole.

---

4 plus 4

_____ 8.

I can solve a word problem by writing an

_____.

© Pearson Education, Inc. 1

My Word Cards

Study the words on the front of the card. Complete the activity on the back.

whole

5

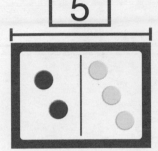

The **whole** is 5.

difference

$4 - 1 = 3$

↑

difference

subtract

$5 - 3 = 2$

minus

$5 \quad - \quad 3$

5 **minus** 3

This means 3 is taken away from 5.

more

The red row has **more**.

fewer

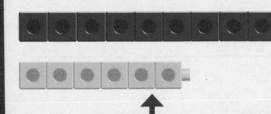

The yellow row has **fewer**.

My Word Cards

Use what you know to complete the sentences.
Extend learning by writing your own sentence using each word.

I use a minus sign to

____________________.

The answer to a subtraction equation is called the

____________________.

When I add all of the parts, I make a

____________________.

The group that has less has

____

objects.

The group with a greater number of objects has

____________________.

5 ________________

3 equals 2.

My Word Cards

Study the words on the front of the card.
Complete the activity on the back.

A-Z
Glossary

addend

$6 + 3 = 9$

addends

In the addition equation $6 + 3 = 9$, the 6 and the 3 are

_____.

© Pearson Education, Inc. 1

Name _____

Solve & Share

Jada has 2 . She adds on 1 more .
How many does she have now?

How can you show this story with cubes and
an addition equation?

Lesson 1-1
Solve Problems: Add To

I can ...
solve word problems about
adding to.

I can also model
with math.

_____ + _____ = _____

Paul has 5 . He snaps on 2 more . How many  does he have now?

I can add to a number to find the sum.

You can show the problem on a part-part mat.

Add to find how many in all.

You can write an addition **equation** to match the problem.

$$5 + 2 = 7$$

5 plus 2 equals 7. Paul now has 7 .

Do You Understand?

Show Me! You have 4 . You snap on 3 more . How can you find how many  you have now?

☆ **Guided Practice** ☆ Write an addition equation to match each problem. Use the pictures to help you.

1. Warren has 3 . He snaps on 3 more . How many  does he have now?

$$3 + 3 = 6$$

2. Anna has 2 . She buys 6 more . How many  does Anna have now?

$$\underline{} + \underline{} = \underline{}$$

Tools   Assessment

Write an addition equation to match each problem.
Use the pictures to help you.

3. 4  are in the garden.
4 more 🐝 join them.
How many 🐝 are there now?

_____ + _____ = _____

4. 3 🐞 are on a leaf.
6 more 🐞 join them.
How many 🐞 are there now?

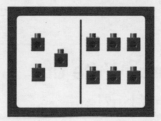

_____ + _____ = _____

Draw a picture to solve the story problem.
Then write an addition equation.

5. **Higher Order Thinking** 6 🦆 are in the pond. 2 more 🦆 join them. 4 🐞 are in the grass. How many 🦆 are in the pond now?

_____ + _____ = _____

6. **A-Z Vocabulary** There are 3 .
4 more join them.
How many are there now?

Write an addition **equation**.

____ + ____ = ____

7. **Model** 8 are playing.
I more joins them.
How many are playing now?

Write an addition equation.

____ + ____ = ____

8. **Higher Order Thinking** Write an addition story about the birds.

Use pictures, numbers, or words.

9. ✓**Assessment** Lisa has 5.
She finds 3 more.
How many does Lisa have now?

Which addition equation matches the story?

Ⓐ 5 + 1 = 6

Ⓑ 5 + 2 = 7

Ⓒ 5 + 3 = 8

Ⓓ 5 + 4 = 9

Name _____

Another Look! You can use addition to solve some word problems.

5  play in the grass.

3 more 🐰 join them.

How many 🐰 are there now?

■■■■■ ■■■ $5 + 3 = 8$

7 🐞 are on a leaf.

2 more 🐞 join them.

How many 🐞 are there now?

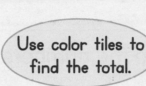
Use color tiles to find the total.

HOME ACTIVITY Gather 9 pennies. Tell your child this story: "6 pennies are in a jar. I put 3 more pennies in the jar. How many pennies are there now?" Have your child write and solve an equation to match the number story.

■■■■■■■ ■■ $7 + 2 = 9$

Write an addition equation to match each problem.
Use the pictures to help you.

1. 3 🐸 are in the pond.

   3 more 🐸 join them.

   How many 🐸 are there now?

   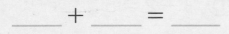   ___ + ___ = ___

2. 2 🐞 are on a rock.

   3 more 🐞 join them.

   How many 🐞 are there now?

      ___ + ___ = ___

Write an addition equation to solve each problem.

3. **Model** 2 🐭 are sleeping.
4 more 🐭 join them.
How many 🐭 are there now?

_____ + _____ = _____

4. **Model** 5 ⚽ are on the field. 5 more ⚽ roll on the field. How many ⚽ are on the field now?

_____ + _____ = _____

5. **Algebra** Read the story. Write the numbers missing from the equation.

3 🐰 are sleeping. 2 more 🐰 join them.
How many 🐰 are there now?

_____ + 2 = _____

6. **Higher Order Thinking** Tell an addition story about the frogs. Then write an equation to show how many in all.

_____ + _____ = _____

7. ✓**Assessment** Which equation describes the picture?

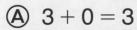

Ⓐ 3 + 0 = 3

Ⓑ 2 + 2 = 4

Ⓒ 3 + 1 = 4

Ⓓ 3 + 2 = 5

Solve & Share

Your 2 bags each have connecting cubes of a different color. Pick out a handful of cubes from each bag.

How can you use numbers to show how many cubes you picked in all? Show your work.

I can ...
solve word problems about putting together.

I can also make sense of problems.

Kenny picks 4  and 2 .

The **parts** are 4 and 2.

4   2

Add the parts to find the **whole**.

4 + 2 = ___

I put the parts together when I add.

Write an addition equation to show the parts and the whole.

4 + 2 = 6

Kenny picks 6 cubes in all.

Do You Understand?

Show Me! You have 2  and 3 . How can you find how many cubes you have in all?

☆ Guided ☆ Practice

Write the parts. Then write an addition equation to match each problem.

1. Cheryl has 3 ▉ and 5 ▉. How many cubes does she have in all?

3 + 5

3 + 5 = 8

2. Jenny sees 1 🐞 and 6 🐝. How many bugs does Jenny see in all?

___ + ___

___ = ___ + ___

Independent Practice

Write the parts. Then write an addition equation to match each problem.

3. The pet store has 3  and 4 🐱. How many pets does the store have in all?

____ + ____

____ + ____ = ____

4. The box holds 3 ⚾ and 3 ⚽. How many balls are in the box?

____ + ____

____ + ____ = ____

5. **Higher Order Thinking** Marco finds 2 brown 🥚, 7 red 🥚, and 3 🐚. How many 🥚 did Marco find in all?

Draw a picture to solve.
Then write an addition equation.

____ + ____ = ____

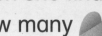

6. **Make Sense** Jen finds 2 .
Then she finds 5 more .
How many did Jen find?

Draw a picture to show that you know what the story means. Then write an addition equation.

_____ + _____ = _____

7. **Higher Order Thinking** Draw a picture to show an addition story about red worms and brown worms. Write an equation to tell how many worms there are in all.

_____ = _____ + _____

8. 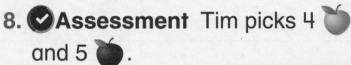**Assessment** Tim picks 4 and 5 .
How many apples did he pick?

Which addition equation matches this story?

Ⓐ 9 + 4 = 13

Ⓑ 4 + 5 = 9

Ⓒ 3 + 6 = 9

Ⓓ 4 + 4 = 8

© Pearson Education, Inc. 1

Help   Tools   Games

Another Look! Use the parts to write an addition equation.

I have 2 red counters and 3 yellow counters. These are the parts. I have 5 counters in all.

Greg has 3 ● and 5 ○. How many counters does he have in all?

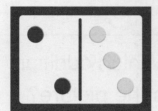

2 + 3
2 + 3 = 5

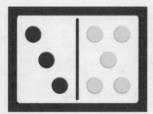

3 + 5
3 + 5 = 8

HOME ACTIVITY Give your child 2 groups of small objects to count (e.g., one group of 3 buttons and one group of 4 buttons of a different color). Together, find the total number of objects and say the corresponding addition equation (e.g., "3 plus 4 equals 7."). Repeat the activity several times with different groupings.

Write the parts. Then write an addition equation to match each problem.

1. Stephanie has 4 ● and 2 ○. How many counters does she have in all?

___ + ___
___ + ___ = ___

2. Glen has 4 ● and 4 ○. How many counters does he have in all?

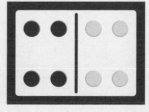

___ + ___
___ + ___ = ___

Write an addition equation for each story.

3. **Model** Ian picks 3 🍎.
   Then he picks 5 more 🍎.
   How many 🍎 did Ian pick in all?

   ____ + ____ = ____

4. **Model** Sara has 2 ⬭.
   Jake has 4 ⬭.
   How many ⬭ do they have in all?

   ____ + ____ = ____

5. **Higher Order Thinking** Circle 2 groups of fruit. Write an addition equation to tell how many pieces of fruit there are in your 2 groups.

   ____ + ____ = ____

6. ✓**Assessment** Which addition equation matches the picture?

   Ⓐ $4 + 4 = 8$

   Ⓑ $4 + 5 = 9$

   Ⓒ $2 + 7 = 9$

   Ⓓ $4 + 6 = 10$

Name _____

Solve & Share

Show how you could place the 5 pencils in these two cups. Complete the equation to show your work. Then talk to a classmate. Are your equations the same?

I can ...
solve word problems by breaking apart the total number of objects.

I can also make math arguments.

$$5 = \underline{\hspace{1cm}} + \underline{\hspace{1cm}}$$

There are 7 penguins. How many can go inside and outside the cave?

Here is one way to show the 7 penguins.

There are still 7 penguins. 4 is one part. 3 is the other part.

You can write an equation to show the whole and the parts.

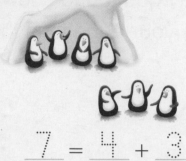

$7 = 4 + 3$

Here is another way to show the 7 penguins.

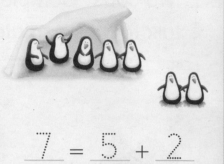

$7 = 5 + 2$

Do You Understand?

Show Me! What are two different ways that 4 penguins could be inside or outside the cave?

☆ **Guided Practice** ☆   Draw a picture to show the parts. Then write an equation.

1. There are 5 🐧 in all. How many are inside and outside the cave?

$5 = 3 + 2$

2. There are 8 🐧 in all. How many are inside and outside the cave?

$\_\_\_ = \_\_\_ + \_\_\_$

     Topic 1 | Lesson 3

Independent Practice   Draw pictures to show how many are inside and outside each cave. Then write an equation.

3. There are 9 🕷 in all.

____ = ____ + ____

4. There are 8 🕷 in all.

____ = ____ + ____

5. There are 5 🕷 in all.

____ = ____ + ____

6. There are 7 🕷 in all.

____ = ____ + ____

7. **Math and Science** There are 8 monkeys. Some are parents and some are babies. How many of each could there be? Show two different ways.

_____ parents and _____ babies

OR

_____ parents and _____ babies

8. **Reasoning** Krista takes 2 photos. Then she takes 5 more. How many photos does Krista take in all? Write an addition equation to show your work.

_____ + _____ = _____

_____ photos

9. **Higher Order Thinking** Andy's team scored a total of 10 goals in two games. They scored 1 or 2 goals in the first game. How many goals could they have scored in the second game? Explain how you know.

10. ✅**Assessment** Jess sees 9 birds. Some are flying and some are sitting in a tree.

Match the number of birds flying with the number of birds Jess could have seen in the tree.

7 flying	3 in the tree
8 flying	1 in the tree
5 flying	2 in the tree
6 flying	4 in the tree

Name _____

Another Look! You can show the same number in different ways.

Ashley has 4 flowers. Some are red and some are white. How many of each color flower does Ashley have?

There are always 4 flowers!

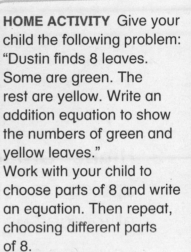

3 red and 1 white
$4 = 3 + 1$

2 red and 2 white
$4 = 2 + 2$

1 red and 3 white
$4 = 1 + 3$

HOME ACTIVITY Give your child the following problem: "Dustin finds 8 leaves. Some are green. The rest are yellow. Write an addition equation to show the numbers of green and yellow leaves."
Work with your child to choose parts of 8 and write an equation. Then repeat, choosing different parts of 8.

Draw a picture to show some frogs by the water and some in the grass. Then write an equation for each problem.

1. 9

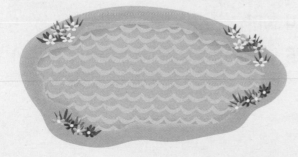

$9 = \underline{\quad} + \underline{\quad}$

Draw a picture to show some frogs by the water and some in the grass. Then write an equation for the problem.

2. **Model** 8

How does your equation show the parts?

$8 = \underline{\hspace{1cm}} + \underline{\hspace{1cm}}$

3. **Higher Order Thinking** Laura picks 7 apples. Some apples are red and some are green. Fewer than 4 of the apples are red. How many of Laura's apples could be green? Explain how you know.

4. ✓**Assessment** Mark sees 6 puppies. Some have spots and some do not.

Match the number of puppies with spots with the number of puppies without spots that Mark could have seen.

I with spots	4 without spots
2 with spots	2 without spots
4 with spots	5 without spots
5 with spots	I without spots

© Pearson Education, Inc. I

Name _____

Solve & Share

6 ducks swim in a pond. 2 ducks fly away.
How can you use connecting cubes to show how
many ducks are left? What subtraction equation
can you write?

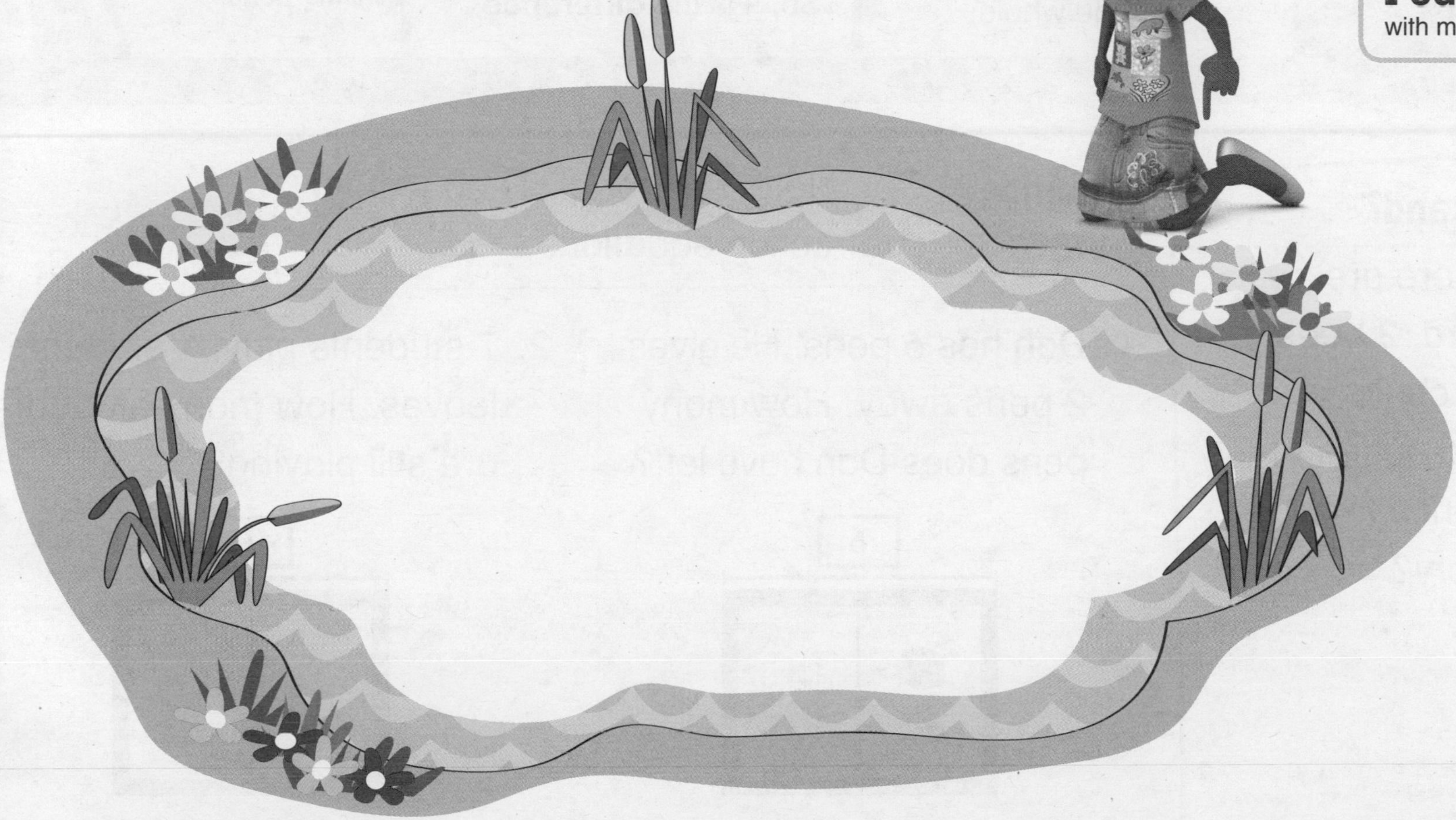

I can ...
solve word problems that
involve taking from a group.

I can also model
with math.

_____ − _____ = _____

7 ducks are in a pond. 3 ducks fly away. How many are still in the pond?

You can use cubes to model the problem.

7 is the whole.

3 is the part that you take from 7.

7

So, 4 is the **difference**.

You can **subtract** to solve the problem.

7 − 3 = 4

7 minus 3 equals 4. There are 4 ducks still in the pond.

Do You Understand?

Show Me! There are 6 bees in a yard. 2 bees fly away. How could you use connecting cubes to find the difference in this subtraction story?

☆ **Guided Practice** ☆ Complete the model. Then write a subtraction equation.

1. Dan has 6 pens. He gives 2 pens away. How many pens does Dan have left?

6

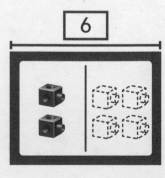

6 − 2 = 4

2. 7 students play. 1 student leaves. How many students are still playing?

7

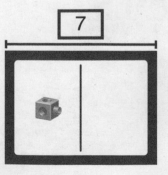

___ − ___ = ___

© Pearson Education, Inc. 1

Topic 1 | Lesson 4

Name _____

Independent Practice   Complete each model. Then write a subtraction equation.

3. 8 frogs sit on a log. 4 frogs jump away. How many frogs are still on the log?

8

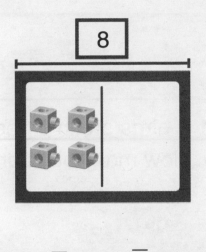

___ – ___ = ___

4. 9 cats play. 6 cats run away. How many cats are still playing?

9

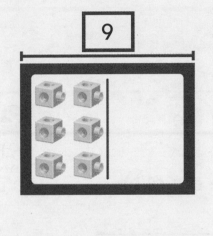

___ – ___ = ___

5. 7 bugs on a leaf. 2 bugs crawl away. How many bugs are still on the leaf?

7

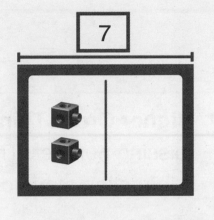

___ – ___ = ___

6. Higher Order Thinking 8 students are in a reading group. Some of the students leave. How many students are still in the group? Do you have enough information to solve this problem? Explain.

_____

_____

_____

_____

7. **Use Tools** Lin has 9 stamps. She gives 4 stamps to Tom. How many stamps does Lin have now?

_____ − _____ = _____

8. **Use Tools** Gloria has 8 flowers. She gives 5 flowers to her mother. How many flowers does Gloria have now?

_____ − _____ = _____

9. **Higher Order Thinking** Find the missing number. Then write a subtraction story to match the equation.

$7 - 2 =$ _____

_____

_____

_____

10. ✓**Assessment** 8 birds are in a tree. 6 birds fly away. How many birds are still in the tree?

Which subtraction equation matches the story?

Ⓐ $8 - 2 = 6$ Ⓑ $8 - 7 = 1$

Ⓒ $7 - 2 = 5$ Ⓓ $8 - 6 = 2$

Name _____

Another Look! You can write a subtraction equation to match a number story.

6 cats are on a fence.
3 cats jump off. How many cats are still on the fence?

$$6 - 3 = 3$$

5 cats are on a fence.
2 cats jump off. How many cats are still on the fence?

$$5 - 2 = 3$$

HOME ACTIVITY Place 8 small objects, such as buttons, on the table. Take away several of the buttons. Ask your child to tell a subtraction story. Then have your child write a subtraction equation to match the story, such as $8 - 2 = 6$. Have your child count the buttons that are left to check if his or her answer is correct.

Write a subtraction equation to match each problem.

1. 9 apples are on a table.
7 apples roll off. How many apples are still on the table?

___ − ___ = ___

2. 10 crayons are in a box.
7 crayons fall out.
How many crayons are still in the box?

___ − ___ = ___

3. Reasoning 6 bees are on a flower. 4 bees fly away. How many bees are still on the flower?

____ − ____ = ____

4. Reasoning 8 ducks are in the pond. 4 ducks get out. How many ducks are still in the pond?

____ − ____ = ____

5. Higher Order Thinking Find the missing number. Then write a subtraction story to match the equation.

$$7 - 3 = \underline{\quad}$$

_____

_____

_____

_____

6. ✓Assessment Jonah has 10 pebbles. He gives 2 pebbles to his sister.

How many pebbles does Jonah have now?

Which subtraction equation matches the story?

Ⓐ $9 - 4 = 5$

Ⓑ $10 - 3 = 7$

Ⓒ $8 - 1 = 7$

Ⓓ $10 - 2 = 8$

Name _____

Solve & Share

Lori sees 5 red cars and 3 blue cars. Did she see more red cars or blue cars? How many more? How can you tell?

I can ...
solve word problems that involve comparing.

I can also use math tools correctly.

5 cats have blue hats.
2 cats have orange hats.
How many more blue hats are
there than orange hats?

You can use cubes to
compare.

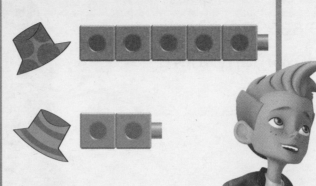

You can write a subtraction
equation to compare.

$$5 - 2 = 3$$

There are
3 more blue hats
than orange hats.

Do You Understand?

Show Me! If you have
2 groups of objects, how
can you tell which group
has more?

Guided Practice Use cubes to write a subtraction equation.
Then write how many more.

I. Peggy draws 6 frogs. Mike draws 3 frogs. How many more
frogs does Peggy draw than Mike?

$$\underline{6} - \underline{3} = \underline{3}$$ _____ more frogs

 **Independent Practice**   Draw cubes to show the subtraction. Then write an equation to match the story. Tell how many.

2. Sue has 3 dogs. Julio has 1 dog. How many more dogs does Sue have?

_____ − _____ = _____

_____ more dogs

3. Tony counts 7 mice. He counts 5 more mice than Marie. How many mice does Marie count?

_____ − _____ = _____

_____ mice

Higher Order Thinking How many more blue birds than yellow birds? Use the picture to find the missing number for each problem.

4.

_____ − 3 = 1

5.

6 − _____ = 1

6. **Number Sense** 4 fish are in a tank. 2 fish are sold. How many fish are still in the tank? Write an equation to match the story. Then tell how many.

_____ − _____ = _____

_____ fish

7. **Model** Luis sees 5 green frogs. He sees 1 blue frog. How many more green frogs does Luis see than blue frogs? Write an equation to match the story. Tell how many more.

_____ − _____ = _____

_____ more green frogs

8. **Higher Order Thinking** Draw some yellow flowers. Draw more red flowers than yellow flowers. Write a subtraction equation that tells how many more red flowers than yellow flowers there are.

_____ − _____ = _____

9. ✅**Assessment** Bill counts 6 gray cats and 4 white cats.

How many more gray cats than white cats did Bill count?

Ⓐ 2

Ⓑ 4

Ⓒ 6

Ⓓ 10

You can draw a picture to help.

Name _____

Help Tools Games

Another Look! Match the red cubes with the blue cubes. Then count how many more.

1 2 3

How many red cubes? __8__

How many blue cubes? __5__

How many more red cubes? __3__

__8__ – __5__ = __3__

HOME ACTIVITY Give your child 5 blue buttons and 2 green buttons. Ask: Are there more blue or green buttons? Have your child tell how many more blue buttons than green buttons he or she has. Repeat with up to 10 blue buttons and 10 green buttons.

Write how many red cubes and blue cubes. Then tell how many more. Write a subtraction equation to match.

1.

____ red cubes

____ blue cubes

Which color has more cubes? _____

How many more? ____

____ – ____ = ____

2.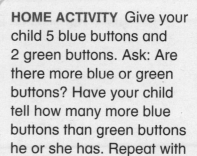

____ blue cubes

____ red cube

Which color has more cubes? _____

How many more? ____

____ – ____ = ____

Solve each problem below.

3. **Number Sense** Sam plays with 5 dogs. 3 dogs go home. How many dogs are still playing with Sam?

Write an equation to match the story. Then tell how many.

_____ – _____ = _____

_____ dogs

4. **Model** David has 6 tickets. Mimi has 2 tickets. How many more tickets does David have than Mimi? Draw cubes to show the subtraction. Then write an equation to match the story. Tell how many more.

_____ – _____ = _____

_____ more tickets

5. **Higher Order Thinking** Draw some red cubes. Draw more blue cubes than red cubes. Write a subtraction equation that shows how many more blue cubes than red cubes you drew.

_____ – _____ = _____

6. ✓**Assessment** Lucy has 6 apples. Julie has 7 apples. How many more apples does Julie have than Lucy?

0   I   6   7
Ⓐ   Ⓑ   Ⓒ   Ⓓ

© Pearson Education, Inc. 1

Name _____

Solve & Share

Amy had 7 stickers. Sheldon had 5 stickers. How many fewer stickers did Sheldon have than Amy?

I can ...
solve word problems by comparing.

I can also model with math.

Troy has 5 toy cars. Brady has 9 toy cars. Who has fewer toy cars? How many fewer?

Troy has fewer toy cars than Brady because 5 is less than 9.

Use cubes to find how many fewer. Start at 9 and count back.

$9 - 5 = 4$

You can also subtract to find how many fewer. Troy has 4 fewer cars.

Do You Understand?

Show Me! If you have 2 groups of objects, how can you tell which group has fewer?

☆ **Guided Practice** ☆ Use the cubes to show the subtraction. Then write an equation. Tell how many fewer.

1. Steven has 8 coins. Sarah has 2 coins. How many fewer coins does Sarah have than Steven?

___ − ___ = ___

____ fewer coins

2. Ann finds 4 bandanas in a box. Stacy finds 7 bandanas. How many fewer bandanas did Ann find than Stacy?

___ − ___ = ___

____ fewer bandanas

Tools Assessment

Independent Practice Use the pictures to show the subtraction. Then write an equation. Tell how many fewer.

3. Cheryl buys 10 apples at the store.

Kristina buys 5 apples at the store.

How many fewer apples did Kristina

buy than Cheryl?

_____ – _____ = _____

_____ fewer apples

4. Beth writes on 3 cards.

Joseph writes on 9 cards.

How many fewer cards did Beth

write on than Joseph?

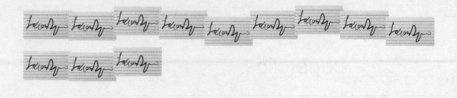

_____ – _____ = _____

_____ fewer cards

5. **Higher Order Thinking** Draw a picture to show the subtraction.

Then write an equation. Tell how many fewer.

Keith makes 4 sandwiches.

Vince makes 8 sandwiches.

How many fewer sandwiches did Keith

make than Vince?

_____ – _____ = _____

_____ fewer sandwiches

6. Reasoning Leah uses 3 paperclips.
Scott uses 6 paperclips.
How many paperclips did Scott and
Leah use in all? Write an equation.
Then tell how many.

_____ + _____ = _____

_____ paperclips

7. Reasoning There are 7 oranges on
a branch. 3 oranges fall off.
How many oranges are still on the branch?
Write a subtraction equation. Then tell
how many.

_____ − _____ = _____

_____ oranges

8. Higher Order Thinking Draw some
blue balloons. Draw fewer yellow
balloons. Write an equation to match
your drawing.

_____ − _____ = _____

9. ✓Assessment An orchard has 8 apple
trees and 6 pear trees. Which of the
following correctly answers how many
more or fewer? Choose all that apply.

☐ 2 more pear trees

☐ 2 more apple trees

☐ 2 fewer pear trees

☐ 2 fewer apple trees

Name _____

Another Look! How many fewer orange cubes are there than purple cubes? Match the purple cubes with the orange cubes. Then count how many fewer. Write a subtraction equation to match.

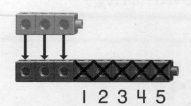

1 2 3 4 5

How many purple cubes? __8__

How many orange cubes? __3__

How many fewer orange cubes? __5__

__8__ − __3__ = __5__

HOME ACTIVITY Give your child 3 buttons and 5 paperclips. Ask: Are there fewer buttons or paperclips? Have your child tell how many fewer buttons than paperclips he or she has. Your child may line them up to compare. Repeat with up to 10 buttons and 10 paperclips.

Write how many orange cubes and purple cubes. Then tell how many fewer. Write a subtraction equation to match.

1.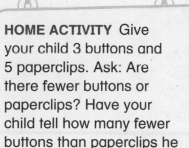

____ purple cubes

____ orange cubes

Which color has fewer cubes? _____

How many fewer? _____

____ − ____ = ____

2.

____ purple cubes

____ orange cubes

Which color has fewer cubes? _____

How many fewer? _____

____ − ____ = ____

Solve the problems below.

3. **Reasoning** Hannah sells 5 muffins for a fundraiser. Then she sells 2 more. How many muffins does Hannah sell in all? Write an equation. Then tell how many.

_____ + _____ = _____

_____ muffins

4. **Reasoning** 6 butterflies are in a tree. 3 butterflies fly away. How many butterflies are left in the tree? Write an equation. Then tell how many.

_____ − _____ = _____

_____ butterflies

5. **Higher Order Thinking** Draw some red cubes. Draw fewer green cubes. Write an equation to match your drawing.

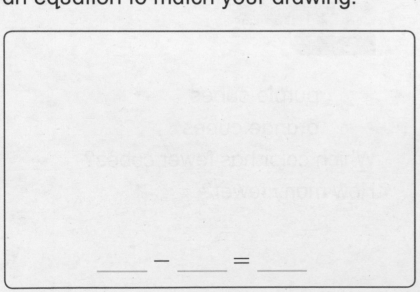

_____ − _____ = _____

6. ✔**Assessment** An animal shelter has 10 cats and 6 dogs. Which of the following correctly answers how many more or fewer? Choose all that apply.

☐ 4 more cats

☐ 4 more dogs

☐ 4 fewer cats

☐ 4 fewer dogs

Name _____

Solve & Share

5 train cars are on the track. Some more train cars join them. Now there are 9 train cars. How many train cars joined the first 5 train cars on the track? Use connecting cubes to model this story. Write an addition equation.

I can ...
use addition or subtraction to help find a missing addend.

I can also model with math.

_____ + _____ = _____

_____ train cars joined.

A station has 7 train cars. Some more train cars roll into the station. Now there are 9 train cars. How many rolled in?

7 plus what is 9?

Use cubes and a model to help find the missing **addend**.

9

You can write an addition equation to match the story.

$$7 + 2 = 9$$

addends   sum

2 more train cars rolled in.

Do You Understand?

Show Me! How do you solve an addition problem if you know only one part and the sum?

☆ **Guided Practice** ☆   Complete the model and the equation. Then tell how many.

1. Bobby has 4 fish. He buys some more fish. Now Bobby has 7 fish. How many fish did Bobby buy?

7

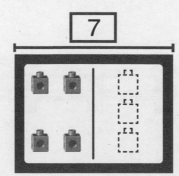

$$4 + \underline{3} = 7$$

_____ fish

Topic I | Lesson 7

Name _____

Tools Assessment

Independent Practice Complete the model. Then write an equation to match. Tell how many.

2. Mary has 4 stickers. Pat gives her some more stickers. Now Mary has 8 stickers. How many stickers did Pat give to Mary?

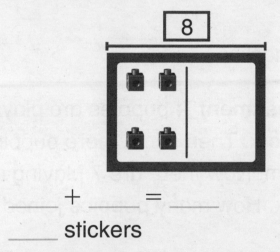

_____ + _____ = _____

_____ stickers

3. Billy reads 4 pages on Monday. He reads some more pages on Tuesday. He reads 10 pages in all. How many pages did Billy read on Tuesday?

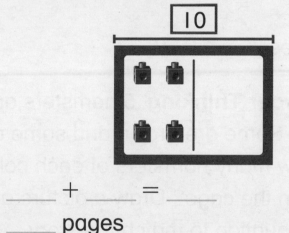

_____ + _____ = _____

_____ pages

4. Higher Order Thinking Megan has 6 shoes in all. Some shoes are on the mat. 2 shoes are in the box. How many shoes are on the mat?

Draw a picture to solve. Then write an equation to match. Tell how many.

_____ + _____ = _____

_____ shoes on the mat

5. **Model** Gabe's dog buries 4 bones on Monday. It buries some more bones on Friday. It buries 10 bones in all. How many bones did Gabe's dog bury on Friday? Write an equation to match the story. Then tell how many.

_____ + _____ = _____

_____ bones

6. **Model** Natalia has 3 pretzels and 7 crackers. How many snacks does she have in all? Write an equation to match the story. Then tell how many.

_____ + _____ = _____

_____ snacks

7. **Higher Order Thinking** 5 hamsters are in a cage. Some are brown and some are black. How many hamsters of each color could be in the cage? Draw a picture and write an equation to match the story.

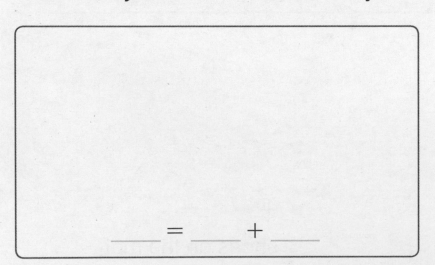

_____ = _____ + _____

8. ✅**Assessment** 4 puppies are playing at the park. Then some more puppies join them. Now there are 7 playing at the park. How many puppies joined the first 4?

Which equation matches the story?

☐ 9 = 4 + 5

☐ 7 = 6 + 1

☐ 7 = 4 + 3

☐ 10 = 7 + 3

Name _____

Help   Tools   Games

Another Look! You can use a model to solve an addition story and to write an equation.

Jim has 4 golf balls. He finds some more golf balls in his bag. Now Jim has 7. How many golf balls did Jim find in his bag?

$$\underline{4} + \underline{3} = \underline{7}$$

____ golf balls

HOME ACTIVITY Give your child a collection of small objects to use as counters. Tell your child this story: 4 ants are on the ground. Some more ants join them. Now there are 8 ants on the ground. How many ants joined the first 4? Have your child use the small objects to solve the addition story. Then have him or her write an equation to match.

Complete the model. Then write an equation to match. Tell how many.

1. 2 cats are playing. Some more cats come to play. Now there are 7 cats playing. How many cats came to play with the first 2 cats?

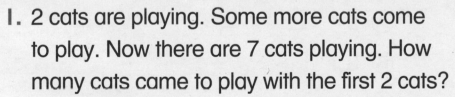

___ + ___ = ___

____ cats

2. 8 friends are eating lunch. Some more friends join them. Now there are 10 friends eating. How many more friends came to lunch?

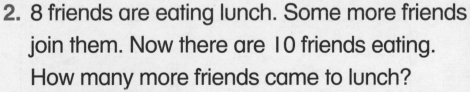

___ + ___ = ___

____ friends

Solve each problem.

3. **Model** Linda has 4 lemons. She buys 4 more lemons. How many lemons does Linda have now? Write an equation to match the story. Then tell how many.

_____ + _____ = _____

_____ lemons

4. **Model** Tia puts 5 berries in a basket. Brad adds some more berries to the basket. Now there are 9 berries in the basket. How many berries did Brad add? Write an equation to match the story. Then tell how many.

_____ + _____ = _____

_____ berries

5. **Higher Order Thinking** Complete the equation. Then write an addition story to match the equation.

$8 + \_\_\_\_ = 10$

6. ✅**Assessment** Rashida has 7 coins. Gary gives her some more. Now Rashida has 10 coins. How many coins did Gary give Rashida?

Ⓐ 2

Ⓑ 3

Ⓒ 4

Ⓓ 5

Solve & Share

Sophie sees 5 small pebbles by the lake. She also sees some big pebbles. She sees a total of 7 pebbles. How many big pebbles did Sophie see? Show how you know.

I can ...
solve word problems that involve putting together or taking apart.

I can also use math tools correctly.

8 cats and dogs are on the dance floor. 5 dogs are dancing. How many cats are dancing?

Think about the whole and the part you know from the story.

8

?

There are 5 dogs dancing.

Subtract to find the missing part.

8

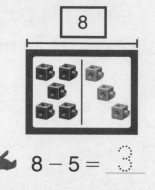

$8 - 5 = 3$

You can also add to find the missing part.

$5 + 3 = 8$

6 7 8

3 cats are dancing.

Do You Understand?

Show Me! If you know the whole and one of the parts, how can you find the missing part?

☆ **Guided Practice** ☆ Complete the model. Then write an addition or subtraction equation.

1. Nick and Roger have 9 robots in all. Nick has 3 robots. How many robots does Roger have?

9

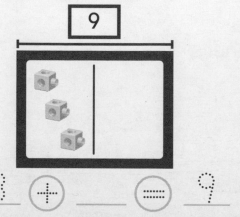

3 ⊕ ___ ⊜ 9

2. Gail has 6 kites. Some are red and some are blue. If 2 kites are red, how many kites are blue?

6

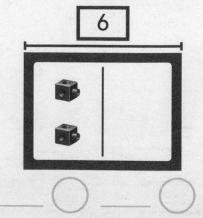

___ ◯ ___ ◯ ___

Tools Assessment

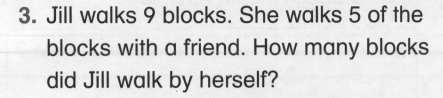

Independent Practice Complete the model. Then write an equation. Tell how many.

3. Jill walks 9 blocks. She walks 5 of the blocks with a friend. How many blocks did Jill walk by herself?

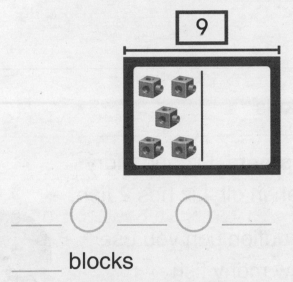

9

____ ◯ ____ ◯ ____

____ blocks

4. Rita has 3 yellow balloons. The rest of her balloons are pink. She has 7 balloons in all. How many pink balloons does Rita have?

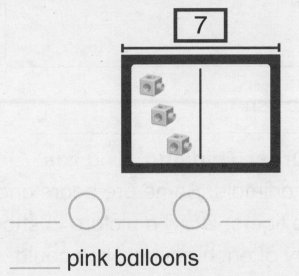

7

____ ◯ ____ ◯ ____

____ pink balloons

5. Higher Order Thinking Henry has 8 shells in all. 3 shells are big. The rest are small. How many small shells does Henry have?

Draw a picture to solve. Then write an equation. Tell how many.

____ ◯ ____ ◯ ____

____ small shells

6. **Make Sense** Joe buys 2 red fish and some blue fish. He buys 9 fish in all. How many blue fish did Joe buy?

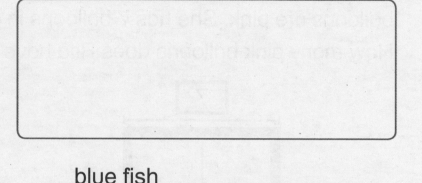

_____ blue fish

7. **Make Sense** Rachel has 8 nickels. She gives 4 nickels away. How many nickels does Rachel have left?

_____ nickels

8. **Higher Order Thinking** Nina has 8 stuffed animals. Some are bears and some are tigers. Draw a picture to show how many of each animal Nina could have. Then write the numbers.

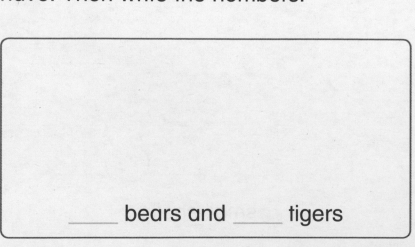

_____ bears and _____ tigers

9. ✔**Assessment** Liz and Mary have 7 fish in all. Liz has 2 fish.

Which equation can you use to find how many fish Mary has?

Ⓐ 9 − 2 = 7

Ⓑ 6 − 1 = 5

Ⓒ 7 − 2 = 5

Ⓓ 8 − 7 = 1

The equation should match the number story.

Name _____

Another Look! The dog has 8 spots on its back.
6 spots are brown. The rest are black. How many
spots are black?

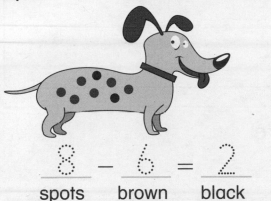

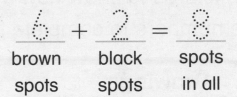
There are 8 spots
in all. Subtract or count on
from 6 to find the number
of black spots.

$$\underline{8} - \underline{6} = \underline{2}$$

spots   brown   black
in all   spots   spots

$$\underline{6} + \underline{2} = \underline{8}$$

brown   black   spots
spots   spots   in all

HOME ACTIVITY Place
6 to 9 small objects in a
paper cup. Have your child
pour some of the objects
onto the table. Ask, "How
many are still in the cup?"
Have your child subtract the
number of objects on the
table from the number he or
she started with. Then have
your child count the objects
that are left to check if his or
her answer is correct.

Each dog has black and brown spots. Draw the missing
brown spots. Write an equation to model the problem.

1. 6 spots in all

◯ ____ ◯ ____

2. 9 spots in all

◯ ____ ◯ ____

3. 7 spots in all

◯ ____ ◯ ____

Solve each problem below.

4. **Model** Juan has 9 shirts. 6 of his shirts are white. The rest are **NOT** white.

Draw a picture and write an equation to show how many of Juan's shirts are **NOT** white.

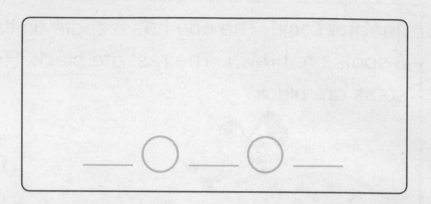

5. **Higher Order Thinking** Draw pictures to show how many there are of each fruit. Then write the numbers to complete the chart.

	Drawings	Bananas	Oranges
Amy has 8 in all.		4	
Joe has 6 in all.			2

6. ✓**Assessment** Pedro and Deb have 9 baseball cards in all. Deb has 1 baseball card. How many baseball cards does Pedro have?

Which equation matches the story?

Ⓐ 9 − 1 = 8   Ⓑ 8 − 1 = 7   Ⓒ 8 − 7 = 1   Ⓓ 7 − 1 = 6

© Pearson Education, Inc. 1

Name _____

Solve & Share

Mia needs 8 movie tickets. She has 5 movie tickets. She buys 3 more. Does she have enough tickets now? Explain how you know with pictures, numbers, or words.

I can ...
construct math arguments using addition and subtraction.

I can also add and subtract to 10.

Thinking Habits

How can I use math to explain my work?

Is my explanation clear?

Does 6 − 2 have the same value as 1 + 3?

Make a math argument using pictures, numbers, or words to explain.

How can I use math to show my thinking?

I can use pictures and numbers to make an argument.

⊠⊠〇〇〇〇 4   ☐ ☐☐☐ 4
  6 - 2   1 + 3

I can use words and numbers to make an argument.

6−2 equals 4 and 1+3 equals 4.

6−2 equals 1+3.
So, they have the same value.

Do You Understand?

Show Me! How are the two different math arguments alike and different?

☆ **Guided** ☆ Use pictures, numbers, or words to
Practice   make an argument.

1. Marlen draws 6 tiles. 4 are red and the rest are green. How many green tiles did Marlen draw? Explain how you know.

Independent Practice ☆ Use pictures, numbers, or words to make an argument.

2. Jan has 7 pennies. She wants to buy a toy car for 3 pennies and a toy plane for 5 pennies. How many more pennies does Jan need? Explain.

3. Lidia has 7 pencils. Jon has 2 pencils. Who has fewer pencils? How many fewer? Explain.

4. **Higher Order Thinking** Max has 3 apples. He buys 2 more apples. He wants to keep 1 apple for himself and give 1 apple to each of his 5 friends.

Will Max have enough apples? Explain.

Lemonade Stand Alex opens a lemonade stand.

The table shows how many cups he sold on certain days. Use this information to solve the problems below.

Cups Sold			
Friday	**Saturday**	**Sunday**	**Monday**
3	5	2	

5. **Explain** How many fewer cups did Alex sell on Friday than on Saturday? Use pictures, words, or numbers to make an argument.

6. **Make Sense** On Monday, Alex sells 4 more cups than he sold on Sunday. How many cups did Alex sell on Monday? Fill in the table. Explain how you know you are right.

Name _____

Another Look! Bill has 3 bananas. He buys 3 more. He wants to keep 1 banana for himself and give bananas to 5 of his friends. Will Bill have enough bananas? Explain.

The picture and equations show that Bill will have enough bananas.

$3 + 3 = \underline{6}$ bananas $1 + 5 = \underline{6}$ people

HOME ACTIVITY Tell your child the following story: "Jack has 2 marbles. He buys 1 more. He wants to keep 1 marble and give marbles to 3 of his friends. Will he have enough marbles?" Have your child use pictures, numbers, and his or her own words to explain whether or not Jack has enough marbles.

 Use pictures, numbers, or words to make an argument.

1. Tim has 7 toy cars. He buys 2 more. He wants to keep 1 toy car for himself and give 1 to each of his 8 friends. Will Tim have enough toy cars? Explain.

Walking Weekend Jada plans to walk a total of 8 miles in three days.

The table shows how many miles Jada walked on Friday and Saturday. How many miles does Jada need to walk on Sunday to reach her goal?

Miles Walked		
Friday	Saturday	Sunday
3	2	

2. **Reasoning** What do the numbers in the table mean? How can they help you solve the problem?

_____

_____

_____

_____

_____

3. **Explain** How many miles does Jada need to walk on Sunday to reach her goal? Complete the table above. Explain how you found your answer. Use pictures, words, or numbers for your argument.

© Pearson Education, Inc. 1

Show the Word

Color these sums and differences. Leave the rest white.

I can ...
add and subtract within 5.

| 4 | 3 | 5 |

8 − 3	0 + 1	0 + 5	5 − 2	3 + 0	5 − 2	5 − 1	2 + 2	3 + 1
2 + 3	0 + 2	7 − 2	1 + 2	0 + 2	4 − 1	1 − 1	4 − 0	5 − 5
10 − 5	5 + 0	3 + 2	3 + 0	5 − 2	3 − 0	0 + 1	1 + 3	5 − 4
4 + 1	5 − 4	5 − 0	4 − 1	4 − 4	2 + 1	2 + 0	4 + 0	0 + 1
9 − 4	1 + 1	1 + 4	3 − 0	4 − 3	0 + 3	3 − 2	0 + 4	3 − 1

The word is

_____   _____   _____

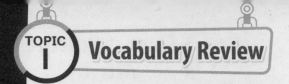

 Glossary

Word List
- add
- addend
- difference
- equal
- equations
- fewer
- minus
- more
- part
- plus
- subtract
- sum
- whole

Understand Vocabulary

1. Write an addition equation.

___ ◯ ___ ◯ ___

2. Write a subtraction equation.

___ ◯ ___ ◯ ___

3. Circle the difference.

$$8 - 2 = 6$$

4. Circle one part.

$$5 + 3 = 8$$

5. Circle the plus sign.

$$3 + 4 = 7$$

Use Vocabulary in Writing

6. Tell how to find $8 - 4$. Use at least one term from the Word List.

Name _____

Set A

You can solve problems about adding to.

Cindy has 3 shells. She finds 1 more. How many shells does Cindy have in all?

3 plus **1** more equals **4**.

$$3 + 1 = 4$$

Write an addition equation to solve.

1. Ethan plants 5 flowers. Then he plants 2 more. How many flowers does Ethan plant in all?

____ + ____ = ____

Set B

You can solve problems about putting together.

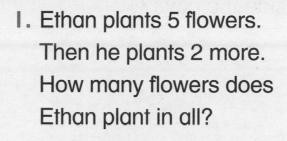

Rick had 3 🔲 and 2 🔲. How many cubes does he have in all? The parts are 3 and 2.

$$3 + 2$$

$$3 + 2 = 5$$

Rick has 5 cubes in all.

Write the parts. Then write an addition equation to match the problem.

2. Brandon has 4 🔲 and 2 🔲. How many cubes does he have in all?

____ + ____

____ + ____ = ____

You can solve problems with
both addends unknown.

There are 7  in all. How many
are inside and outside the cave?

7 is the whole.
If 5 is one part,
2 is the other part.

$\underline{7} = \underline{5} + \underline{2}$

Draw a picture and write
an equation to solve.

3. There are 6 in all.
What is one way they
could be inside and
outside the cave?

____ + ____ = ____

4. There are 9 in all.
What is one way they
could be inside and
outside the cave?

____ = ____ + ____

You can use cubes to model problems
about taking from.

Rob has 8 pears. He gives
3 pears to Sal. How many
pears does Rob have left?

8

?

$\underline{8} - \underline{3} = \underline{5}$

Use cubes to help you complete the
model. Then write an equation to match.

5. 7 carrots are in the garden.
Karl picks 3 carrots. How
many carrots are still in the
garden?

7

____ − ____ = ____

Name _____

You can use cubes to solve problems about comparing.

Carla has 4 blue pencils. She has 3 yellow pencils. How many more blue pencils than yellow pencils does Carla have?

$4 - 3 = 1$

Write an equation to match each problem.

6. Mosi has 4 pens. Holly has 1 pen. How many more pens does Mosi have than Holly?

____ − ____ = ____

7. Martin has 7 baseballs and 3 soccer balls. How many more baseballs than soccer balls does he have?

____ − ____ = ____

Set F

You can use a model to solve problems about adding to.

Ty has 4 grapes. He takes some more grapes. Now he has 9 grapes. How many more grapes did Ty take?

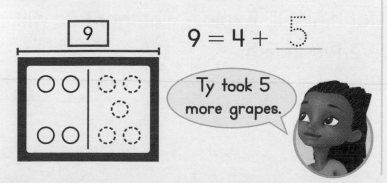

$9 = 4 + 5$

Ty took 5 more grapes.

Complete the model to solve the addition story.

8. Ivy has 2 fish in a bowl. She adds some more fish. Now Ivy has 5 fish in the bowl. How many fish did she add to the bowl?

$2 + \underline{} = 5$

You can write an equation to find a missing part in a put together or take apart problem.

Tom has 9 shirts. Some are blue and some are red. If Tom has 4 red shirts, how many blue shirts does he have?

| 9 |

$9 - 4 = 5$

Complete the model. Then write an equation to solve.

9. John and Jenny have 8 pairs of shoes in all. Jenny has 4 pairs of shoes. How many pairs of shoes does John have?

| 8 |

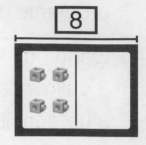

____ ◯ ____ ◯ ____

Thinking Habits

Construct Arguments

How can I use math to explain my work?

Is my explanation clear?

Use pictures, numbers, or words to make an argument. Explain.

10. Luc has 4 goldfish and 2 guppies. He buys 2 more guppies. He wants to give 2 of each fish to a friend and keep 2 of each fish for himself. Explain whether Luc will have enough fish.

Name _____

1. There are 8 penguins. Some go inside the cave and some stay outside.

   Match the number of penguins inside the cave with the number of penguins outside.

Inside:	5 penguins	4 penguins	7 penguins
Outside:	1 penguin	3 penguins	4 penguins

2. Sage had 8 peppers. She cooked 3 of them. How many peppers does Sage have left?

   Write an equation that tells about the story.

   ____ − ____ = ____

3. Use the model to write the parts. Then write and solve an equation.

   ____ + ____

   ____ + ____ = ____

4. Trina has 4 markers. Her mother gives her 5 more markers.

Which addition equation shows how many markers Trina has in all?

Ⓐ $5 + 2 = 7$

Ⓑ $4 + 3 = 7$

Ⓒ $4 + 4 = 8$

Ⓓ $4 + 5 = 9$

5. George had 7 postcards. Then he gets some more. Now he has 9 postcards.

How many new postcards did George get?

Ⓐ 1

Ⓑ 2

Ⓒ 3

Ⓓ 4

6. Dante has 5 books. He wants to have 7 books in his collection. How many more books does Dante need to buy in order to have 7 in all?

7	5	4	2
Ⓐ	Ⓑ	Ⓒ	Ⓓ

7. Lucy and Ellie have 6 cubes in all. Ellie has 5 cubes. How many cubes does Lucy have?

Which equations show the story? Choose all that apply.

$6 - 4 = 2$ $6 - 5 = 1$ $5 + 1 = 6$ $3 + 3 = 6$

☐   ☐   ☐   ☐

---

8. Trina has 6 ribbons. Julie has 2 ribbons.
Which addition equation shows how many ribbons they have in all?

Ⓐ $7 = 5 + 2$

Ⓑ $8 = 5 + 3$

Ⓒ $8 = 6 + 2$

Ⓓ $9 = 6 + 3$

---

9. Draw the missing cubes. Then write an equation that shows the story.

Owen has 5 blocks. He gives 1 to Jordan.
How many blocks does Owen have left?

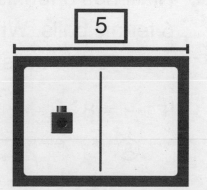

____ − ____ = ____

10. Hannah sees 7 flowers. Carrie sees 6 flowers. Which equation shows how many fewer flowers Carrie sees than Hannah?

$7 - 7 = 0$ $7 - 6 = 1$ $7 + 1 = 8$ $7 + 2 = 9$

    Ⓐ   Ⓑ   Ⓒ   Ⓓ

---

11. Laura has 4 pears. She buys 3 more pears. She wants to keep 2 pears for herself and give one to 6 of her friends.

Use pictures and words to explain whether Laura will have enough pears.

---

12. Nikki has 8 tennis balls. Thomas has 6 tennis balls. Which equation shows many more tennis balls Nikki has than Thomas?

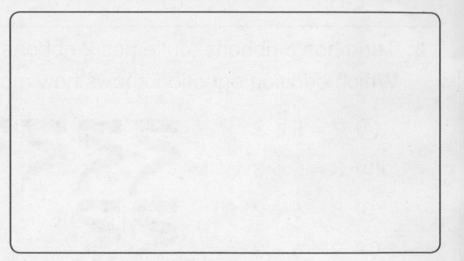

$4 + 4 = 8$ $8 - 3 = 5$ $2 - 0 = 2$ $8 - 6 = 2$

    Ⓐ   Ⓑ   Ⓒ   Ⓓ

Name _____

Skating Ribbons

Marta is an ice skater.

She wins ribbons for her skating.

1. Marta wins 2 blue ribbons and 4 red ribbons.

   How many blue and red ribbons does she win in all?

   _____ ribbons

2. Marta has 4 red ribbons.
   She wins some more red ribbons.
   Now she has 7 red ribbons.

   How many more red ribbons did Marta win?

   _____ more

   Write an equation to show why your answer is correct.

3. Marta has 8 yellow ribbons. What are 2 different ways she can place the ribbons on her door or her wall?

Write two different addition equations to show how she can put the ribbons on her door or her wall.

4. Marta has 8 yellow ribbons and 2 blue ribbons. How many more yellow ribbons than blue ribbons does Marta have?

_____ more

5. Explain why your answer to Item 4 is correct. Use numbers, pictures, or words.

Fluently Add and Subtract Within 10

Essential Question: What strategies can you use while adding and subtracting?

Digital Resources

Solve   Learn   Glossary

Tools   Assessment   Help   Games

The cap of an acorn protects it when it falls.

What could people wear to protect themselves from a fall?

Wow! Let's do this project and learn more.

Math and Science Project: Protect Yourself

Find Out Think of other things that help plants and animals survive. What helps humans survive? Do we make things to help protect us?

Journal: Make a Book Show what you found out. In your book, also:

- Make a list of some things that humans make to protect themselves.

- Make up and solve addition and subtraction problems about these things.

Name _____

Review What You Know

A-Z Vocabulary

1. Circle the numbers that are the **parts**.

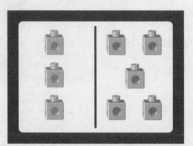

$$3 + 5 = 8$$

2. Circle the number that is the **whole**.

$$3 + 5 = 8$$

3. Circle the symbol for **equals**.

$$+ \quad - \quad =$$

Understanding Addition

4. Write an addition sentence to match the picture.

_____ + _____ = _____

5. Bob sees 5 bees. Ella sees some bees. They see 9 bees in all. How many bees did Ella see?

Write an addition sentence to solve.

_____ + _____ = _____

Making Numbers

6. Draw counters to show one way to make 8.

My Word Cards Study the words on the front of the card. Complete the activity on the back.

A-Z Glossary

number line

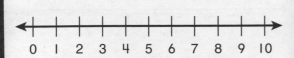

0 1 2 3 4 5 6 7 8 9 10

This **number line** shows the numbers 1 through 10.

doubles fact

4 + 4 = 8

This is a **doubles fact**.

near doubles fact

4 + 5 = 9

This is a **near doubles fact**.

Use what you know to complete the sentences.
Extend learning by writing your own sentence using each word.

An addition fact where one addend is 1 or 2 more than the other addend is a

_____

_____.

An addition fact where one addend is the same as the other addend is a

_____.

A _____

_____

shows numbers in order from left to right.

© Pearson Education, Inc. 1

Solve & Share

The rabbit puts 5 carrots in a pot. He needs to add 1 more. Can you find how many there will be in all without counting all the carrots?

I can ...
add by counting on from a number.

I can also reason about math.

___ + ___ = ___

There are 4 tomatoes in the pot. Add 2 more. How many in all?

4

You can add to join the two groups.

$$4 + 2 = 6$$

2 more than 4 is 6. There are 6 tomatoes in all!

You can also use a **number line** to count on and find the sum.

Start at 4 and count on 2 more.

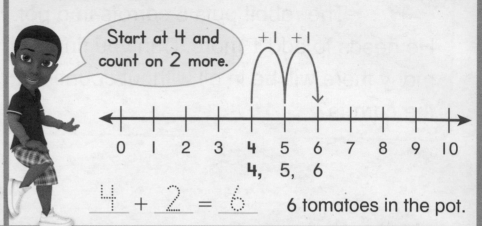

+1 +1

0 1 2 3 4 5 6 7 8 9 10

4, 5, 6

$$4 + 2 = 6$$

6 tomatoes in the pot.

Do You Understand?

Show Me! How do you add 1 to any number? How do you add 2 to any number?

Guided Practice   Count on to find the sum.

1.

3

$$3 + 2 = 5$$

2.

8

___ + ___ = ___

3.
3

___ + ___ = ___

4.
7

___ + ___ = ___

Topic 2 | Lesson 1

Independent Practice ☆ Count on to add. Use the number line to help.

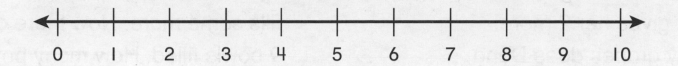

0 1 2 3 4 5 6 7 8 9 10

5. $3 + 2 =$ _____

6. $8 + 1 =$ _____

7. $7 + 1 =$ _____

8. $9 + 1 =$ _____

9. $4 + 3 =$ _____

10. $9 = 6 +$ _____

11. $2 + 6 =$ _____

12. $6 = 5 +$ _____

13. $5 + 3 =$ _____

14. **Number Sense** Circle **True** or **False**. Count on to help you.

$8 + 0 = 8$	True	False	$3 + 1 = 5$	True False
$7 + 1 = 7$	True	False	$6 = 4 + 0$	True False
$8 = 6 + 2$	True	False	$5 + 2 = 7$	True False

15. **Model** Dana has 8 grapes. Her sister gives her 2 more. How many grapes does Dana have now?

_____ + _____ = _____

Dana has _____ grapes.

16. **Model** Anna fills 6 bowls. Jason fills some more. Now there are 9 bowls filled. How many bowls did Jason fill?

_____ + _____ = _____

Jason filled _____ bowls.

17. **Higher Order Thinking** Max has 1 more carrot than Jena. Jena has 3 more carrots than Sal. Sal has 4 carrots.

Write how many carrots each person has.

_____ _____ _____

Max   Jena   Sal

18. ✓**Assessment** Maria is 2 years older than Tim. She is 7 years old.

Which addition equation helps you find Tim's age?

Ⓐ $2 + 7 = 9$

Ⓑ $5 + 1 = 6$

Ⓒ $5 - 2 = 3$

Ⓓ $5 + 2 = 7$

Name _____

Another Look! Count on to find the sum.

Add 1 and the sum is 1 more.

3, 4

$3 + 1 = 4$

Add 2 and the sum is 2 more.

3, 4, 5

$3 + 2 = 5$

Add 3 and the sum is 3 more.

3, 4, 5, 6

$3 + 3 = 6$

HOME ACTIVITY Place between 1 and 7 small objects on a table. Have your child count the objects. Then add 0, 1, or 2 more. Ask your child to add the objects. Have your child write an addition equation to correspond with the objects on the table. Repeat with a different number of objects.

Count on to complete the addition facts.

1.

6, _____

$6 + 1 = $ _____

2.

5, _____, _____, _____

$5 + 3 = $ _____

3.

7, _____, _____

$7 + 2 = $ _____

4. Max earns 5 dollars for washing dishes. Then he earns some more dollars for walking the dog. In all, Max earns 7 dollars. How many dollars did Max earn for walking the dog?

Draw a picture. Write the number.

_____ dollars

5. Emma reads 7 books in one week. Then she reads 3 more books. How many books did Emma read in all?

Draw a picture. Write the number.

_____ books

6. Higher Order Thinking Write the missing number.

$3 + 2 = 2 + \underline{\quad}$

Use the picture to help!

7. ✓**Assessment** There are 6 bees in a hive. 3 more bees fly in. Count on to find how many bees are in the hive now.

Which addition fact matches the story?

Ⓐ $6 + 2 = 8$

Ⓑ $6 + 3 = 9$

Ⓒ $6 + 0 = 6$

Ⓓ $8 + 0 = 8$

Name _____

Solve & Share

Emily and I each have 3 toys. How many toys do we have in all? Use cubes to find the answer. Then write an equation to match the story.

I can ...
use doubles to solve problems.

I can also look for things that repeat.

_____ + _____ = _____

This is a **doubles fact**.

$$2 + 2 = 4$$

The addends are the same.

Every cube in this group

$$\begin{array}{r} 2 \\ +\ 2 \\ \hline 4 \end{array}$$

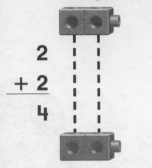

has a partner in this group.

This is not a doubles fact. Every cube does not have a partner.

$$2 + 1 = 3$$

The addends are not the same.

Think of doubles when both addends are the same.

$$\begin{array}{r} 2 \\ +\ 2 \\ \hline 4 \end{array} \qquad \begin{array}{r} 1 \\ +\ 1 \\ \hline 2 \end{array}$$

Do You Understand?

Show Me! Is $6 + 4$ a double? Explain.

☆ **Guided Practice** ☆ Write the addition equation for each double.

1.

$$4 + 4 = 8$$

2.

$$\underline{} + \underline{} = \underline{}$$

3.

$$\underline{} = \underline{} + \underline{}$$

4.

$$\underline{} + \underline{} = \underline{}$$

Topic 2 | Lesson 2

Name _____

Independent Practice ☆ Write the sum for each doubles fact.

5.

_____ + _____ = _____

6.

_____ + _____ = _____

7.

_____ + _____ = _____

8.   2
   + 2
   ☐

9.   4
   + 4
   ☐

10.   0
    + 0
    ☐

11. **A-Z Vocabulary** Draw a picture to show a **doubles fact**.
Write the addition equation to match your drawing.

_____ + _____ = _____

12. Make Sense Neela makes 4 pies. John makes the same number of pies.

How many pies do Neela and John make in all?

_____ pies

13. Make Sense Kim has 2 pockets. She has 5 pennies in each pocket.

How many pennies does Kim have in all?

_____ pennies

14. Higher Order Thinking Is there a doubles fact that has a sum of 9? Draw a picture to find out.
Circle **Yes** or **No**.

Yes   **No**

15. ✓Assessment Danny has 2 baskets. He has the same number of pencils in each basket. He has 6 pencils in all.

How many pencils does Danny have in each basket?

3   4   5   6
Ⓐ   Ⓑ   Ⓒ   Ⓓ

Name _____

Another Look! When the addends are the same, it is a doubles fact. Here are some doubles facts.

HOME ACTIVITY Have your child use small objects to show 2 groups of 4. Then ask your child to write an addition equation to show the double (4 + 4 = 8). Repeat for other doubles of 1 + 1 through 5 + 5.

$$\begin{array}{r} 2 \\ +2 \\ \hline 4 \end{array}$$

$$2 + 2 = 4$$

↑ addend   ↑ addend   ↑ sum

$$\begin{array}{r} 3 \\ +3 \\ \hline \boxed{6} \end{array}$$

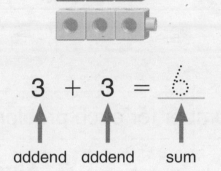

$$3 + 3 = 6$$

↑ addend   ↑ addend   ↑ sum

Write the sum for each doubles fact.

1.

$$\begin{array}{r} 1 \\ +1 \\ \hline \end{array}$$

2.

$$\begin{array}{r} 4 \\ +4 \\ \hline \end{array}$$

3.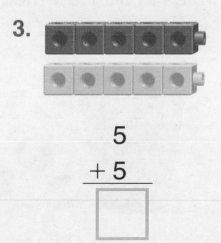

$$\begin{array}{r} 5 \\ +5 \\ \hline \end{array}$$

Write an addition equation to solve each problem.

4. Reasoning Owen paints 5 pictures. Luis paints 5 pictures, too. How many pictures did Owen and Luis paint in all?

_____ + _____ = _____

5. Reasoning Tess and Maya grow 6 flowers in all. Tess grows 3 flowers. How many flowers does Maya grow?

_____ = _____ + _____

Write the missing number for each problem.

6. Algebra

$4 = 2 +$ _____

7. Algebra

_____ $+ 4 = 8$

8. Algebra

$0 +$ _____ $= 0$

9. Higher Order Thinking There are 6 marbles in all. How many marbles are inside the cup?

_____ marbles are inside the cup.

10. ✓**Assessment** There are 10 marbles in all. There are 5 marbles outside the cup. How many marbles are inside the cup?

Ⓐ 2

Ⓑ 4

Ⓒ 5

Ⓓ 10

Name _____

Solve & Share

Emily has 4 shells and I have 5 shells. How can you use counters to show how many we would have in all? Write an equation.

I can ...
solve problems using near doubles facts.

I can also model with math.

____ + ____ = ____

You can use a doubles fact to solve a **near doubles fact**.

$4 + 5 = ?$
$4 + 6 = ?$

> I can use the doubles fact $4 + 4$ to solve.

$4 + 5$ is $4 + 4$ and I more.

8 and I more is 9.

$4 + 6$ is $4 + 4$ and 2 more.

8 and 2 more is 10.

$$\begin{array}{r} 4 \\ + 5 \\ \hline 9 \end{array} \qquad \begin{array}{r} 4 \\ + 6 \\ \hline 10 \end{array}$$

> Knowing doubles facts can help solve near doubles facts.

Do You Understand?

Show Me! How does knowing the sum of $3 + 3$ help you find the sum of $3 + 4$?

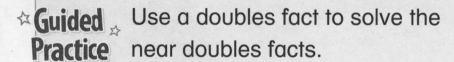

☆ **Guided** ☆ Use a doubles fact to solve the
Practice near doubles facts.

1. $2 + 3 = ?$

   $\underline{2} + \underline{2} = \underline{4}$

   So, $\underline{2} + \underline{3} = \underline{5}$

   ---

2. $2 + 4 = ?$

   $\underline{} + \underline{} = \underline{}$

   So, $\underline{} + \underline{} = \underline{}$

Independent Practice Use a doubles fact to solve the near doubles facts.

3. $3 + 4 = ?$

_____ + _____ = _____

So, _____ + _____ = _____

4. $3 + 5 = ?$

_____ + _____ = _____

So, _____ + _____ = _____

5.   4
    $+ 5$

☐

6.   2
    $+ 4$

☐

7.   2
    $+ 1$

☐

Think of a doubles fact and add 1 or 2 more.

8. $3 + 2 = $ _____

9. $1 + 3 = $ _____

Number Sense Write the missing numbers.

10. If $2 + $ _____ $= 4$, then $2 + $ _____ $= 5$.

11. If $4 + $ _____ $= 8$, then $4 + $ _____ $= 9$.

12. **Reasoning** Omar eats 2 pears. Jane eats 2 pears and then I more. How many pears did Omar and Jane eat in all?

_____ + _____ = _____

Omar and Jane eat _____ pears.

13. **Reasoning** Sam finds 3 shells and Jack finds 4 shells. How many shells did they find in all?

_____ + _____ = _____

Sam and Jack find _____ shells.

14. **Higher Order Thinking** Write a story problem about a near double. Then draw a picture to show the story.

15. ✓**Assessment** Patty plays 4 games of jump rope. Mary plays 4 games of jump rope and then I more.

How many games of jump rope did Patty and Mary play in all?

Ⓐ 10

Ⓑ 9

Ⓒ 8

Ⓓ 7

You can use a near doubles fact to help solve the problem.

© Pearson Education, Inc. I

Name _____

Another Look! You can use doubles to add near doubles.

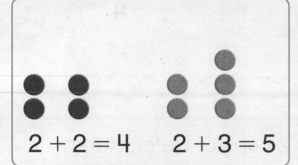

$2 + 2 = 4$ $2 + 3 = 5$

If $2 + 2 = 4$, then $2 + 3$ is 1 more.

$2 + 3 = 5$

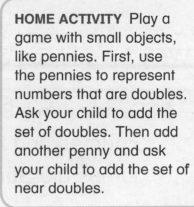

$3 + 3 = 6$ $3 + 4 = 7$

If $3 + 3 = 6$, then $3 + 4$ is 1 more.

$3 + 4 = 7$

HOME ACTIVITY Play a game with small objects, like pennies. First, use the pennies to represent numbers that are doubles. Ask your child to add the set of doubles. Then add another penny and ask your child to add the set of near doubles.

Add the doubles. Then add the near doubles.

1.

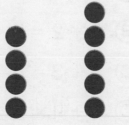

___ + ___ = ___   ___ + ___ = ___

2.

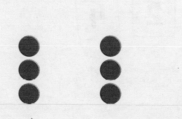

___ + ___ = ___   ___ + ___ = ___

Find the number to complete each near doubles fact.

3. Algebra

$3 + \underline{\quad} = 7$

4. Algebra

$9 = 4 + \underline{\quad}$

5. Algebra

$1 + \underline{\quad} = 4$

Write an addition equation to solve each problem.

6. Sandy plays 3 games. Bill plays 3 games and then 1 more. How many games did Sandy and Bill play in all?

$\underline{\quad} = \underline{\quad} + \underline{\quad}$

Sandy and Bill played __ games.

7. Nina drinks 2 cups of water. Karen drinks 4 cups of water. How many cups did they drink in all?

$\underline{\quad} + \underline{\quad} = \underline{\quad}$

Nina and Karen drank __ cups.

8. **Higher Order Thinking** Use each card once to write addition equations using doubles and near doubles.

   5 4

$\underline{\quad} + \underline{\quad} = \underline{\quad}$

$\underline{\quad} + \underline{\quad} = \underline{\quad}$

9. **Assessment** Which doubles fact can help you solve $4 + 5 = ?$

Ⓐ $1 + 1 = 2$

Ⓑ $2 + 2 = 4$

Ⓒ $3 + 3 = 6$

Ⓓ $4 + 4 = 8$

© Pearson Education, Inc. 1

Name _____

Solve & Share

Put some counters on the bottom row of the ten-frame. What addition equation can you write to match the counters?

I can ...
use a ten-frame to help solve addition facts with 5 and 10.

I can also model with math.

____ + ____ = ____

You can use a ten-frame to show an addition fact with 5.

$5 + 3 = ?$

Start with 5. Then add 3 more.

5 and 3 more is 8.

There are 8 counters in the ten-frame.

$5 + 3 = 8$

The ten-frame shows another addition fact. You have 8. Make 10.

2 boxes are empty. Add 2.

8 plus 2 more is 10.

$8 + 2 = 10$

Do You Understand?

Show Me! How does a ten-frame help you add $5 + 4$?

☆ Guided Practice ☆

Look at the ten-frames.
Write an addition fact with 5.
Then write an addition fact for 10.

1.
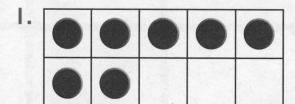

$5 + \underline{2} = 7$

$7 + \underline{3} = 10$

2.
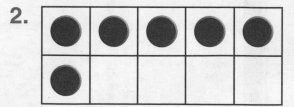

$5 + \underline{} = \underline{}$

$\underline{} + \underline{} = 10$

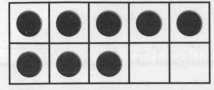 Look at the ten-frames. Write an addition fact with 5. Then write an addition fact for 10.

3.

5 + ___ = ___

___ + ___ = 10

4.

5 + ___ = ___

___ + ___ = 10

5.

5 + ___ = ___

___ + ___ = 10

6. **Higher Order Thinking** Using 2 colors, draw counters in the ten-frames to match the addition equations. Then write the missing numbers.

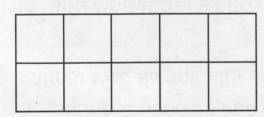

8 + ___ = 10

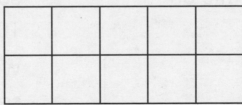

7 + ___ = 10

Which number will make 10?

7. **Model** A team has 5 softballs. The coach brings 3 more. How many softballs does the team have now?

Draw counters in the ten-frame. Then write an addition fact to solve.

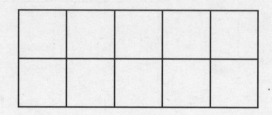

_____ + _____ = _____   _____ softballs

8. **Model** Kami reads 5 books. Sue reads 4 books. How many books did the girls read in all?

Draw counters in the ten-frame. Then write an addition fact to solve.

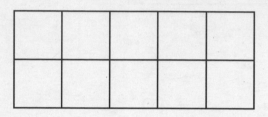

_____ + _____ = _____   _____ books

9. **Higher Order Thinking** Write a new story about adding to 10 in the ten-frame in Item 7. Then write an equation for your story.

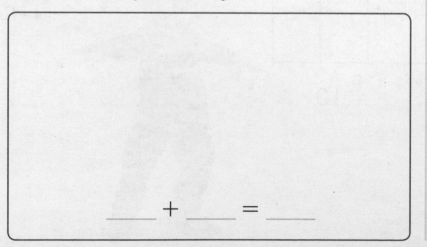

_____ + _____ = _____

10. ✅**Assessment** Todd's team has 5 soccer balls. Todd's coach brings some more. Todd's team now has 10 soccer balls.

Which addition fact shows how many soccer balls Todd's coach brought?

Ⓐ 5 + 5 = 10

Ⓑ 10 + 3 = 13

Ⓒ 7 + 3 = 10

Ⓓ 10 + 7 = 17

Another Look! You can write an addition fact with 5 using a ten-frame. You can also write an addition fact for 10 using a ten-frame.

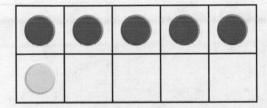

$$5 + 1 = 6$$

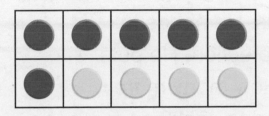

$$6 + 4 = \underline{10}$$

HOME ACTIVITY Play a game using ten-frames drawn on a sheet of paper. Draw circles on each ten-frame. Then ask your child to write an accompanying equation using 5 or 10 below each ten-frame.

Look at the ten-frames.
Write an addition fact with 5.
Then write an addition fact for 10.

I.
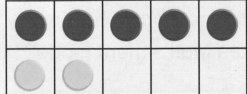

$$5 + 2 = \underline{}$$

$$\underline{} + \underline{} = 10$$

2.
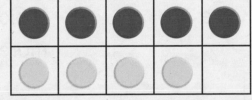

$$5 + 4 = \underline{}$$

$$\underline{} + \underline{} = 10$$

3.
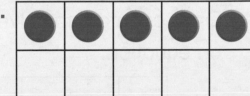

$$5 + 0 = \underline{}$$

$$\underline{} + \underline{} = 10$$

4. 5 + ___ = ___

   6 + ___ = 10

5. 5 + ___ = ___

   9 + ___ = 10

6. 5 + ___ = ___

   8 + ___ = 10

7. **Math and Science** Rich is going rock climbing with his friends. He needs to pack 10 helmets for protection. He puts 4 helmets in the van. How many more helmets does Rich need to pack?

Draw counters to solve. Then write an equation.

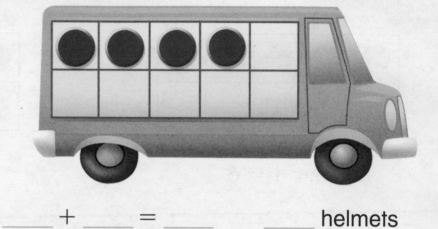

___ + ___ = ___   ___ helmets

8. **Higher Order Thinking** A camp has 7 tents in all. First, the campers set up 5 tents. How many more tents did the campers set up?

Draw counters to solve. Then write an equation.

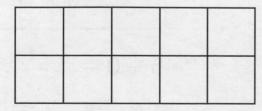

___ = ___ + ___   ___ tents

9. ✓**Assessment** Matt's mom makes 10 pancakes in all. First, she makes 6 pancakes. Then she makes some more.

Which addition fact shows how many more pancakes Matt's mom made?

(A) 6 + 1 = 7

(B) 6 + 4 = 10

(C) 10 + 4 = 14

(D) 6 + 6 = 12

Name _____

Write an addition equation for the green and yellow cubes in each cube tower. How are the addition equations the same? How are they different?

___ + ___ = ___   ___ + ___ = ___

4 and 2 is 6.

2 and 4 is 6.

$$4 + 2 = 6$$
$$2 + 4 = 6$$

You can change the order of the addends. The sum is the same.

You can write 2 addition equations.

4 plus 2 equals 6.
2 plus 4 equals 6.

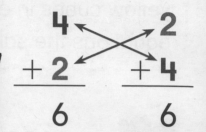

Do You Understand?

Show Me! How can you use cubes to show that $5 + 3$ is the same as $3 + 5$?

★ **Guided Practice** ★ Color to change the order of the addends. Then write the addition equations.

1.

$$\underline{3} + \underline{4} = \underline{7}$$

___ + ___ = ___

2.

___ + ___ = ___

___ + ___ = ___

Independent Practice Write the sum. Then change the order of the addends. Write the new addition equation.

3. 2 + 3 = ___

___ + ___ = ___

4. 1 + 6 = ___

___ + ___ = ___

5. ___ = 3 + 6

___ = ___ + ___

6. 5 + 2 = ___

___ + ___ = ___

7. 4 + 5 = ___

___ + ___ = ___

8. 6 + 2 = ___

___ + ___ = ___

 **Number Sense** Use the numbers on the cards to write two addition equations.

9. **3**  **8** **5**

___ + ___ = ___

___ + ___ = ___

10. **4** **6** **2**

___ = ___ + ___

___ = ___ + ___

11. **Model** Liza and Anna collect 6 cans on Monday. On Tuesday, they collect 4 cans. How many cans did they collect in all?

Draw a picture. Then write two different addition equations.

_____ + _____ = _____

_____ + _____ = _____

12. **Higher Order Thinking**
Draw a picture of 5 birds.
Make some blue.
Make the rest red.

Write two addition equations to tell about the picture.

_____ + _____ = _____

_____ + _____ = _____

13. ✓**Assessment** Look at the two addition equations. Which is the missing addend?

$$9 = \underline{\ ?\ } + 2$$

$$9 = 2 + \underline{\ ?\ }$$

Ⓐ 6

Ⓑ 7

Ⓒ 8

Ⓓ 9

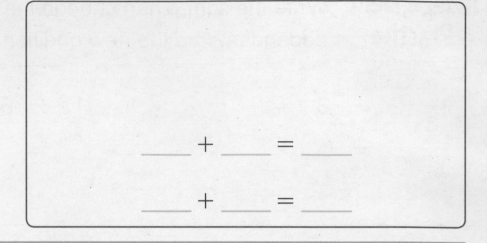

Both equations have a 2 and a 9.

© Pearson Education, Inc. 1

Help   Tools   Games

Another Look! When you change the order of addends, the sum is the same.

$4 + 2 = 6$

$2 + 4 = 6$

HOME ACTIVITY Write several addition equations for your child. Have him or her change the order of addends and write the new addition equation. Ask, "How are the addition equations the same? How are they different?"

$\underline{5} + \underline{2} = \underline{7}$

$\underline{2} + \underline{5} = \underline{7}$

Add. Write addition equations with addends in a different order.

1.

___ + ___ = ___

___ + ___ = ___

2.

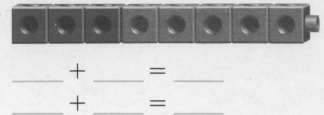

____ + ____ = ____

____ + ____ = ____

3.

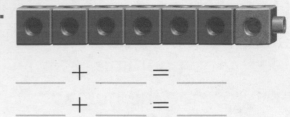

____ + ____ = ____

____ + ____ = ____

4. **Higher Order Thinking** Use the cubes below.
Pick two colors of cubes. Write an addition story.
Then write two addition equations for your story.

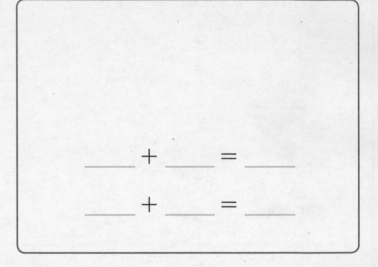

____ + ____ = ____

____ + ____ = ____

5. ✓**Assessment** Which shows two ways
to add the cubes in the cube train?

Ⓐ 4 + 3, 3 + 4

Ⓑ 2 + 6, 6 + 2

Ⓒ 2 + 7, 7 + 2

Ⓓ 5 + 2, 2 + 5

6. ✓**Assessment** Which has the same
value as 5 + 1?

Ⓐ 1 + 2

Ⓑ 5 + 3

Ⓒ 2 + 6

Ⓓ 1 + 5

Solve & Share

There are 5 people on a bus. It stops and 2 people get off. Use the number line to show how many people are still on the bus. Write the number.

Solve

Lesson 2-6
**Count Back
to Subtract**

I can ...
count back to solve
subtraction problems.

I can also model
with math.

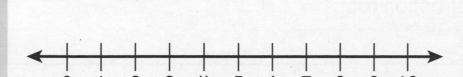

0 1 2 3 4 5 6 7 8 9 10

_____ people are left on the bus.

You can use the number line to help you subtract.

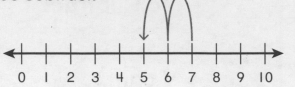

7, 6, 5 $7 - 2 =$ __5__

If I start at 7 and count back 2, I end at 5.

When you subtract 3, you count back 3.

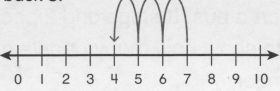

7, __6__, __5__, __4__

$$\begin{array}{r} 7 \\ -\ 3 \\ \hline \boxed{4} \end{array}$$

When you subtract 0, you count back 0.

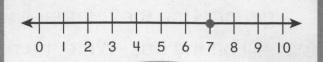

$$\begin{array}{r} 7 \\ -\ 0 \\ \hline \boxed{7} \end{array}$$

 If I start at 7 and don't count back any, I stay at 7!

Do You Understand?

Show Me! Write subtraction equations to show counting back by 1, 2, or 3.

☆ **Guided Practice** ☆ Count back to complete each subtraction fact.

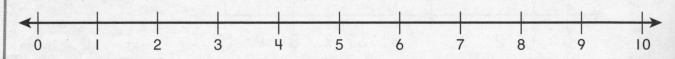

1.
$$\begin{array}{r} 4 \\ -\ 1 \\ \hline \boxed{3} \end{array} \qquad \begin{array}{r} 4 \\ -\ 0 \\ \hline \boxed{4} \end{array}$$

2.
$$\begin{array}{r} 6 \\ -\ 0 \\ \hline \boxed{} \end{array} \qquad \begin{array}{r} 6 \\ -\ 2 \\ \hline \boxed{} \end{array}$$

3.
$$\begin{array}{r} 9 \\ -\ 5 \\ \hline \boxed{} \end{array} \qquad \begin{array}{r} 9 \\ -\ 3 \\ \hline \boxed{} \end{array}$$

---

110 one hundred ten

Topic 2 | Lesson 6

Independent Practice

Complete each subtraction fact. Count back or use the number line to help you.

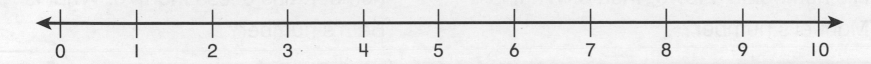

0   1   2   3   4   5   6   7   8   9   10

4.   6
    − 5
    ☐

5.   8
    − 0
    ☐

6.   10
    − 8
    ☐

7.   7
    − 3
    ☐

8.   9
    − 4
    ☐

Draw a picture to solve. Write a subtraction equation.

9. **Higher Order Thinking** Amy and Ryan buy pencils at the store. Amy buys 10 pencils. Ryan buys 8 pencils. How many fewer pencils did Ryan buy?

_____ − _____ = _____ fewer pencils

10. **Reasoning** Manuel picks a number. His number is 4 fewer than 8. What is Manuel's number?

_____ − _____ = _____

Manuel's number is _____.

11. **Reasoning** Beth is thinking of a number. It is 0 less than 10. What is Beth's number?

_____ − _____ = _____

Beth's number is _____.

12. **Higher Order Thinking** Complete the subtraction equation. Then write a story to match the equation.

5 − 1 = _____

_____

_____

_____

13. ✓ **Assessment** Jan has 10 tickets. She gives 2 tickets to her friends. How many tickets does Jan have left?

Ⓐ 8
Ⓑ 6
Ⓒ 4
Ⓓ 2

You can write an equation to help you solve the problem.

Name _____

Another Look! You can count back to solve subtraction problems.

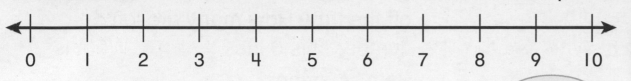

0 1 2 3 4 5 6 7 8 9 10

$4 - 2 = ?$

Start at 4.

Count back 2.   **4,** 3, 2

Solve the problem.

$4 - 2 = 2$

$6 - 1 = ?$

Start at 6.

Count back 1.   **6,** __5__

Solve the problem.

$6 - 1 = \underline{5}$

Count back to subtract.

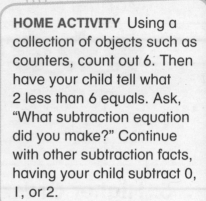

HOME ACTIVITY Using a collection of objects such as counters, count out 6. Then have your child tell what 2 less than 6 equals. Ask, "What subtraction equation did you make?" Continue with other subtraction facts, having your child subtract 0, 1, or 2.

Count back or use a number line to help you subtract.

1.

9

Count back 1.   Solve the problem.

$9 - 1 = \underline{}$

____

2.

10

Count back 0.   Solve the problem.

$10 - 0 = \underline{}$

____

3. There are 9 apples in Maya's basket. She eats 1 apple. How many apples are left?

_____ − _____ = _____

4. There are 6 cups on a tray. 4 cups fall off the tray. How many are left?

_____ − _____ = _____

5. **Higher Order Thinking** Write a subtraction equation. Then write a story to match your equation.

_____ = _____ − _____

_____

_____

_____

_____

6. ✓**Assessment** Nicole has 8 pages to read in her book. She reads 3 pages on the bus. Which equation shows how many pages Nicole has left to read?

Ⓐ 10 − 5 = 5

Ⓑ 10 − 2 = 8

Ⓒ 8 − 2 = 6

Ⓓ 8 − 3 = 5

Name _____

Solve & Share

Jenna has 6 beachballs. 4 of them blow to the other side of the pool. How many does she have left?

How can you use an addition fact to find the answer to $6 - 4 =$ _____ ? Use counters to help you solve the problem.

I can ...
use addition facts I know to help me solve subtraction problems.

I can also look for patterns.

_____ + _____ = _____   So, _____ − _____ = _____.

You can use addition to help you subtract.

$7 - 3 = \boxed{?}$

$3 + \boxed{?} = 7$

What can I add to 3 to make 7?

$3 + \boxed{4} = 7$

The missing part is 4.

Think of the addition fact to solve the subtraction equation.

$7 - 3 = \boxed{4}$

$3 + 4 = 7$

Do You Understand?

Show Me! How can an addition fact help you solve $7 - 6$?

Guided Practice Think addition to help you subtract. Draw the missing part. Then write the numbers.

1.

$5 - 4 = ?$

$4 + \underline{} = 5$

So, $5 - 4 = \underline{}$.

2.

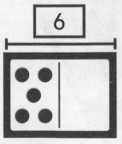

$6 - 5 = ?$

$5 + \underline{} = 6$

So, $6 - 5 = \underline{}$.

Topic 2 | Lesson 7

Tools Assessment

Independent Practice Think addition to help you subtract. Draw the missing part. Then write the numbers.

3.

8

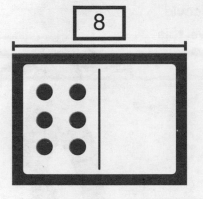

6 + ___ = 8

So, 8 − 6 = ___.

4.

7

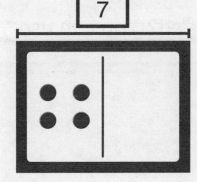

4 + ___ = 7

So, 7 − 4 = ___.

5.

4

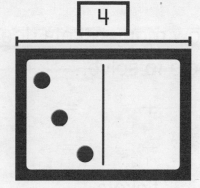

3 + ___ = 4

So, 4 − 3 = ___.

6. **Higher Order Thinking** Draw the shape to complete the equation.

If ⬤ + ▲ = ◼,

then ◼ − ⬤ = ___.

7. **Use Tools** Pam needs 8 tickets to get on a ride. She has 2 tickets. She needs some more tickets.

   How many tickets does Pam still need? You can use tools to solve.

   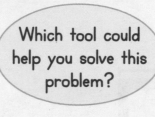

   Which tool could help you solve this problem?

   ____ + ____ = ____

   ____ − ____ = ____

   ____ tickets

8. **Higher Order Thinking** Kathy has a box that holds 6 crayons. 4 crayons are inside the box. She uses addition to find how many are missing. Is Kathy correct? Explain.

   $6 + 4 = 10$

   10 crayons are missing.

9. ✅**Assessment** Which addition facts can help you solve the problem? Choose all that apply.

   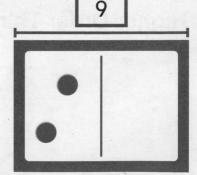

   9

   $9 - 2 = ?$

   ☐ $7 + 2 = 9$

   ☐ $5 + 4 = 9$

   ☐ $2 + 7 = 9$

   ☐ $8 + 1 = 9$

Help Tools Games

Another Look! Use addition to help you subtract.

I know that
2 + 6 = 8.
So, 8 – 6 = 2.

$\underline{3} + \underline{6} = \underline{9}$

So, $\underline{9} - \underline{6} = \underline{3}$.

HOME ACTIVITY Fold a sheet of paper in half so you have 2 equal boxes. Put 1–8 pennies in the box on the left. Say a number greater than the number of pennies in the box, but not greater than 9. Ask: "What subtraction equation can you write? What addition equation is related?" Continue with different number combinations.

Write an addition fact that will help you write and solve the subtraction fact.

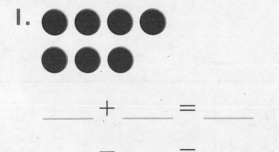

1. _____ + _____ = _____

_____ – _____ = _____

2. _____ + _____ = _____

_____ – _____ = _____

3. _____ + _____ = _____

_____ – _____ = _____

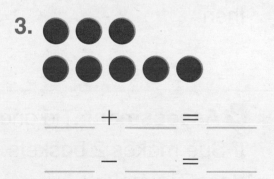

Write a subtraction and an addition equation to solve.

4. Look for Patterns Draw counters.

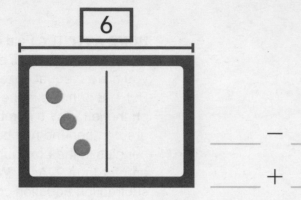

6

___ − ___ = ___

___ + ___ = ___

5. Reasoning Rosi buys 10 beads to make a bracelet. She buys 3 blue beads and some white beads.

How many white beads does Rosi buy?

_____ white beads

___ + ___ = ___

___ − ___ = ___

Higher Order Thinking Draw the shapes to complete each equation.

6. If △ + ○ = ▢ ,

then ___ − ___ = ___ .

7. If ▯ = ▭ + ▭ ,

then ___ = ___ − ___ .

8. ✓Assessment Tia and Sue make 8 baskets. If Sue makes 2 baskets, how many baskets does Tia make?

Which addition facts can help you subtract? Choose all that apply.

☐ $8 + 6 = 14$

☐ $2 + 8 = 10$

☐ $6 + 2 = 8$

☐ $2 + 6 = 8$

© Pearson Education, Inc. 1

Name _____

Solve & Share

How can you use an addition fact to find the answer to 8 − 5 = _____? Use counters to help you solve the problem.

I can ...
use addition facts to 10 to solve subtraction problems.

I can also reason about math.

_____ + _____ = _____   So, _____ − _____ = _____.

Think addition to help you subtract.

$9 - 5 = \boxed{?}$

9

5	?

$5 + \boxed{?} = 9$

What can I add to 5 to make 9?

9

5	?

$5 + \boxed{4} = 9$

4 is the missing part.

9

5	4

Think of the addition fact to solve the subtraction fact.

$5 + 4 = 9$, so $9 - 5 = 4$.

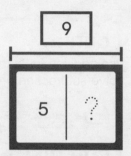

Do You Understand?

Show Me! What 2 subtraction facts can $4 + 6 = 10$ help you solve?

Think addition to help you subtract.
Write the missing part.

1.

9

7	2

$9 - 7 = ?$

$7 + \underline{2} = 9$

So, $9 - 7 = \underline{2}$.

2.

10

6	

$10 - 6 = ?$

$6 + \underline{} = 10$

So, $10 - 6 = \underline{}$.

© Pearson Education, Inc. 1   **Topic 2** | Lesson 8

Tools Assessment

Independent Practice ☆ Think addition to help you subtract. Write the missing part.

3.
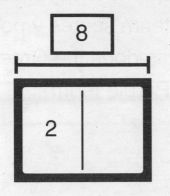

$2 +$ ____ $= 8$

So, $8 - 2 =$ ____.

4.
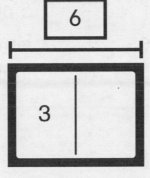

$3 +$ ____ $= 6$

So, $6 - 3 =$ ____.

5.
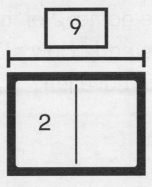

$2 +$ ____ $= 9$

So, $9 - 2 =$ ____.

6. **Math and Science** Turtles have shells to protect them from dangers in the ocean. 10 turtles are on the beach. Then some turtles swim away. Now there are 7 turtles on the beach. How many turtles swam away?

Write an addition and a subtraction equation to match the story.

____ $+$ ____ $=$ ____

____ $-$ ____ $=$ ____   ____ turtles

> You can think addition to help you subtract!

7. Generalize Jamie brings 7 baseballs to the game. 2 of the balls are hit out of the park. How many baseballs does Jamie have left?

____ + ____ = ____

____ − ____ = ____

____ baseballs

8. Generalize The Purple team scores 5 points. The Green team scores 9 points. How many more points does the Green team score than the Purple team?

____ + ____ = ____

____ − ____ = ____

____ points

9. Higher Order Thinking Write a subtraction story about the fish.

_____

_____

____ ◯ ____ = ____

____ ◯ ____ = ____

10. ✓Assessment Mrs. Kane has 9 students. Some are drawing pictures. 6 are reading books. How many students are drawing pictures?

Which addition facts can you use to find the answer? Choose all that apply.

☐ 3 + 5 = 8

☐ 3 + 6 = 9

☐ 6 + 3 = 9

☐ 4 + 6 = 10

Name _____

Another Look! You can use addition facts to help you subtract. Look at the subtraction fact. Then look at the addition fact that can help.

$9 - 1 = 8$

$8 + 1 = 9$

$8 - 2 = 6$

$6 + 2 = 8$

HOME ACTIVITY Give your child a subtraction fact to solve. Have him or her use pennies or other objects, such as counters, to solve the problem. Then have your child tell you the addition problem that is related. Continue with several subtraction facts.

Subtract. Then write the addition fact that helped you subtract.

1.

$10 - \underline{} = 8$

$8 + \underline{} = 10$

2.

$9 - \underline{} = 5$

$5 + \underline{} = 9$

3.

$8 - \underline{} = 1$

$1 + \underline{} = 8$

Think addition to help you subtract. Write the missing part.

4.

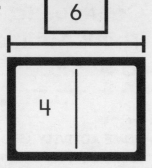

6

4

$4 + \underline{\hspace{1.5em}} = 6$

So, $6 - 4 = \underline{\hspace{1.5em}}$.

5.

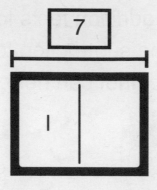

7

1

$1 + \underline{\hspace{1.5em}} = 7$

So, $7 - 1 = \underline{\hspace{1.5em}}$.

6. Higher Order Thinking Write a number story for $10 - 3$. Then write the addition fact that helped you subtract.

7. ✅ **Assessment** Miguel and Andy pick apples. Miguel picks 9 apples. Andy picks 4 apples. How many fewer apples did Andy pick than Miguel?

Which addition facts can help you solve this number story? Choose all that apply.

☐ $5 + 4 = 9$

☐ $4 + 4 = 8$

☐ $6 + 3 = 9$

☐ $4 + 5 = 9$

© Pearson Education, Inc. 1

Topic 2 | Lesson 8

Name _____

Solve & Share

6 fish swim by. Some more fish join them. Now there are 10 fish. How many fish joined the fish swimming by?

Draw a picture to solve the problem. Then write an equation.

I can ...
draw pictures and write equations to help solve word problems.

I can also make sense of problems.

____ + ____ = ____

Slater has 7 books. He gives some books to Anna. Now Slater has 2 books. How many books did he give Anna?

You can write an equation to model the problem.

$$7 - \underline{\quad ? \quad} = 2$$

Slater's books minus the books he gives Anna equals 2. So, Slater gives Anna 5 books.

You can also count back from 7 to 2 to solve.

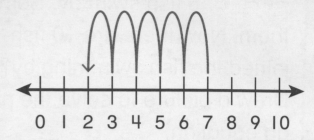

Count each jump from 7 when you count back. There are 5 jumps.

Do You Understand?

Show Me! 7 cubes are on a table. Some cubes fall on the floor. Now there are 3 cubes on the table. How many fell on the floor?

Guided Practice

Draw a picture. Then write an addition or a subtraction equation.

1. Maria sees 3 blue birds. Then she sees some red birds. Maria sees 9 birds in all. How many red birds did Maria see?

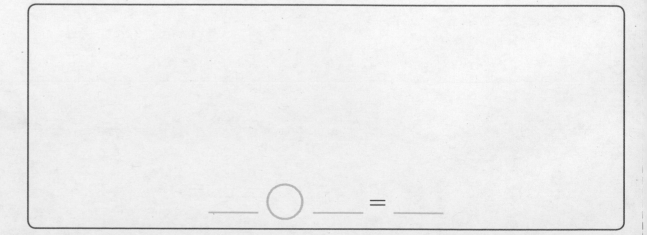

$$\underline{\quad} \underline{\quad} \bigcirc \underline{\quad} = \underline{\quad}$$

© Pearson Education, Inc. 1

Name _____

Independent Practice ☆ Draw a picture. Then write an addition or a subtraction equation.

2. Jamal picks 9 berries. Then Ed picks more berries. Jamal and Ed pick 12 berries in all. How many berries did Ed pick?

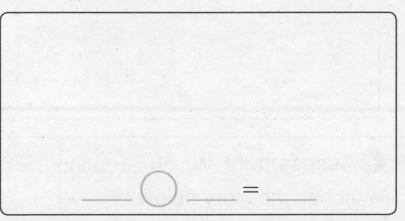

____ ◯ ____ = ____

3. There are 8 flowers in Vicky's garden. She picks some flowers. Now there are 4 flowers in Vicky's garden. How many flowers did Vicky pick?

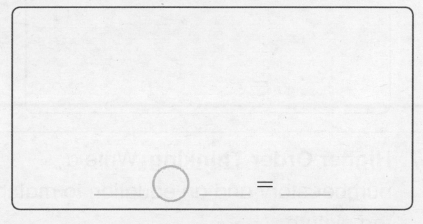

____ ◯ ____ = ____

4. **Higher Order Thinking** Write a number story to match the picture. Then write an equation.

_____

_____

_____

____ ____ = ____ ◯ ____

5. **Make Sense** Charlie draws 7 stars. Joey draws 4 stars. How many fewer stars did Joey draw than Charlie?

_____ = _____ ◯ _____

6. **Make Sense** Brian finds 3 rocks on Monday. He finds 7 rocks on Friday. How many more rocks did Brian find on Friday than on Monday?

_____ = _____ ◯ _____

7. **Higher Order Thinking** Write a number story and an equation to match the picture.

_____

_____

_____

_____

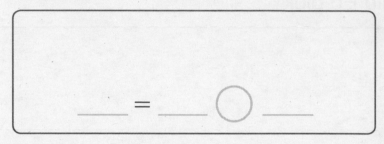

8. ✓**Assessment** Which equation matches the story below?

5 ducks are in a row.
More ducks join them.
Now there are 8 ducks.
How many ducks join them?

Ⓐ 5 − 3 = 2

Ⓑ 5 + 5 = 10

Ⓒ 6 − 3 = 3

Ⓓ 5 + 3 = 8

© Pearson Education, Inc. 1   **Topic 2** | Lesson 9

Name _____

Another Look! You can use pictures to solve a number story.

Linda has 4 buttons.
She buys some more.
Now Linda has 7 buttons.

How many buttons did Linda buy?

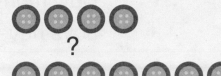

4 ⊕ 3 = 7

3 buttons

HOME ACTIVITY Tell your child a story that involves adding or subtracting. Say, "Draw a picture and write an equation for this story." Check to make sure the drawing and the equation match the story. Repeat with 1 or 2 different stories.

Draw a picture to solve. Then write an equation to match.

1. Abby has 6 apples. Judy has 9 apples.

How many more apples does Judy have?

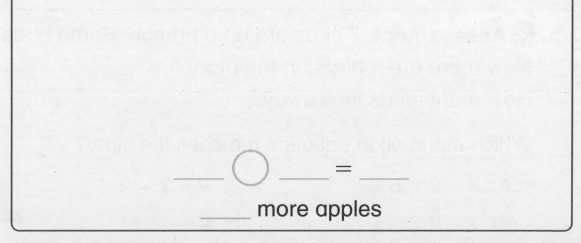

____ ◯ ____ = ____

____ more apples

2. Tim has 9 pears.

3 pears are yellow.

The rest are green.

How many pears are green?

____ ◯ ____ = ____

3. Ian has 5 red balloons.

Max has 6 blue balloons.

How many balloons do the

boys have in all?

____ ◯ ____ = ____

4. Higher Order Thinking Use the chart. Write a number story. Then write an addition or a subtraction equation to match your story.

Fruit	How Many?
Blueberries	
Raspberries	

____ ◯ ____ = ____

5. ✓**Assessment** 7 birds are on a branch. Some birds fly away.

Now there are 4 birds on the branch.

How many birds flew away?

Which subtraction equation matches the story?

Ⓐ 7 − 2 = 5   Ⓒ 9 − 7 = 2

Ⓑ 7 − 4 = 3   Ⓓ 4 − 3 = 1

Solve & Share

Use counters and the part-part-whole mat to show different ways to make 10. Write the different ways in the table.

Problem Solving

Lesson 2-10
Look For and Use Structure

I can ...
look for patterns and use structure to solve problems.

I can also make 10 in different ways.

10

Thinking Habits

Is there a pattern?

How can I describe the pattern?

$10 = \boxed{} + \boxed{}$

$10 = \boxed{} + \boxed{}$

$10 = \boxed{} + \boxed{}$

$10 = \boxed{} + \boxed{}$

The bears and lions want to cross the sea. Only 10 animals can fit on the boat. Show all the ways they can go on the boat.

How can I use structure to help me solve this problem?

Bears	Lions
0	10
1	9

I can look for patterns to help me find how many bears and how many lions.

There is a pattern in the table. The parts in each row add up to 10. As the number of bears increases, the number of lions decreases.

Bears	Lions
0	10
1	9
2	8
3	7
4	6
5	5
6	4
7	3
8	2
9	1
10	0

The table shows all the ways the bears and lions can go on the boat.

Do You Understand?

Show Me! What is a pattern in the table that shows how many bears and how many lions there are?

Guided Practice

Use a pattern to help you solve the problem.

1. Patty has 4 dog stickers and 4 cat stickers. She wants to put 6 stickers on a page of her book.

Use structure to show 3 different ways Patty can put stickers on the page.

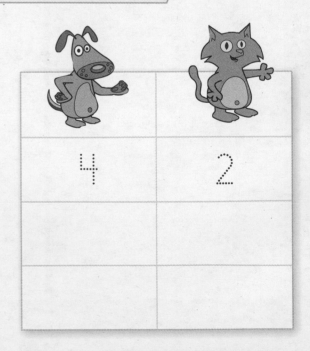

4	2

© Pearson Education, Inc. 1 **Topic 2 | Lesson 10**

Tools Assessment

Independent Practice ☆ Use a pattern to help you solve each problem.

2. Max has 5 markers. He can put the markers in his desk or in his bag.

Complete the table to show all the ways Max can put the markers away.

Desk	Bag
0	___
___	4
2	3
3	___
___	1
___	___

3. Mrs. Davis fills a box with prizes. She has 7 balls and 7 balloons. She wants to put 10 prizes in the box.

Complete the table to show all the ways Mrs. Davis can fill the box.

7	3
6	4
5	___
4	___
___	___

Use a pattern to help you solve the problem.

4. Higher Order Thinking Julie is planting 10 flowers. She can plant them by a tree or in a box. Use structure to help you find 3 different ways Julie can plant the flowers.

_____ by a tree and _____ in a box

_____ by a tree and _____ in a box

_____ by a tree and _____ in a box

Problem Solving

Pieces of Fruit

Ed eats 7 pieces of fruit. He can eat strawberries or grapes. Fill in a table to show how many different ways Ed can pick which fruit to eat.

Student A and Student B solved the number story. Each student's table is shown at the right.

5. **Model** Fill in the missing numbers in each table. Use cubes to help you.

Student A

🍓	🍇
0	
1	
2	
3	
4	
5	
6	
7	

Student B

🍓	🍇
	6
	1
	4
	3
	2
	5
	0
	7

6. **Look for Patterns** Describe a pattern used in each table.

_____

_____

_____

Help   Tools   Games

Another Look! Karen has 5 purple marbles and 4 yellow marbles. She can only fit 5 marbles in her pocket. What are the different ways she can put purple and yellow marbles in her pocket? Use a pattern to help you solve the problem. Then complete the table to show all the ways Karen can put the marbles in her pocket.

The sum of the numbers in each row is __5__.

5	0
4	1
3	2
2	3
1	4

HOME ACTIVITY Collect 5 each of two small objects, such as buttons and paperclips. Put 5 buttons in a row. Ask your child, "How many buttons? How many paperclips?" Then replace 1 button with a paperclip and ask the questions again. Continue replacing buttons with paperclips one at a time, asking the questions after each turn. Then ask, "What is the total each time?"

Use structure to find patterns to help you solve the problems below.

1. Tom has 5 toy cars. He can put them away in his toy box or on a shelf. Complete the table to show all the ways Tom can put away his toy cars.

Box	Shelf
5	___
___	1
2	___
___	4
___	___

2. Kathy has 5 tulips and 5 roses. She wants to plant 5 flowers in her garden. Complete the table to show all the ways Kathy can plant the flowers in her garden.

0	___
___	3
3	___
___	1
5	___

Making a Fruit Bowl

Bill has 5 apples and 5 bananas.
He can only put 5 pieces of fruit in
a bowl. How can Bill make a table
to show the different ways he can
put fruit in the bowl?

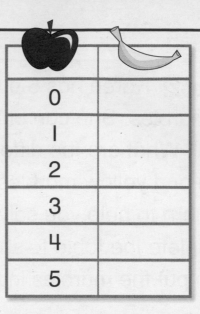

🍎	🍌
0	
1	
2	
3	
4	
5	

3. **Generalize** What will be the same in each row of the table?

_____

_____

4. **Reasoning** Will the number of bananas get smaller or larger as you move down the table? How do you know?

_____

_____

_____

5. **Look for Patterns** Write the missing numbers in the table. How do you know your answers are correct?

_____

_____

_____

_____

_____

_____

_____

© Pearson Education, Inc. 1

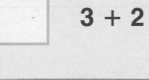

Find a partner. Point to a clue. Read the clue.

Look below the clues to find a match. Write the clue letter in the box next to the match.

Find a match for every clue.

I can ...
add and subtract within 10.

Clues

A 3 + 1

B 8 + 2

C 4 + 3

D 2 + 3

E 1 + 2

F 5 − 3

G 9 − 1

H 5 + 4

| ☐ 3 + 2 | ☐ 2 + 8 | ☐ 2 + 1 | ☐ 4 + 5 |
| ☐ 3 + 4 | ☐ 4 − 2 | ☐ 1 + 3 | ☐ 8 − 0 |

TOPIC 2 — Vocabulary Review

Word List
- doubles fact
- fewer
- more
- near doubles fact
- number line

Understand Vocabulary

1. Circle the addition equation that is shown on the number line.

   $1 + 1 = 2$ $2 + 1 = 3$ $2 + 4 = 6$ $3 + 3 = 6$

2. Cross out the parts that do **NOT** show doubles facts.

   $3 + 7$

   $2 + 2$

   $1 + 2$

3. Circle the near doubles facts.

   $4 + 5$

   $2 + 7$

   $3 + 6$

4. Circle the word that completes the sentence. Sam has 6 pens and Bev has 4 pens. Bev has 2 _____ pens than Sam.

   more   red   fewer

Use Vocabulary in Writing

5. Write and solve a story problem. Use at least one term from the Word List.

Answers for Find a Match *on page 139*

C	F	A	G
D	B	E	H

© Pearson Education, Inc. 1

Name _____

Set A _____

There are 8 peppers in the pot. You can add I more by counting I more.

I more than 8 is 9.

8 + 1 = 9

Add I, 2, or 0 to find the sum. Write the addition fact.

1.

____ + ____ = ____

2.

____ + ____ = ____

Set B _____

You can use doubles facts to add.

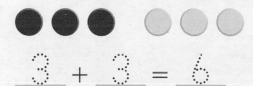

2 + 2 = 4

3 + 3 = 6

Both addends are the same. They are doubles.

Write an addition equation for each doubles fact.

3.

____ + ____ = ____

4.

How many coins are there in all?

____ + ____ = ____

Topic 2 | Reteaching

one hundred forty-one 141

You can use doubles facts to add near doubles.

$2 + 2$

2 + 2 and
1 more

$2 + 2 = 4$ $2 + 3 = 5$

Find each sum.

5.

___ + ___ = ___

___ + ___ = ___

You can use a ten-frame to learn facts with 5.

Look at the addition equation.
Draw counters in the frame.

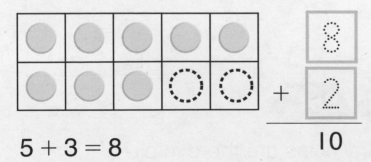

$5 + 3 = 8$

$\begin{array}{r} 8 \\ +\ 2 \\ \hline 10 \end{array}$

Draw counters and complete the addition problems.

6.

$5 + 1 = $ ___

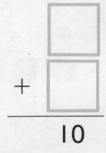

$\begin{array}{r} \square \\ +\ \square \\ \hline 10 \end{array}$

Name _____

Set E

Find the sum.

$$2 + 5 = \underline{7}$$
sum

Write the sum. Then change the order of the addends and write a new addition equation.

You can change the order of the addends.

Write the new addition equation.

$$\underline{5} + \underline{2} = \underline{7}$$
sum

The sum is the same.

7. $1 + 4 =$ _____

_____ + _____ = _____

8. $6 + 3 =$ _____

_____ + _____ = _____

When you change the order of the addends, the sum is the same.

Set F

You can subtract by counting back.

2 less than 9 is $\underline{7}$.

Write the subtraction fact.

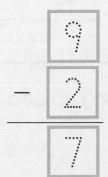

$$\begin{array}{r} 9 \\ -\ 2 \\ \hline 7 \end{array}$$

Count back to find the difference. Write the subtraction fact.

9.

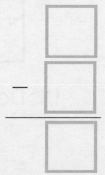

1 less than 4 is ____.

10.

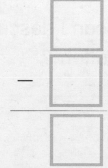

0 less than 6 is ____.

You can think addition to help you subtract.

| Think addition to help you subtract. |

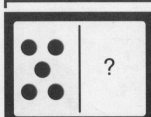

The missing part is 3.

$5 + \underline{3} = 8$

So, $8 - 5 = \underline{3}$.

11.

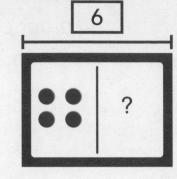

6

$4 + \underline{} = 6$

So, $6 - 4 = \underline{}$.

12.

7

$6 + \underline{} = 7$

So, $7 - 6 = \underline{}$.

Thinking Habits

Look For and Use Structure

Is there a pattern?

How can I describe the pattern?

Dani's family can foster 3 animals. She made a list of the number of cats and dogs they can foster.

13. Complete the table below.

Dogs	0	1	2	3
Cats				

14. Describe a pattern you see in the table.

_____

_____

Name _____

1. Molly has 5 toy cars. She got 2 more as a gift. How many toy cars does Molly have now?

Ⓐ 5

Ⓑ 6

Ⓒ 7

Ⓓ 8

2. Brad has 5 books. His mother gives him 4 more. How many books does Brad have in all?

Ⓐ 1

Ⓑ 4

Ⓒ 5

Ⓓ 9

3. Sammy earns 4 stars in gym class. He earns 3 stars in music class. How many stars did Sammy earn in all? How can you count on to find the answer?

_____ stars

4. Count back to find the difference. Show your work.

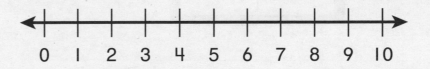

$8 - 2 =$ _____

5. Write the doubles fact that will help you find $3 + 4$. Find the missing number.

___ + ___ = ___

$3 + 4 =$ ___

6. Yuri is thinking of a number. His number is 0 less than 9. Use the subtraction equation to find his number.

$9 - 0 =$ ___

7. Find the missing part.

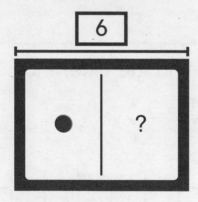

$1 +$ ___ $= 6$

$6 - 1 =$ ___

8. Which addition equation matches the picture? Choose all that apply.

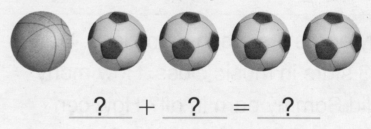

___ ? ___ $+$ ___ ? ___ $=$ ___ ? ___

☐ $1 + 4 = 5$

☐ $2 + 2 = 4$

☐ $3 + 1 = 4$

☐ $4 + 1 = 5$

© Pearson Education, Inc. 1

9. Which addition equations help you solve $9 - 3$? Choose all that apply.

☐ $6 + 3 = 9$

☐ $9 + 3 = 12$

☐ $3 + 6 = 9$

☐ $9 + 1 = 10$

10. Find $5 + 4$. Use the number line to count on.

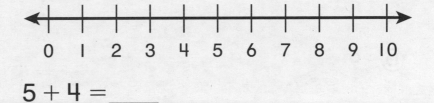

$5 + 4 =$ _____

11. Paul has 5 grapes. His friend gives him 3 more. How many grapes does Paul have in all?

Ⓐ 8

Ⓑ 9

Ⓒ 10

Ⓓ 11

12. 3 frogs sit on a rock. 3 more join them. How many frogs in all? Draw a picture and write an equation.

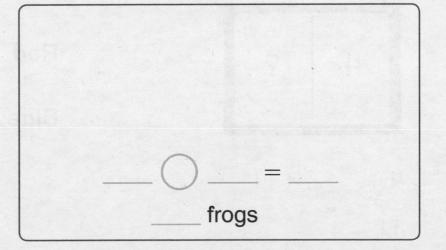

_____ ◯ _____ = _____

_____ frogs

13. Add the doubles.
Find the missing number.

$4 + 4 = \underline{\quad?\quad}$

Ⓐ 6

Ⓑ 7

Ⓒ 8

Ⓓ 9

14. Erin is thinking of a number. Her number is 5 less than 10. What doubles fact could Erin use to solve the problem?

$10 - 5 = \underline{\quad?\quad}$

$\underline{\quad} + \underline{\quad} = \underline{\quad}$

15. Think addition to help you subtract. Find the missing part. Write the numbers.

$4 + \underline{\quad} = 11$

$11 - 4 = \underline{\quad}$

16. Tina wants to buy 6 beads. She can buy red or blue beads. Show the different ways she can buy beads. Write the numbers in the table.

Red	●			2	3		5	
Blue	●	6	5					0

Name _____

Favorite Fruits

The first-grade students at Park School took a survey of their favorite fruits. They made this chart.

Our Favorite Fruits	
Fruit	**Number of Votes**
Apple	5
Orange	4
Banana	6
Strawberry	2
Blueberry	3
Cherry	3
Peach	4
Grape	1

1. How many fewer students voted for **Strawberry** than **Apple**? Draw a picture and write an equation to solve.

2. Laura says that she can use near doubles to find the total number of votes for **Banana** and **Strawberry**. Do you agree?

Circle **Yes** or **No**.

Show your work to explain.

3. 2 girls voted for **Orange**. Some boys voted for **Orange**.
How many boys voted for **Orange**?

Draw a picture to solve. Then write an addition or a subtraction equation.

Write how many boys voted for **Orange**.

_____

4. Fewer girls voted for **Banana** than boys. Complete the chart. Show the different ways boys and girls could have voted.

Girls	Boys

5. Gina says that **Blueberry** and **Orange** have the same total number of votes as **Cherry** and **Peach**. Is she correct? Explain how you know.

© Pearson Education, Inc. I

Addition Facts to 20: Use Strategies

Essential Question: What strategies can you use for adding to 20?

Some animals have special teeth to eat plants.

Some animals have special teeth to eat meat.

Wow! Let's do this project and learn more.

Digital Resources

Solve Learn Glossary

Tools Assessment Help Games

Math and Science Project: What Do They Eat?

Find Out Talk to friends and relatives about the things different animals eat. Ask how their teeth help them survive and meet their needs.

Journal: Make a Book Show what you found out. In your book, also:

- Draw pictures of animals and what they eat.

- Make up and solve addition problems about animals and what they eat.

Name _____

Review What You Know

A-Z Vocabulary

1. Circle the problem that shows a **double**.

   $$5 + 5 = 10$$

   $$5 + 6 = 11$$

   $$5 + 7 = 12$$

2. Circle the word that tells which strategy can be used to add the numbers.

   $$7 + 8 = ?$$

   doubles

   near doubles

   count back

3. Circle the **sum** in the problem below.

   $$7 + 4 = 11$$

Addition and Subtraction

4. Robin has 9 stamps. Joe gives her 4 stamps. How many stamps does Robin have now?

   _____ stamps

5. Jen has 18 treats for her cat. She feeds some treats to her cat. Jen has 9 treats left. How many treats did Jen give her cat?

   _____ treats

Doubles Facts

6. Solve this doubles fact.

   $$7 + 7 = \underline{\quad}$$

My Word Cards

Study the words on the front of the card.
Complete the activity on the back.

A-Z
Glossary

open number line

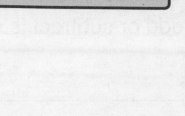

doubles-plus-1 fact

the addends are 1 apart

 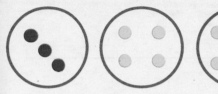

$$3 + 4 = 7$$

addends

doubles-plus-2 fact

the addends are 2 apart

$$3 + 5 = 8$$

addends

My Word Cards

Use what you know to complete the sentences.
Extend learning by writing your own sentence using each word.

When adding numbers that are 2 apart, you can use a

_____

_____.

When adding numbers that are 1 apart, you can use a

_____

_____.

One tool you can use to add or subtract is an

_____

_____.

Name _____

Solve & Share

Abby has 5 cubes.
Salina gives her 7 more cubes.
How many cubes does Abby have now?
Show your thinking on the number line below.

I can ...
count on to add using a number line.

I can also model with math.

⟵ | | | | | | | | | | | | | | | | | | | | | ⟶
0 1 2 3 4 5 6 7 8 9 10 11 12 13 14 15 16 17 18 19 20

_____ cubes

Solve **7 + 8 = ?** using a number line.

This number line has numbers from 0 to 20.

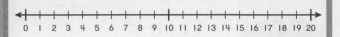

Find 7 on the number line. Then count on 8 more to add 7 + 8.

Start at 7 and make 8 jumps. You land on 15.

So, 7 + 8 = 15.

If you start at 8 and make 7 jumps, you land on the same number.

So, 8 + 7 = 15 too!

Do You Understand?

Show Me! How do you know where to start counting on? How do you know how many to count on?

☆ **Guided Practice** ☆ Use the number line to count on and find each sum.

1. 9 + 7 = __16__

2. 9 + 9 = ____

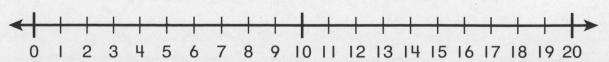

© Pearson Education, Inc. 1

Topic 3 | Lesson 1

Name _____

Independent Practice   Use a number line to count on and find each sum.

3. $7 + 4 = $ _____

4. $6 + 8 = $ _____

5. $9 + 4 = $ _____

6. $9 + 6 = $ _____

7. $7 + 7 = $ _____

8. $9 + 8 = $ _____

9. $6 + 4 = $ _____

10. $8 + 5 = $ _____

11. $3 + 9 = $ _____

Use a number line to count on to solve.

12. **Math and Science** Kim works at a zoo. She feeds
the big cats 9 pounds of meat. She feeds the tortoises
7 pounds of leaves and berries.

How many pounds of food does Kim feed the animals?

_____ pounds of food

13. **Reasoning** Scott walks 6 blocks. Then he walks 3 more blocks. Write the numbers that will help find out how many blocks Scott walked in all.

$6 + 3 =$ ____

Start at ____ .   Count on ____ more.

14. **Reasoning** Ramona mails 7 letters. Then she mails 8 more letters. Write the numbers that will help find out how many letters Ramona mailed in all.

$7 + 8 =$ ____

Start at ____ .   Count on ____ more.

15. **Higher Order Thinking** Write and solve a story problem. Show your work on a number line.

_____

_____

_____   ____ + ____ = ____

16. ✓**Assessment** Solve $5 + 9 = ?$ on the number line. Show your work.

0 1 2 3 4 5 6 7 8 9 10 11 12 13 14 15 16 17 18 19 20

Name _____

Another Look! There is more than one way to count on to add $2 + 8$.

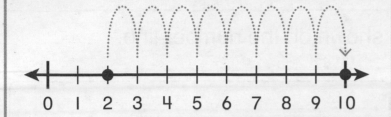

0 1 2 3 4 5 6 7 8 9 10

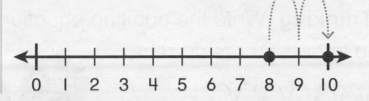

0 1 2 3 4 5 6 7 8 9 10

Start at 2, then take 8 jumps.

Start at 8, then take 2 jumps.

If you start at 8 instead of 2, you don't have to count on as many. Remember, you get the same answer both ways.

$2 + 8 = \underline{10}$

HOME ACTIVITY Draw a number line and label it from 0–20. Give your child an addition fact, such as $5 + 9$. Have your child use the number line to show counting on to add 5 and 9. Ask, "Can you show me more than one way to add these numbers ($5 + 9$ and $9 + 5$)?" Repeat with other addition facts.

Use a number line to count on and find each sum.

1. $9 + 4 = \underline{\quad}$

2. $4 + 8 = \underline{\quad}$

3. $9 + 7 = \underline{\quad}$

Use a number line to count on and find each sum.

4. $9 + 6 = $ ____

5. $7 + 4 = $ ____

6. $8 + 5 = $ ____

---

7. Higher Order Thinking Write the addition equation shown on the number line. Explain how you know you are correct.

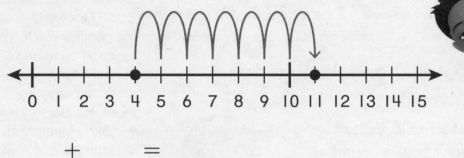

0 1 2 3 4 5 6 7 8 9 10 11 12 13 14 15

____ + ____ = ____

---

8. ✓**Assessment** Daryl showed an equation on the number line below. Which of the following could be Daryl's equation?

0 1 2 3 4 5 6 7 8 9 10 11 12 13 14 15 16 17 18 19 20

Ⓐ $9 + 9 = 18$ Ⓑ $7 + 10 = 17$ Ⓒ $9 + 8 = 17$ Ⓓ $10 + 7 = 17$

© Pearson Education, Inc. 1

Solve

Solve & Share

Arnie runs 8 miles on Thursday. He runs 9 more miles on Friday. How many miles did Arnie run in all? Use the number line to show how you know.

I can ...
count on to add using an open number line.

I can also make math arguments.

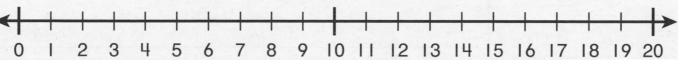

_____ miles

An **open number line** can help you add.

$$7 + 6 = ?$$

7

Start by placing the 7 on the number line.

Counting on by 1s is one way to add 6 more. Start at 7. Then count on 6 more.

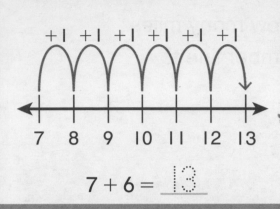

+1 +1 +1 +1 +1 +1

7 8 9 10 11 12 13

$$7 + 6 = \underline{13}$$

You can also break apart the 6. Adding 3 and 3 is one way to add 6 more.

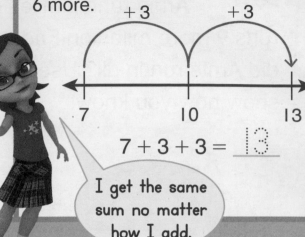

+3   +3

7   10   13

$$7 + 3 + 3 = \underline{13}$$

I get the same sum no matter how I add.

Do You Understand?

Show Me! What number is always included on an open number line?

☆ **Guided Practice** ☆ Use the open number line to solve the problems. Show your work.

1. $7 + 5 = \underline{12}$

+3   +2

7   10   12

2. $6 + 2 = \underline{}$

© Pearson Education, Inc. 1

Name _____

Tools Assessment

3. 4 + 7 = _____

4. 8 + 8 = _____

5. 6 + 6 = _____

6. 9 + 7 = _____

7. A-Z **Vocabulary** Solve the problem. Show your work on the **open number line** below.

8 + 6 = _____

Think about what numbers to include on your number line.

8. **Use Tools** Marco rides his bike 7 miles. Then he rides 9 more miles. How many miles did Marco ride in all?

____ + ____ = ____

____ miles

9. **Use Tools** Ana reads 10 books in January. She reads 10 books in February. How many books did Ana read in all?

____ + ____ = ____

____ books

10. **Higher Order Thinking** Kate has 8 roses. She picks some more roses. Now Kate has 17 roses. How many roses did Kate pick? Use words or pictures to explain how you know.

11. ✅**Assessment** Solve the equation. Show your work on the open number line below.

$9 + 6 =$ ____

⟷

Name _____

Another Look! You can count on to solve addition problems using an open number line.

8 + 9 = ?

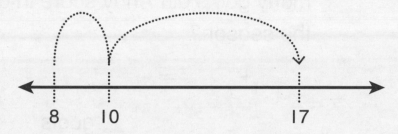

8   10   17

Start at __8__ and count on __9__ more.

8 + 9 = _17_

HOME ACTIVITY Draw an open number line. Give your child an addition fact, such as 6 + 8. Ask, "Which number can you put at the beginning of the number line?" Have him or her show 2 different ways to add 8 to 6. Repeat with different addition facts.

Use the open number line to solve the problems. Show your work.

1. 8 + 4 = ____

2. 8 + 7 = ____

← ─────────────→   ← ─────────────→

3. Laura reads 8 pages on Monday. She reads 6 pages on Tuesday. How many pages did Laura read in all?

_____ + _____ = _____

_____ pages

How many pages did Laura read on both Monday and Tuesday?

4. Andy scores 6 goals in the first half of his soccer season. He scores 7 goals in the second half of the season. How many goals did Andy score in all during the season?

_____ + _____ = _____

_____ goals

5. **Higher Order Thinking** Sam has 9 stamps in his collection. He gets some more. Now he has 18 stamps. How many more stamps did Sam get? Use words or pictures to show how you know.

6. ✅**Assessment** Solve the equation. Show your work on the open number line below.

$5 + 7 =$ _____

<————————————————————>

© Pearson Education, Inc. I

Name _____

Solve & Share

Carlos and Alisa each have 6 books. If they put their books together, how many books will they have in all? Show your thinking below.

I can ...
memorize doubles facts.

I can also model with math.

_____ + _____ = _____

Let's look at some doubles facts that you may know.

$3 + 3 = 6$

$5 + 5 = 10$

Here are ways we can show these facts.

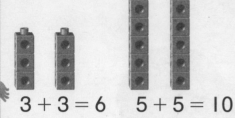

$3 + 3 = 6$ $5 + 5 = 10$

You can represent the doubles fact $6 + 6$ the same way.

$6 + 6 = 12$

This isn't a doubles fact.

$6 + 5 = 11$

Do You Understand?

Show Me! Becca shows $6 + 7$ with cubes and says it is not a doubles fact. Is she correct? How do you know?

☆ **Guided Practice** ☆ Decide if each set of cubes shows a doubles fact. Circle your answer. Then write an equation to match the cubes.

1.

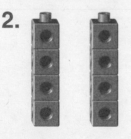

Doubles Fact   **NOT** Doubles Fact

$5 + 6 = 11$

2.

Doubles Fact   **NOT** Doubles Fact

___ + ___ = ___

© Pearson Education, Inc. 1

Topic 3 | Lesson 3

Tools Assessment

Independent Practice Decide if each set of cubes shows a doubles fact. Circle your answer. Then write an equation to match the cubes.

3.

Doubles Fact   **NOT** Doubles Fact   ____ + ____ = ____

4.

Doubles Fact   **NOT** Doubles Fact   ____ + ____ = ____

5.

Doubles Fact   **NOT** Doubles Fact   ____ + ____ = ____

6.

Doubles Fact   **NOT** Doubles Fact   ____ + ____ = ____

 Complete each doubles fact.

7. $0 + 0 =$ ☐   **8.** ☐ $= 9 + 9$ **9.** $8 + 8 =$ ☐   **10.** $5 + 5 =$ ☐

11. Make Sense Andrew and his sister each pick 10 flowers. How many flowers did they pick in all?

Write an equation to match the problem.

____ + ____ = ____

____ flowers

12. Make Sense Pearl and Charlie each get 5 books for their birthday. How many books did they get in all?

Write an equation to match the problem.

____ + ____ = ____

____ books

13. Higher Order Thinking Max plays in 2 hockey games. He scores the same number of goals in each game. He scores 8 goals in all. How many goals did Max score in each game? Show your work below. Then write the equation you used to solve the problem.

____ = ____ + ____

14. ✓**Assessment** Carrie takes the same number of pictures on both Saturday and Sunday. Which equations show the number of pictures Carrie could have taken? Choose all that apply.

☐ $7 + 7 = 14$

☐ $8 + 6 = 14$

☐ $8 + 8 = 16$

☐ $9 + 7 = 16$

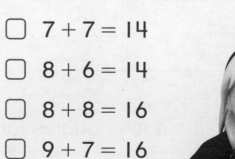

Use cubes to help if you need to!

© Pearson Education, Inc. 1

Name _____

Help Tools Games

Another Look! Some facts are doubles facts. Some facts are not.

This is not a doubles fact.

This is a doubles fact.

The addends are not the same.

HOME ACTIVITY Divide a strip of paper into 6–10 parts so that it looks like a cube tower. Ask your child to count the parts. Then cut the strip in half vertically so you have 2 strips each with 6–10 parts. Ask your child how many are in each tower. Have him or her tell you the doubles fact that is represented. Repeat with other numbers (1–10).

In a doubles fact, both addends are the same.

$3 + 2 =$ __5__

$2 + 2 =$ __4__

Decide if each set of cubes shows a doubles fact. Circle your answer. Then write an equation to match the cubes.

1.

Doubles Fact

NOT Doubles Fact

___ + ___ = ___

2.

Doubles Fact

NOT Doubles Fact

___ + ___ = ___

Solve each fact. Circle the doubles. Use cubes if you need to.

3.

_____ $= 8 + 5$

4.

$5 + 5 =$ _____

5.

$9 + 5 =$ _____

6.

$10 + 10 =$ _____

7.

_____ $= 7 + 6$

8.

_____ $= 9 + 9$

9.

$8 + 8 =$ _____

10.

_____ $= 3 + 4$

11.

$7 + 7 =$ _____

12. Higher Order Thinking Simone built the same number of model cars and model airplanes. Show how Simone could have built 14 models. Explain how you know.

13. ✔Assessment Mike picks the same number of red apples and green apples. How many apples could Mike have picked? Choose all that apply.

☐ 19

☐ 18

☐ 17

☐ 16

© Pearson Education, Inc. 1

Name _____

Solve & Share

Carlos and I each pick 5 strawberries. What doubles fact shows how many strawberries we have in all?

If I pick 1 more strawberry, how could you find how many strawberries there are in all?

I can ...
use doubles facts to help solve doubles-plus-1 facts.

I can also make sense of problems.

____ + ____ = ____   ____ + ____ = ____

Double

You can use doubles to find **doubles-plus-1 facts**.

$$6$$
$$+7$$
$$?$$

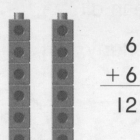

Doubles-plus-1 facts are also called near doubles.

You already know 6 + 6.

$$6$$
$$+6$$
$$12$$

6 + 7 is 6 + 6 and 1 more.

$$6$$
$$+6$$
$$12$$
and 1 more

$$6$$
$$+7$$
$$13$$

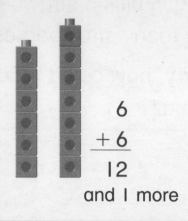

12 and 1 more is 13.

Do You Understand?

Show Me! How does knowing 7 + 7 help you find 7 + 8?

☆ **Guided Practice** ☆ Add the doubles. Then use the doubles facts to help you solve the doubles-plus-1 facts.

1.

$$\underline{5} + \underline{5} = \underline{10}$$

So, 5 + 6 = $\underline{11}$.

2.

$$\underline{} + \underline{} = \underline{}$$

So, 8 + 9 = $\underline{}$.

Tools Assessment

Independent Practice Add the doubles. Then use the doubles facts to help you solve the doubles-plus-1 facts.

3. $\begin{array}{r} 7 \\ +7 \\ \hline \square \end{array}$ $\begin{array}{r} 8 \\ +7 \\ \hline \square \end{array}$

4. $\begin{array}{r} 4 \\ +4 \\ \hline \square \end{array}$ $\begin{array}{r} 4 \\ +5 \\ \hline \square \end{array}$

5. $\begin{array}{r} 5 \\ +5 \\ \hline \square \end{array}$ $\begin{array}{r} 5 \\ +6 \\ \hline \square \end{array}$

6. $\begin{array}{r} 9 \\ +9 \\ \hline \square \end{array}$ $\begin{array}{r} 9 \\ +10 \\ \hline \square \end{array}$

7. $\begin{array}{r} 6 \\ +6 \\ \hline \square \end{array}$ $\begin{array}{r} 6 \\ +7 \\ \hline \square \end{array}$

8. $\begin{array}{r} 3 \\ +3 \\ \hline \square \end{array}$ $\begin{array}{r} 3 \\ +4 \\ \hline \square \end{array}$

 Use a doubles-plus-1 fact to help you write an equation for the problem. Then draw a picture to show your work.

9. **Higher Order Thinking** Max has some blue marbles. Tom has some red marbles. Tom has 1 more marble than Max. How many marbles do they have in all?

_____ + _____ = _____

10. Reasoning Carrie and Pete each pick 7 cherries. Then Pete picks 1 more. How many cherries do they have in all?

Write an equation to match the problem.

_____ + _____ = _____

_____ cherries

11. Reasoning Manny and Pam each buy 5 apples. Then Pam buys 1 more. How many apples do they have in all?

Write an equation to match the problem.

_____ + _____ = _____

_____ apples

12. Higher Order Thinking Laura has to solve $9 + 8$. Explain how she could use $8 + 8$ to find the sum.

_____

_____

_____

_____

13. ✓**Assessment** Juan eats 8 grapes after lunch. Then he eats some more grapes after dinner. He ate 17 grapes in all. How many grapes did Juan eat after dinner?

Ⓐ 8

Ⓑ 9

Ⓒ 7

Ⓓ 1

You can use doubles and a doubles-plus-1 fact to help you solve the problem.

Name _____

Another Look! You can use doubles facts to solve doubles-plus-1 facts.

$4 + 5 = ?$

$5 = 4 + 1$, so you can write

$4 + 5$ as $4 + 4 + 1$.

| 4 | + | 4 | | + | 1 |

$4 + 4 = 8$

8 and 1 more is 9. So, $4 + 5 = 9$.

$2 + 3 = ?$

$3 = \underline{2} + \underline{1}$

| 2 | + | 2 | | + | 1 |

$\underline{2} + \underline{2} = \underline{4}$

So, $\underline{2} + \underline{3} = \underline{5}$.

HOME ACTIVITY Give your child a doubles fact, such as $3 + 3$. Have your child use objects to show the doubles fact, such as two groups of 3 buttons. Ask, "How many in all?" Then add 1 more object to one of the groups. Ask, "What is the doubles-plus-1 fact? How many in all now?" Repeat with other doubles facts.

 Add the doubles. Then use the doubles facts to help you solve the doubles-plus-1 facts.

1.
$\begin{array}{r} 3 \\ + 3 \\ \hline \square \end{array}$

$\begin{array}{r} 3 \\ + 4 \\ \hline \square \end{array}$

2.
$\begin{array}{r} 6 \\ + 6 \\ \hline \square \end{array}$

$\begin{array}{r} 6 \\ + 7 \\ \hline \square \end{array}$

Draw I more cube. Use a doubles fact to help you add.

3.

Think: _____ + _____ = _____.

So, 7 + 8 = _____.

4.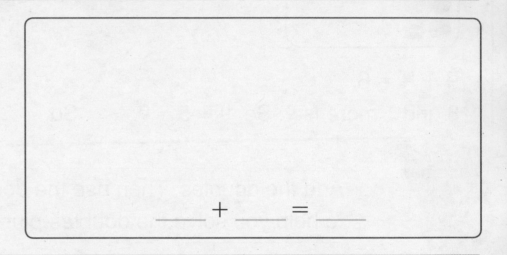

Think: _____ + _____ = _____.

So, 9 + 10 = _____.

5. **Higher Order Thinking** Use a doubles-plus-I fact to help you write an equation for the problem. Then draw a picture to show your work.

Dan saw some cats and dogs.
He saw I more dog than cat.
How many dogs and cats did Dan see?

_____ + _____ = _____

6. ✓**Assessment** Which doubles-plus-I fact should you use to solve 9 + 8?

 Ⓐ 7 + 7 and I more

 Ⓑ 8 + 8 and I more

 Ⓒ 6 + 6 and I more

 Ⓓ 9 + 9 and I more

7. ✓**Assessment** Which doubles-plus-I fact should you use to solve 5 + 6?

 Ⓐ 6 + 6 and I more

 Ⓑ 4 + 5 and I more

 Ⓒ 5 + 5 and I more

 Ⓓ 4 + 4 and I more

© Pearson Education, Inc. I

Solve

Solve & Share

Carlos and I each find 5 seashells. What doubles fact shows how many seashells we have in all?

If Carlos finds 2 more seashells, how could you find how many seashells there are in all?

I can ...
use doubles facts to help solve doubles-plus-2 facts.

I can also reason about math.

____ + ____ = ____

Double

____ + ____ = ____

These are called **doubles-plus-2 facts**.

$$6 \qquad 9$$
$$\underline{+8} \qquad \underline{+7}$$
$$? \qquad ?$$

Doubles-plus-2 facts are also called near doubles.

There are different ways to solve a doubles-plus-2 fact.

$$6$$
$$\underline{+8}$$
$$?$$

Double the lesser number. Then add 2.

Think $6 + 6 = 12$ and 2 more.

Double 6 is 12. 2 more than 12 is 14.

$$6 + 8 = 14$$

Or, double the number between.

7 is between 6 and 8. Double 7 is 14.

Do You Understand?

Show Me! Which doubles facts can help you solve $7 + 9$? Explain.

☆ **Guided Practice**   Use the doubles fact to help you add.

1.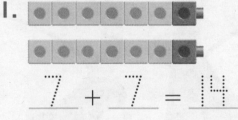

$$\underline{7} + \underline{7} = \underline{14}$$

So, $6 + 8 = \underline{14}$.

2.

$$\underline{} + \underline{} = \underline{}$$

So, $5 + 7 = \underline{}$.

3.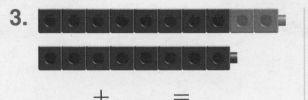

$$\underline{} + \underline{} = \underline{}$$

So, $10 + 8 = \underline{}$.

4.

$$\underline{} + \underline{} = \underline{}$$

So, $7 + 9 = \underline{}$.

Tools Assessment

Independent Practice Draw 2 more cubes. Use a doubles fact to help you add.

5.

___ + ___ = ___

So, 10 + 8 = ___.

6.

___ + ___ = ___

So, 9 + 11 = ___.

7.

___ + ___ = ___

So, 8 + 6 = ___.

8.

___ + ___ = ___

So, 7 + 5 = ___.

9.

___ + ___ = ___

So, 4 + 6 = ___.

10.

___ + ___ = ___

So, 3 + 5 = ___.

Use a doubles or a doubles-plus-2 fact to help you write an equation for the problem. Draw cubes to help you.

11. **Number Sense** Dan makes a red cube train. Kay makes a yellow cube train. Kay's train has 2 more cubes than Dan's train. How many cubes do they have in all?

___ = ___ + ___

12. Reasoning Kelly and Eric each make 6 sand castles. Then Kelly makes 2 more. How many sand castles did the two friends make in all?

Write an addition equation.

_____ + _____ = _____

_____ sand castles

13. Reasoning Mark finds 8 shells. Sue finds 2 more than Mark. Together, they find 18 shells. How many shells did Sue collect?

Write an addition equation.

_____ + _____ = _____

Sue collected _____ shells.

14. Higher Order Thinking Use a doubles-plus-2 fact to help you write an equation for the problem. Then solve.

There are some fish in a pond. Some fish are silver. Some fish are gold. There are 2 more gold fish than silver fish. How many fish are there in all?

_____ + _____ = _____

silver gold fish
fish fish

15. ✓**Assessment** Ben sees 7 crabs. Jamie sees 9 crabs. How many crabs did they see in all?

Which should you use to find how many crabs Ben and Jamie saw in all?

Ⓐ 7 + 7 and 1 more

Ⓑ 7 + 9 and 1 more

Ⓒ 7 + 7 and 2 more

Ⓓ 9 + 9 and 2 more

Name _____

 Help Tools Games

Another Look! You can use doubles facts to solve doubles-plus-2 facts.

$6 + 8 = ?$

$8 = 6 + 2$, so you can write
$6 + 8$ as $6 + 6 + 2$.

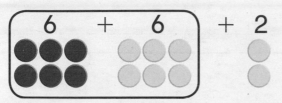

6 + 6

+ 2

$6 + 6 = 12$

12 and 2 more is 14. So, $6 + 8 = 14$.

$2 + 4 = ?$

$4 = \underline{2} + \underline{2}$

2 + 2 + 2

$\underline{2} + \underline{2} = \underline{4}$

So, $\underline{2} + \underline{4} = \underline{6}$.

HOME ACTIVITY Give your child a doubles fact, such as $4 + 4$. Have your child use objects to show the doubles fact, such as two groups of 4 paper clips. Ask, "How many in all?" Then add 2 more paper clips to one of the groups. Ask, "What is the doubles-plus-2 fact? How many in all now?" Repeat with other doubles facts.

 Add the doubles. Then use the doubles to help you solve the doubles-plus-2 facts.

1. $\begin{array}{r} 3 \\ + 3 \\ \hline \square \end{array}$ $\begin{array}{r} 3 \\ + 5 \\ \hline \square \end{array}$

2. $\begin{array}{r} 4 \\ + 4 \\ \hline \square \end{array}$ $\begin{array}{r} 6 \\ + 4 \\ \hline \square \end{array}$

Draw 2 more cubes. Then use the doubles to help you solve the doubles-plus-2 facts.

3.

Think: ____ + ____ = ____.
So, 5 + 7 = ____.

4.

Think: ____ + ____ = ____.
So, 3 + 5 = ____.

5. Higher Order Thinking Use a doubles-plus-2 fact to help you write an equation for the problem. Then draw a picture to show your work.

Tanya and Kyle feed the same number of birds at the zoo. Then Kyle feeds 2 more birds. How many birds did they feed in all?

____ = ____ + ____

6. ✓**Assessment** Max's team scores 8 runs on Monday and 10 runs on Tuesday. How many runs did the team score in all?

Which doubles fact will help you solve the problem?

Ⓐ 7 + 7   Ⓒ 9 + 9

Ⓑ 6 + 6   Ⓓ 10 + 10

7. ✓**Assessment** Which should you use to solve 7 + 9?

Ⓐ 7 + 7 and 1 more

Ⓑ 7 + 7 and 2 more

Ⓒ 8 + 8 and 1 more

Ⓓ 8 + 8 and 2 more

© Pearson Education, Inc. 1

Solve & Share

How can thinking about 10 help you find the answer to the addition fact 9 + 5?

Show your work and explain.

Solve

Lesson 3-6
Make 10 to Add

I can ...
make 10 to add numbers to 20.

I can also make math arguments.

_____ + _____ = _____

Make 10 to help you add.

$$7 \\ +4 \\ \hline ?$$

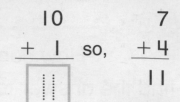

Move 3 counters from the 4 to the 7.

Now I have 10 and 1.

10 + 1 is the same as 7 + 4.

$$10 \\ +1 \\ \hline \boxed{11}$$

10 + 1 so, 7 + 4

$$10 \\ +1 \\ \hline \boxed{11}$$

$$7 \\ +4 \\ \hline 11$$

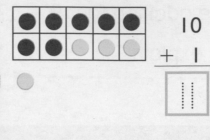

The sums are the same!

Do You Understand?

Show Me! How would you make 10 to find the sum of 9 + 4?

☆ Guided Practice ☆

Draw counters to make 10. Then write the sums.

1.
$$7 \\ +6 \\ \hline ?$$

$$10 \\ +3 \\ \hline \boxed{13}$$ so, $$7 \\ +6 \\ \hline \boxed{}$$

2.
$$8 \\ +6 \\ \hline ?$$

$$10 \\ +4 \\ \hline \boxed{}$$ so, $$8 \\ +6 \\ \hline \boxed{}$$

© Pearson Education, Inc. 1

Topic 3 | Lesson 6

Tools Assessment

Independent Practice   Draw counters to make 10. Then write the sums.

3. 7
     +8
     ?

10   7
+ 5   so, + 8
[ ]   [ ]

4. 9
     +6
     ?

10   9
+ 5   so, + 6
[ ]   [ ]

5. 7
     +7
     ?

10   7
+ 4   so, + 7
[ ]   [ ]

Draw counters to make 10. Use 2 different colors.
Then write the sums.

6. 4
     +8
     ?

10   4
+ 2   so, + 8
[ ]   [ ]

7. 6
     +5
     ?

10   6
+ 1   so, + 5
[ ]   [ ]

8. 5
     +9
     ?

10   5
+ 4   so, + 9
[ ]   [ ]

9. **Model** Carlos sees 7 yellow birds in a tree. Then he sees 6 white birds in a tree. How many birds does Carlos see in all?

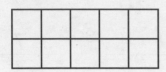

_____ birds

10. **Model** Emily picks 8 red flowers. Then she picks 8 yellow flowers. How many flowers does Emily pick in all?

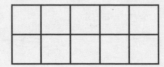

_____ flowers

11. **Higher Order Thinking** Look at the model. Complete the equations to match what the model shows.

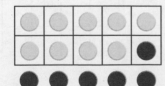

10 + _____ = _____

So, _____ + _____ = _____

12. ✓**Assessment** Which number belongs in the ⬜ ?

10 + 1 = 11

So, 6 + ⬜ = 11

| 16 | 11 | 6 | 5 |
| Ⓐ | Ⓑ | Ⓒ | Ⓓ |

Help   Tools   Games

Another Look! You can make 10 to help you add.

7 and 5 more.

$7 + 5 = ?$ Make 10.

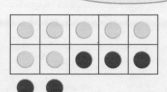
10 and 2 more.

So, $7 + 5$ and $10 + 2$ have the same sum.

$10 + 2 = \underline{12}$ so, $7 + 5 = \underline{12}$.

HOME ACTIVITY Have your child use small objects to show $7 + 6$. Tell your child to move some objects to make 10. Then have your child give the 2 equations: $10 + 3 = 13$ so, $7 + 6 = 13$.

Draw counters to make 10. Then write the sums.

1.   9
    +6
    ___
     ?

    10   9
   + 5 so, +6
   ___   ___
   [ ]   [ ]

2.   7
    +6
    ___
     ?

    10   7
   + 3 so, +6
   ___   ___
   [ ]   [ ]

3.   5
    +6
    ___
     ?

    10   5
   + 1 so, +6
   ___   ___
   [ ]   [ ]

Draw counters to make 10. Use 2 different colors. Then write the sums.

4.   9
        +5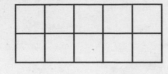
         ?

10   9
+ 4 so, + 5

5.   8
        +3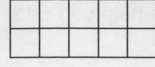
         ?

10   8
+ 1 so, + 3

6.   4
        +9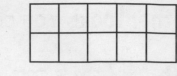
         ?

10   4
+ 3 so, + 9

---

7. Higher Order Thinking Circle 2 numbers.

 5   **6** **7** **8** **9**

Draw counters to make 10 using the numbers
circled. Use 2 different colors. Then write 2 addition
equations to match.

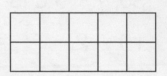

10 + _____ = _____.

So, _____ + _____ = _____.

© Pearson Education, Inc. 1

Name _____

Solve & Share

How can you make 10 to solve the addition fact 8 + 5? Show your work and explain.

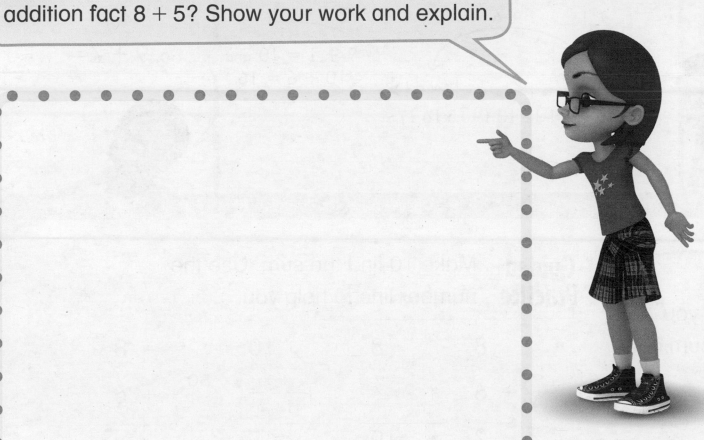

Make 10 to help you add.

$9 + 7 = ?$

9 is really close to 10. How can that help me find 9 + 7?

Think about the problem on a number line to help you make 10.

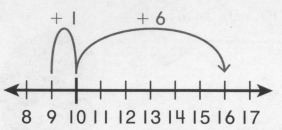

+1   +6

8 9 10 11 12 13 14 15 16 17

9 + 1 = 10 and 10 + 6 = 16.

You can think about $9 + 7$ as $9 + 1 + 6$, because $7 = 1 + 6$.

So, $9 + 7 = \underline{16}$

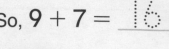

Do You Understand?

Show Me! How can you make 10 to find the sum of $7 + 6$?

☆ Guided Practice ☆

Make 10 find the sum. Use the number line to help you.

1.
$$\begin{array}{r} 8 \\ + 6 \\ \hline ? \end{array}$$
$$\begin{array}{r} 8 \\ + \boxed{2} \\ \hline 10 \end{array}$$
$$\begin{array}{r} 10 \\ + \boxed{4} \\ \hline \boxed{14} \end{array}$$
so,
$$\begin{array}{r} 8 \\ + 6 \\ \hline \boxed{} \end{array}$$

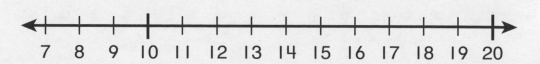

7 8 9 10 11 12 13 14 15 16 17 18 19 20

Topic 3 | Lesson 7

Independent Practice ☆ Make 10 to find the sum. Use a number line to help you.

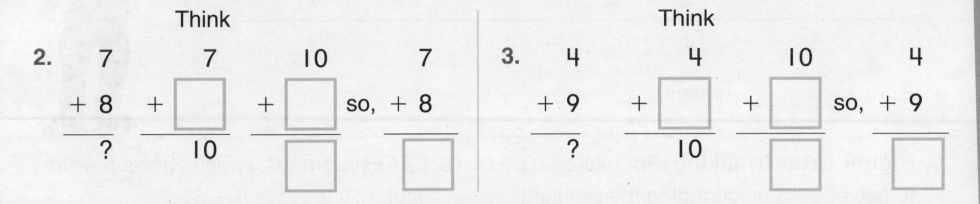

0 1 2 3 4 5 6 7 8 9 10 11 12 13 14 15 16 17 18 19 20

Think

2.
$$\begin{array}{c} 7 \\ + 8 \\ \hline ? \end{array}$$
$$\begin{array}{c} 7 \\ + \square \\ \hline 10 \end{array}$$
$$\begin{array}{c} 10 \\ + \square \\ \hline \square \end{array}$$
so,
$$\begin{array}{c} 7 \\ + 8 \\ \hline \square \end{array}$$

Think

3.
$$\begin{array}{c} 4 \\ + 9 \\ \hline ? \end{array}$$
$$\begin{array}{c} 4 \\ + \square \\ \hline 10 \end{array}$$
$$\begin{array}{c} 10 \\ + \square \\ \hline \square \end{array}$$
so,
$$\begin{array}{c} 4 \\ + 9 \\ \hline \square \end{array}$$

Think

4.
$$\begin{array}{c} 8 \\ + 4 \\ \hline ? \end{array}$$
$$+ \begin{array}{c} 10 \\ \square \\ \hline \square \end{array}$$
so,
$$\begin{array}{c} 8 \\ + 4 \\ \hline \square \end{array}$$

Think

5.
$$\begin{array}{c} 9 \\ + 7 \\ \hline ? \end{array}$$
$$+ \begin{array}{c} 10 \\ \square \\ \hline \square \end{array}$$
so,
$$\begin{array}{c} 9 \\ + 7 \\ \hline \square \end{array}$$

Think

6.
$$\begin{array}{c} 6 \\ + 7 \\ \hline ? \end{array}$$
$$+ \begin{array}{c} 10 \\ \square \\ \hline \square \end{array}$$
so,
$$\begin{array}{c} 6 \\ + 7 \\ \hline \square \end{array}$$

7. **Number Sense** Jon adds 8 + 5.
First, he adds 8 + 2 to make 10.
What should he do next?

_____

_____

8. **Look for Patterns** Conrad has 8 apples. Sam gives him 4 more. How many apples does Conrad have now? Use the open number line to show your work.

Can you break the problem into simpler parts?

⟵――――――――――――――――――――⟶

Conrad has ____ apples.

9. **Higher Order Thinking** Pat makes 10 to solve $7 + 5$ by changing the problem to $7 + 3 + 2$. How does Pat make 10?

_____

_____

_____

_____

10. ✅**Assessment** Which shows how to make 10 to solve $9 + 6$?

Ⓐ $9 + 4 + 2$

Ⓑ $9 + 3 + 3$

Ⓒ $9 + 1 + 5$

Ⓓ $9 + 0 + 6$

Name _____

Help   Tools   Games

Another Look! You know how to add 10 to a number. So making 10 to add can be a helpful addition strategy.

$3 + 9 = ?$

You can break apart either addend to help you make 10.

I broke apart the 3 into 1 and 2 to make 10.

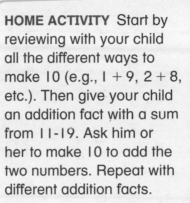

HOME ACTIVITY Start by reviewing with your child all the different ways to make 10 (e.g., 1 + 9, 2 + 8, etc.). Then give your child an addition fact with a sum from 11-19. Ask him or her to make 10 to add the two numbers. Repeat with different addition facts.

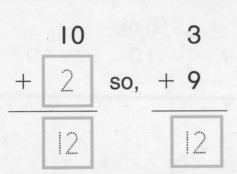

$$\begin{array}{c} 3 \\ + 9 \\ \hline ? \end{array} \qquad \begin{array}{c} 9 \\ + \boxed{1} \\ \hline 10 \end{array} \qquad \begin{array}{c} 10 \\ + \boxed{2} \\ \hline \boxed{12} \end{array} \quad \text{so,} \quad \begin{array}{c} 3 \\ + 9 \\ \hline \boxed{12} \end{array}$$

Fill in the missing numbers to solve each addition problem.

Think

1. $\begin{array}{c} 9 \\ + 8 \\ \hline ? \end{array} \qquad \begin{array}{c} 9 \\ + \boxed{} \\ \hline 10 \end{array} \qquad \begin{array}{c} 10 \\ + \boxed{} \\ \hline \boxed{} \end{array} \quad \text{so,} \quad \begin{array}{c} 9 \\ + 8 \\ \hline \boxed{} \end{array}$

Think

2. $\begin{array}{c} 2 \\ + 9 \\ \hline ? \end{array} \qquad \begin{array}{c} 9 \\ + \boxed{} \\ \hline 10 \end{array} \qquad \begin{array}{c} 10 \\ + \boxed{} \\ \hline \boxed{} \end{array} \quad \text{so,} \quad \begin{array}{c} 2 \\ + 9 \\ \hline \boxed{} \end{array}$

Fill in the missing numbers to solve each addition problem.

3.
Think

$\begin{array}{r} 7 \\ + 5 \\ \hline ? \end{array}$
$\begin{array}{r} 10 \\ + \square \\ \hline \square \end{array}$
so,
$\begin{array}{r} 7 \\ + 5 \\ \hline \square \end{array}$

4.
Think

$\begin{array}{r} 4 \\ + 9 \\ \hline ? \end{array}$
$\begin{array}{r} 10 \\ + \square \\ \hline \square \end{array}$
so,
$\begin{array}{r} 4 \\ + 9 \\ \hline \square \end{array}$

5.
Think

$\begin{array}{r} 8 \\ + 9 \\ \hline ? \end{array}$
$\begin{array}{r} 10 \\ + \square \\ \hline \square \end{array}$
so,
$\begin{array}{r} 8 \\ + 9 \\ \hline \square \end{array}$

6.
Think

$\begin{array}{r} 7 \\ + 8 \\ \hline ? \end{array}$
$\begin{array}{r} 10 \\ + \square \\ \hline \square \end{array}$
so,
$\begin{array}{r} 7 \\ + 8 \\ \hline \square \end{array}$

7.
Think

$\begin{array}{r} 9 \\ + 9 \\ \hline ? \end{array}$
$\begin{array}{r} 10 \\ + \square \\ \hline \square \end{array}$
so,
$\begin{array}{r} 9 \\ + 9 \\ \hline \square \end{array}$

8.
Think

$\begin{array}{r} 5 \\ + 6 \\ \hline ? \end{array}$
$\begin{array}{r} 10 \\ + \square \\ \hline \square \end{array}$
so,
$\begin{array}{r} 5 \\ + 6 \\ \hline \square \end{array}$

9. **Higher Order Thinking** Jazmin says she can make 10 to solve $6 + 3$. Is she correct? Explain how you know.

_____

_____

_____

10. ✓**Assessment** Which one shows how to make 10 to solve $8 + 8$?

Ⓐ $8 + 8 + 2 = 8 + 10 = 18$

Ⓑ $8 + 2 + 6 = 10 + 6 = 16$

Ⓒ $8 + 1 + 8 = 9 + 10 = 19$

Ⓓ $8 + 5 + 4 = 8 + 9 = 17$

© Pearson Education, Inc. 1

Name _____

$9 + 6 = ?$

Choose a strategy to solve the problem. Use words, objects, or pictures to explain your work.

Doubles   Near Doubles   Make 10

____ + ____ = ____

You can use different ways to remember addition facts.

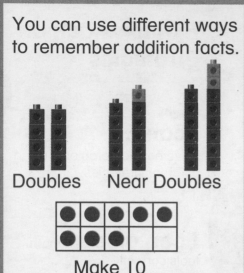

Doubles   Near Doubles

Make 10

4
$+4$

Doubles

Both addends are the same. These are doubles.

$6 + 7$

Near Doubles

The addends are 1 apart. These are near doubles.

$8 + 5$

Make 10

10
$+3$

One addend is close to 10. You can make 10.

Do You Understand?

Show Me! What strategy could you use to solve $7 + 8$? Why is it a good strategy?

☆ **Guided Practice** ☆   Find each sum. Circle the strategy that you used.

1. $\begin{array}{r} 6 \\ + 6 \\ \hline \end{array}$ $\boxed{12}$ — Doubles — / Near Doubles / Make 10 / My Way

2. $\begin{array}{r} 9 \\ + 7 \\ \hline \end{array}$ $\square$ Doubles / Near Doubles / Make 10 / My Way

3. $\begin{array}{r} 6 \\ + 7 \\ \hline \end{array}$ $\square$ Doubles / Near Doubles / Make 10 / My Way

4. $\begin{array}{r} 8 \\ + 9 \\ \hline \end{array}$ $\square$ Doubles / Near Doubles / Make 10 / My Way

Topic 3 | Lesson 8

Tools Assessment

Independent Practice Find each sum.

5. 6
   + 8
   ☐

6. 8
   + 8
   ☐

7. 4
   + 9
   ☐

8. 9
   + 9
   ☐

9. 7
   + 6
   ☐

10. 8
    + 3
    ☐

11. 9
    + 8
    ☐

12. 6
    + 5
    ☐

13. 8
    + 5
    ☐

14. 6
    + 9
    ☐

15. 7
    + 4
    ☐

16. 7
    + 7
    ☐

Find the missing number. Explain the strategy you used.

17. **Algebra** Jan has 9 green marbles and
some red marbles. She has 11 marbles
in all.

_____

_____

9 + ____ = 11

Jan has ____ red marbles.

18. **Make Sense** Brett has 8 shirts in his closet. He puts more shirts in the dresser. Now he has 16 shirts. How many shirts did Brett put in the dresser?

Brett put _____ shirts in the dresser.

Circle the strategy you used to find the missing number.

Doubles   Near Doubles   Make 10   My Way

19. **Higher Order Thinking** Manuel and Jake have 13 pencils in all. How many pencils could each boy have?

Circle the strategy you used to choose the missing addends.

Draw a picture to help you solve the problem.

$13 = \underline{\hspace{1cm}} + \underline{\hspace{1cm}}$

Doubles   Make 10
Near Doubles   My Way

20. ✓**Assessment** Sara has 7 big books. She has 8 small books. Which strategies could help you find how many books Sara has in all? Choose all that apply.

Doubles   Near Doubles   Make 10   My Way
☐   ☐   ☐   ☐

© Pearson Education, Inc. 1

Name _____

Another Look! You can use different strategies to solve problems.

5 and 6 are 1 apart. They are near doubles.

5
+ 6
?

5
+ 5
[10]

5
+ 6
[11]

9 is close to 10. Make 10.

9
+ 5
?

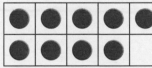

10
+ 4
[14]

so

9
+ 5
[14]

HOME ACTIVITY Have your child use small objects to show 8 + 9. Tell him or her to use one of the following strategies to find the sum: Doubles, Near Doubles, Make 10, or My Way. Ask your child to explain how he or she used that strategy to find the answer.

Find each sum. Circle the strategy that you used.

1.   5
  + 7
  [ ]

Think: 5 and 7 are 2 apart.

Doubles
Near Doubles
Make 10
My Way

2.   8
  + 3
  [ ]

Think: 8 is close to 10.

Doubles
Near Doubles
Make 10
My Way

Find each sum. Circle the strategy that you used.

3.   9
      + 3
      [ ]

Doubles
Near Doubles
Make 10
My Way

4.   7
      + 7
      [ ]

Doubles
Near Doubles
Make 10
My Way

5.   7
      + 9
      [ ]

Doubles
Near Doubles
Make 10
My Way

6. Higher Order Thinking Write a story problem that can be solved by making 10. Then explain how to solve the problem.

---

7. 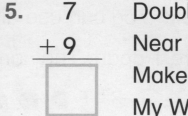 **Assessment** Choose the equations that are **NOT** correct ways to solve the problem below by making 10. Choose all that apply.

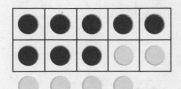

☐ 6 + 4 = 10; 10 + 0 = 10

☐ 7 + 3 = 10; 10 + 1 = 11

☐ 8 + 2 = 10; 10 + 4 = 14

☐ 9 + 1 = 10; 10 + 3 = 13

© Pearson Education, Inc. 1

Solve & Share

Caleb collects stickers. He has 4 more stickers than Zoe. Zoe has 5 stickers. How many stickers does Caleb have? Use objects, drawings, or an equation to show your thinking.

I can ...
solve different types of addition word problems.

I can also make math arguments.

Caleb has _____ stickers.

Tonya reads 5 books. She reads 7 fewer books than Seth. How many books did Seth read?

What do you know?

Tonya read 5 books. Tonya has read 7 fewer books than Seth.

This also means that Seth read 7 more books than Tonya.

What do you need to find out?

How many books Seth read

Seth read 7 more books than Tonya. So I need to add 5 + 7 to solve this problem.

To find out how many books Seth read, you can write an equation.

$5 + 7 = 12$

Seth read 12 books!

Do You Understand?

Show Me! Could you find out how many books Seth has by using objects or a drawing? Explain.

✩ Guided Practice ✩ Read the story. Then solve the problem with an equation.

1. Tim writes 9 stories. Tim writes 3 fewer stories than Daisy. How many stories did Daisy write?

Tim writes [3] fewer stories than Daisy.

Daisy writes [3] more stories than Tim.

[9] [+] [3] = [ ]

2. Sherry reads 6 comic books. Dally reads 5 more comic books than Sherry. How many comic books did Dally read?

Dally reads [ ] more comic books than Sherry.

[ ] ◯ [ ] = [ ]

   Topic 3 | Lesson 9

Name _____

Independent Practice

Solve the problems with objects, drawings, or an equation.
Show your work.

3. Tracy buys 10 buttons on Monday.
   She buys more buttons on Tuesday.
   Now she has 19 buttons.
   How many buttons did Tracy buy on Tuesday?

   _____ buttons

4. Jen has 9 coins.
   Jen has 6 fewer coins than Owen.
   How many coins does Owen have?

   _____ coins

5. 14 cans are on the table.
   5 cans are big and the rest are small.
   How many small cans are on the table?

   _____ small cans

6. **Model** Leland cuts out 12 flowers. How many can he color red and how many can he color yellow?

Draw a picture and write an equation to model and solve the problem.

_____ red flowers   _____ yellow flowers

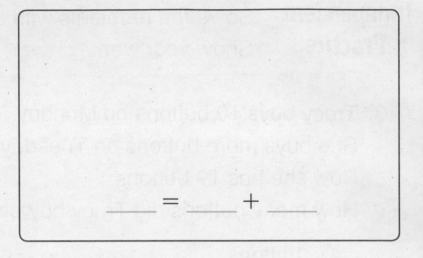

_____ = _____ + _____

---

7. **Higher Order Thinking** Nicole scored 8 goals this season. She scored 9 fewer goals than Julien. How many goals did Julien score?

Restate this problem using the word *more*.

Nicole scored 8 goals this season. Julien scored _____

_____

_____

8. ✓**Assessment** Dan drinks 6 more glasses of water than Becky. Becky drinks 5 glasses of water. How many glasses of water did Dan drink?

Which equation would you use to solve this problem?

Ⓐ $6 - 5 = 1$

Ⓑ $6 + 5 = 11$

Ⓒ $11 + 6 = 17$

Ⓓ $11 - 6 = 5$

© Pearson Education, Inc. 1

Name _____

Help   Tools   Games

Another Look! You can use counters and equations to solve problems.

Jake hits 8 baseballs.

He hits 5 fewer baseballs than Andy.

How many baseballs did Andy hit?

Jake hit 8 baseballs.

Jake hit 5 fewer baseballs than Andy.

That means Andy hit 5 more baseballs than Jake.

$8 + 5 = \underline{13}$

Andy hit $\underline{13}$ **baseballs.**

HOME ACTIVITY Tell your child a number story using either the word *more* or the word *fewer*. Then ask him or her to model the number story using counters and write an equation to solve. Sample story: "John has 4 sweaters. Chris has 5 more sweaters than John. How many sweaters does Chris have?" $4 + 5 = 9$. Chris has 9 sweaters.

Draw counters and write equations to solve.

1. Maude sees 3 more foxes than Henry. Henry sees 4 foxes. How many foxes did Maude see?

2. Desiree has 2 fewer cards than Wendy. Desiree has 9 cards. How many cards does Wendy have?

___ + ___ = ___   ___ foxes

___ + ___ = ___   ___ cards

Model Draw a picture and write an equation to solve.

3. 3 green grapes and 10 red grapes are in a bowl.
How many grapes are in the bowl?

_____ + _____ = _____   _____ grapes

4. 8 cats play. Some more cats come to play. 15 cats are playing now. How many cats came to play with the 8 cats?

_____ + _____ = _____   _____ cats

---

5. Higher Order Thinking Complete the story for the equation below using the words **James**, **fewer**, and **Lily**. Then solve the equation.

$9 + 4 = ?$

James sees 4 _____ birds than Lily. _____ sees 9 birds. How many birds does _____ see?

_____ + _____ = _____

---

6. ✓**Assessment** Chad made 6 fewer sandwiches than Sarah. Chad made 7 sandwiches. How many sandwiches did Sarah make?

Which equation would you use to solve this problem?

$7 - 6 = 1$ $7 - 1 = 6$ $7 + 6 = 13$ $6 + 10 = 16$
   Ⓐ   Ⓑ   Ⓒ   Ⓓ

© Pearson Education, Inc. 1

Solve

Solve & Share

A pet store has 9 frogs. 5 of the frogs are green and the rest are brown. Lidia adds 5 + 9 and says that the store has 14 brown frogs.

Circle if you **agree** or **do not agree** with Lidia's thinking. Use pictures, words, or equations to explain.

I can ...
critique the thinking of others by using pictures, words, or equations.

I can also add and subtract correctly.

Agree   **Do Not Agree**

Thinking Habits
Can I improve on Lidia's thinking?

Are there mistakes in Lidia's thinking?

5 dogs are playing. Some more dogs join. Now 8 dogs are playing. Joe says 3 more dogs joined because $5 + 3 = 8$.

Do You Understand?

Show Me! What question would you ask Joe to have him explain his thinking?

☆ **Guided Practice** ☆ Circle your answer. Use pictures, words, or equations to explain.

1. 9 cats chase a ball. Some cats stop to eat. Now there are 4 cats chasing the ball.

Stan says 13 cats stop to eat because $9 + 4 = 13$.

Do you **agree** or **not agree** with Stan?

Agree   **Not Agree**

© Pearson Education, Inc. 1

Topic 3 | Lesson 10

Name _____

Tools Assessment

2. 14 grapes sit in a bowl. 9 are green. The   **Agree**   **Not Agree**
   rest are purple. How many are purple?

   Steve says 6 grapes are purple because
   $9 + 6 = 14$. Do you **agree** or **not agree**
   with Steve?

---

3. 11 oranges are in a bag. 8 oranges fall out.
   How many oranges are left in the bag?   **Agree**   **Not Agree**

   Maria says 3 oranges are left because
   $11 - 3 = 8$. Do you **agree** or **not agree**
   with Maria?

Flower Vases Jill has 15 roses. She wants to put some in a red vase and some in a blue vase.

Jill solved the problem. Answer the items below to check her thinking. Use pictures, words, or equations to explain.

4. **Explain** Jill says she can put an equal number of roses in each vase. She says she can write a doubles fact to match the flowers in the blue and red vases. Do you agree? Explain.

_____

_____

_____

_____

5. **Model** How could Jill have used words or drawings to show the problem?

_____

_____

_____

_____

_____

_____

© Pearson Education, Inc. 1

Name _____

Another Look! Lidia has 10 pennies. Jon has 8 pennies. Sheila says Jon has 2 fewer pennies than Lidia because $10 - 8 = 2$.

Do you agree or not agree with Sheila?

Lidia ○○○○○○○○○○
Jon ○○○○○○○○

$10 - 8 = 2$

I used a picture and equation to show that Sheila is correct. Jon does have 2 fewer pennies than Lidia. I agree with Sheila.

HOME ACTIVITY Take turns writing your own addition problems involving single digit numbers. Show how you solved the problem using objects or pictures. Make mistakes in some of your problems and challenge each other to find the correct work and the mistakes.

Circle your answer. Use pictures, words, or equations to explain.

1. Anna says that $7 + 4$ is equal to $3 + 9$ because both are equal to 11. Do you **agree** or **not agree** with Anna?

Agree   **Not Agree**

The Birds

9 birds land on a fence. Some more come. Now there are 18 birds on the fence. How many birds came to the fence?

Max solved the problem. Answer the items below to check his thinking. Use pictures, words, or equations to explain.

2. **Explain** Max says that he can use a doubles fact to solve this problem. Do you agree? Explain.

3. **Model** How could Max have used words or drawings to show the problem?

© Pearson Education, Inc. 1

Topic 3 | Lesson 10

Name _____

Point&Tally

Find a partner. Get paper and a pencil.

Each partner chooses a different color: light blue or dark blue.

Partner 1 and Partner 2 each point to a black number at the same time. Both partners add those numbers.

If the answer is on your color, you get a tally mark.

Work until one partner gets twelve tally marks.

I can ...
add and subtract within 10.

Partner 1							Partner 2
2	3	7	4	10	9	2	4
0							6
3	5	1	0	8	3	6	5
1							0
4							1
2							2

Tally Marks for Partner 1	Tally Marks for Partner 2

Word List
- doubles-plus-1 fact
- doubles-plus-2 fact
- open number line
- whole

Understand Vocabulary

1. Circle **True** or **False**.

$10 + 5 = 15$ is a doubles-plus-1 fact.

True   False

2. Circle **True** or **False**.

In the equation below, 8 is the whole.

$$10 + 8 = 18$$

True   False

---

3. Write a doubles-plus-1 fact.

4. Write a doubles-plus-2 fact.

5. Show 15 on the open number line.

Use Vocabulary in Writing

6. How can you use a doubles fact to help you solve $7 + 8 = 15$. Explain.

TOPIC
3

Set A

You can use an open number line to help solve an addition equation. Kara has 10 coins. She gets 8 more coins from her friend. How many coins does Kara have now?

$$10 + 8 = \underline{}?$$

+1 +1 +1 +1 +1 +1 +1 +1

10 11 12 13 14 15 16 17 18

$$10 + 8 = \underline{18}$$

Now, Kara has __18__ coins.

Use an open number line to solve the problem. Show your work.

1. Carmen recycles some cans on Monday. She recycles 4 cans on Tuesday. She recycles 13 cans in all. How many cans did Carmen recycle Monday?

_____ cans

Set B

A doubles-plus-1 fact is a doubles fact and 1 more.

8	8
+ 7	+ 7
?	15

$7 + 7 = 14$.

14 and 1 more is 15.

Add the doubles. Then use the doubles fact to help you add 1 more.

2.
5	6
+ 5	+ 5
☐	☐

3.
8	8
+ 8	+ 9
☐	☐

A doubles-plus-2 fact is a
doubles fact and 2 more.

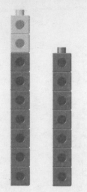

$$9 \atop +7 \over ?$$

$$9 \atop +7 \over \boxed{16}$$

$7 + 7 = 14.$

14 and 2 more is 16.

Add the doubles. Then use the doubles
fact to help you add 2 more.

4.
$$5 \atop +5 \over \Box$$

$$7 \atop +5 \over \Box$$

5.
$$6 \atop +6 \over \Box$$

$$8 \atop +6 \over \Box$$

You can make 10 to add.

$$8 \atop +6 \over ?$$

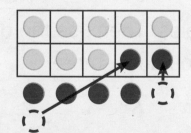

$$10 \atop +4 \over \boxed{14}$$ so $$8 \atop +6 \over \boxed{14}$$

Make 10 to add. Draw counters in
the ten-frame to help you.

6.
$$7 \atop +8 \over ?$$

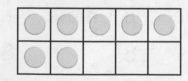

$$10 \atop +5 \over \Box$$ so $$7 \atop +8 \over \Box$$

© Pearson Education, Inc. 1

Name _____

Set E

You can choose different ways to add.

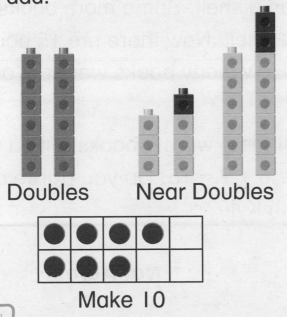

Doubles   Near Doubles

Make 10

Find each sum. Circle the strategy that you used.

7.
$$\begin{array}{r} 8 \\ +\ 4 \\ \hline \square \end{array}$$

Doubles   Make 10

Near Doubles   My Way

8.
$$\begin{array}{r} 7 \\ +\ 8 \\ \hline \square \end{array}$$

Doubles   Make 10

Near Doubles   My Way

Set F

You can write an equation to help you solve addition problems.

Sean plays in 8 soccer matches. Kieran plays in 3 more matches than Sean. In how many matches does Kieran play?

Kieran plays in ___ soccer matches.

Write an equation to solve the problem.

9. Leslie has 8 pencils. She has 9 fewer pencils than Michelle. How many pencils does Michelle have?

Michelle has ___ pencils.

Thinking Habits

Critique Reasoning

What questions can I ask to understand other people's thinking?

Are there mistakes in other people's thinking?

Can I improve on other people's thinking?

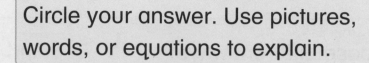

Circle your answer. Use pictures, words, or equations to explain.

10. 6 books are on a shelf. Some more books are put on the shelf. Now there are 15 books on the shelf. How many books were put on the shelf?

Kyle says that there were 9 books put on the shelf because $6 + 9 = 15$. Do you **agree** or **not agree** with Kyle?

Agree   **Not Agree**

Name _____

1. Frank has 7 paper airplanes.
   He makes 9 more.
   How many paper airplanes does
   Frank make in all?

   Ⓐ 18

   Ⓑ 17

   Ⓒ 16

   Ⓓ 15

2. Mark has 7 red marbles.
   He has 8 blue marbles.
   How many marbles does
   Mark have in all?

   Ⓐ 14

   Ⓑ 15

   Ⓒ 16

   Ⓓ 17

3. Use the open number line. Show how to count on to find the sum.

   7 + 9 = _____

   ←——————————————————————————→

4. Is each addition fact below a doubles fact? Fill in the circle for **Yes** or **No**.

$4 + 5 = 9$ ○ Yes   ○ No

$10 + 5 = 15$ ○ Yes   ○ No

$7 + 7 = 14$ ○ Yes   ○ No

$10 + 10 = 20$ ○ Yes   ○ No

5. 8 birds are in a tree.
9 more birds join them.
How many birds are in the tree now?
Write an equation to solve the problem.

____ ○ ____ = ____ birds

6. Gloria has 7 yellow pencils. She has 9 red pencils.
How many pencils does Gloria have in all?
Choose all the strategies that could help you solve the problem.

☐ Doubles Plus 1

☐ Make 10

☐ Doubles Plus 2

☐ My Way

Think about the strategies you have learned!

Name _____

7. Nina bakes 8 corn muffins on Tuesday. She bakes 8 corn muffins on Wednesday. How many corn muffins does Nina bake in all?

Which number line shows the problem?

Ⓐ

Ⓑ

Ⓒ

Ⓓ

8. Sandy makes 9 bracelets.
Then she makes 5 more bracelets.
How many bracelets does Sandy have now?

Solve the problem. Explain the strategy you used.

9. Ming has 8 books.
She buys 5 more books.
How many books does
she have in all?

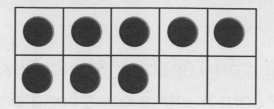

Make 10 to add.

11 books	13 books	15 books	17 books
Ⓐ	Ⓑ	Ⓒ	Ⓓ

---

10. Maria has 8 more scarves than Lucy.
Lucy has 8 scarves.
How many scarves does Maria have?
Write an equation to solve.

_____ + _____ = _____   _____ scarves

---

11. There were 19 limes on the table.
10 fell to the floor. Nicky says there
are 9 limes left on the table.

Do you **agree** or **not agree** with
Nicky's thinking? Use pictures, words,
or equations to explain.

Agree   **Not Agree**

© Pearson Education, Inc. 1

Name _____

Roger's Reading Record

Roger loves to read!
The chart shows how many books he read for six months.

Roger's Reading	
Month	**Number of Books**
January	9
February	7
March	6
April	8
May	5
June	8

1. How many books did Roger read in all in April and June? Write an equation to solve.

_____ + _____ = _____

_____ books

2. Roger read 4 more books in July than he did in January. How many books did he read in July? Draw a picture to solve. Then write an equation to match.

_____ + _____ = _____

He read _____ books in July.

3. In February, Tracy and Roger read 15 books in all. How many books did Tracy read in February?

Explain the strategy that you used to solve the problem.

_____

_____

_____

_____

_____

_____ books

4. Sharon read 8 books in March.

She said that she read 2 fewer books than Roger in March.

Do you **agree** or **not agree** with Sharon? Circle your answer.

Use pictures, words, or equations to explain.

Agree   **Not Agree**

Digital Resources

Solve · Learn · Glossary

Tools · Assessment · Help · Games

TOPIC 4

Subtraction Facts to 20: Use Strategies

Essential Question: What strategies can you use while subtracting?

During the day, the sun appears to move across the sky.

At night, the sun is gone and the moon and stars appear.

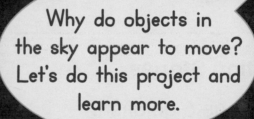

Why do objects in the sky appear to move? Let's do this project and learn more.

Math and Science Project: Pattern of Day and Night

Find Out Talk to friends or relatives about how day and night changes on Earth. How do day and night change as the Earth turns?

Journal: Make a Book Draw pictures of the day sky and the night sky. In your book, also:

- Draw objects that appear in the day and night skies.
- Write subtraction problems about objects that appear in the sky.

Name _____

Review What You Know

A-Z Vocabulary

1. Circle the number that is 4 **fewer** than 8.

   10

   6

   4

   0

2. Circle the **doubles-plus-1 fact**.

   $3 + 7 = 10$

   $8 + 0 = 8$

   $3 + 4 = 7$

   $6 + 6 = 12$

3. Circle the **doubles-plus-2 fact**.

   $4 + 5 = 9$

   $3 + 5 = 8$

   $2 + 5 = 7$

   $2 + 2 = 4$

Subtraction Stories

4. Molly has 6 goldfish. She gives 3 goldfish to Nick.

   How many goldfish does Molly have now?

   Write an equation to show the difference.

   ____ − ____ = ____

5. Katie has 7 stamps. She gives 2 stamps to Jamie.

   How many stamps does Katie have now?

   Write an equation to show the difference.

   ____ − ____ = ____

Parts and Whole

6. Write the parts and the whole for $9 − 1 = 8$.

   Whole: ____

   Part: ____

   Part: ____

My Word Cards Study the words on the front of the card.
Complete the activity on the back.

A-Z
Glossary

related facts

$2 + 3 = 5$

$5 - 2 = 3$

fact family

$3 + 5 = 8$
$5 + 3 = 8$
$8 - 3 = 5$
$8 - 5 = 3$

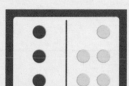

A group of related addition and subtraction facts is called a

_____

_____.

If a subtraction fact and an addition fact have the same whole and the same parts, they are called

_____

_____.

© Pearson Education, Inc. 1

Name _____

 Solve

Solve & Share

Marc has 13 erasers. He gives 5 of them to Troy. How many erasers does Marc have now? Show your thinking on the number line below.

I can …
subtract using a number line.

I can also use math tools correctly.

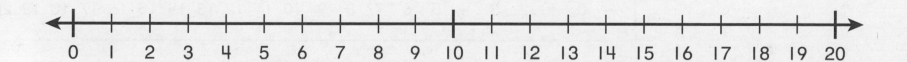

0 1 2 3 4 5 6 7 8 9 10 11 12 13 14 15 16 17 18 19 20

Marc has ____ erasers now.

You can count back or count on to subtract.

Let's try with 11 − 5.

You can count back on a number line to subtract 11 − 5.

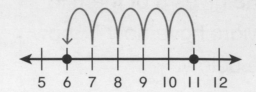

I start at 11 and count back 5.

11 − 5 = 6

You can also count on to subtract 11 − 5 on a number line.

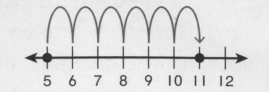

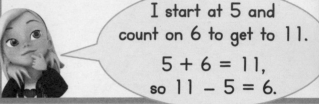

I start at 5 and count on 6 to get to 11.

5 + 6 = 11, so 11 − 5 = 6.

Do You Understand?

Show Me! How can you use a number line to solve 9 − 5?

☆ **Guided Practice** ☆ Use the number line to count back or count on and find the difference.

1. 11 − 3 = __8__

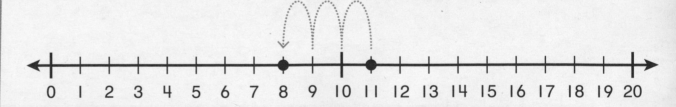

2. ____ = 15 − 6

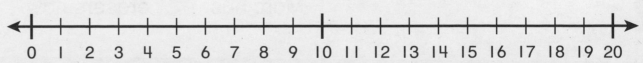

232 two hundred thirty-two

© Pearson Education, Inc. 1

Topic 4 | Lesson 1

Independent Practice

Use the number line to count back or count on and find the difference. Show your work.

3. $11 - 6 =$ _____

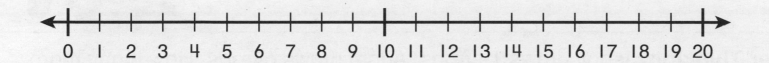

4. _____ $= 7 - 7$

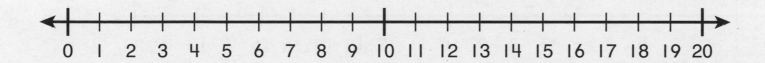

5. $15 -$ _____ $= 7$

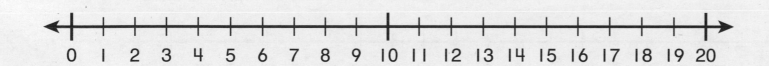

6. **Use Tools** David finds $16 - 7$ on a number line. Write where David starts. Write how many he counts back. Then write the difference.

Start at _____.

Count back _____.

$16 - 7 =$ _____

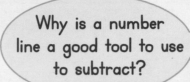

Why is a number line a good tool to use to subtract?

7. **Higher Order Thinking** Jenny draws 14 frogs. Adam draws 6 frogs. How many more frogs does Jenny draw than Adam? Use the number line to show how you can count back or count on to solve. Then write an equation to show the problem.

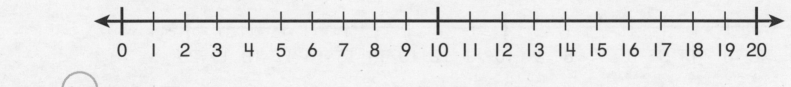

_____ ◯ _____ = _____

8. ✓**Assessment** Use the number line to find the difference. Show your work.

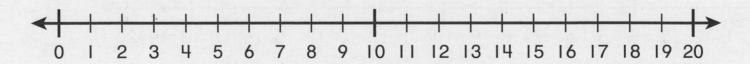

$15 - 9 =$ _____

Name _____

Another Look! You can count back on a number line to subtract.

$$12 - 5 = ?$$

Start at the number you are subtracting from.
Count back the number that you are subtracting.

I started at 12.
Then I counted back 5.
I ended at 7.

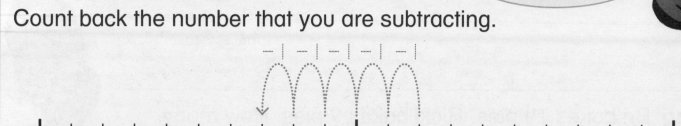

$$12 - 5 = \underline{7}$$

HOME ACTIVITY Draw a number line and label it 0-20. Give your child a subtraction fact, such as 11 − 4. Ask, "How can you use counting back to subtract?" Have your child use the number line to show counting back to subtract 4 from 11. Repeat with other subtraction facts.

 Use the number line to count back or count up and find the difference.

1. $13 - 8 =$ _____

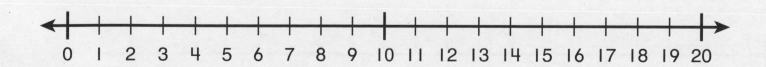

Solve the problems below.

2. **Make Sense** Patty finds $11 - 4$ on a number line. Where does she start? How many does she count back? Then write the difference.

Start at _____.

Count back _____.

$11 - 4 =$ _____

How can you check that your solution makes sense?

3. **Higher Order Thinking** Bri bakes 14 pies. Ricki bakes 9 pies. How many more pies did Bri bake than Ricki? Use the number line to show how you can count back or count on to solve. Then write an equation to show the problem.

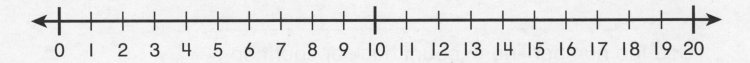

_____ ◯ _____ = _____   _____ more pies

4. ✓ **Assessment** Use the number line to find the difference. Show your work.

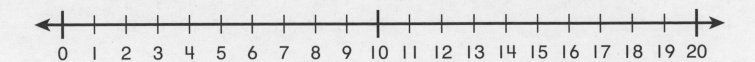

$13 - 8 =$ _____

© Pearson Education, Inc. 1

Name _____

☆ Solve & Share

How can thinking about 10 help you find the answer to the subtraction fact 13 − 7?

I can ...
make subtraction easier by making 10 to subtract.

I can also make math arguments.

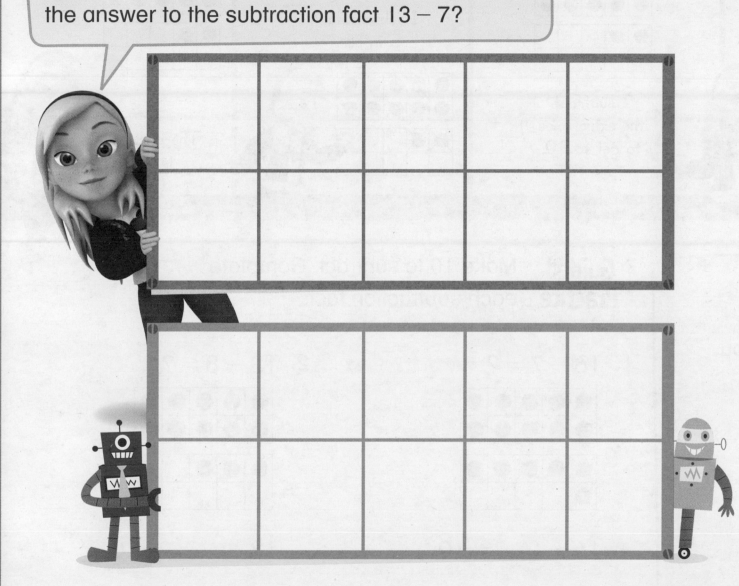

_____ − _____ = _____

You can make 10 to help you subtract.

$12 - 5 = ?$

Start with 12.

Subtract 2 to get to 10.

I subtract the extra ones to get to 10.

Subtract 3 more because $5 = 2 + 3$.

I subtracted 5 in all.

There are 7 left.

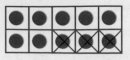

The answer is 7!

Do You Understand?

Show Me! How can finding $14 - 4$ help you find $14 - 6$?

☆ **Guided Practice** ☆ Make 10 to subtract. Complete each subtraction fact.

1. $16 - 7 = ?$

$16 - \underline{6} = 10$

$10 - \underline{1} = \underline{9}$

So, $16 - 7 = \underline{9}$.

2. $13 - 8 = ?$

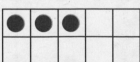

$13 - \underline{} = 10$

$10 - \underline{} = \underline{}$

So, $13 - 8 = \underline{}$.

© Pearson Education, Inc. 1

Tools   Assessment

Independent Practice   Make 10 to subtract. Complete each subtraction fact.

3.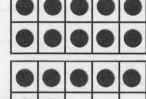

12 − 4 = _____

4.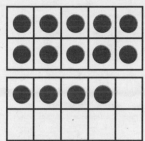

14 − 6 = _____

5.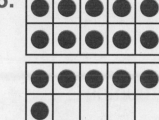

16 − 9 = _____

6.

17 − 8 = _____

7.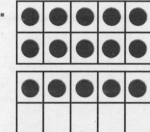

15 − 7 = _____

8.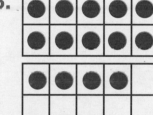

14 − 9 = _____

Draw counters in the ten-frames to show your work.

9. **Number Sense** Show how you can make 10 to find 13 − 6.

13 − 6 = _____

10. **Use Tools** Kyle bakes 12 muffins. His friends eat 6 muffins.
    How many muffins are left? Make 10 to subtract.

    $12 - \underline{\quad} = 10$

    $10 - \underline{\quad} = \underline{\quad}$

    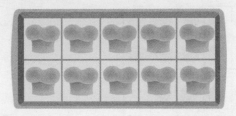

    What tool can you use to help?

    $\underline{\quad}$ muffins

11. **Higher Order Thinking** Zak makes 10 to solve $12 - 5$ by changing the problem to
    $12 - 2 - 3$. How does Zak make 10?

    _____

    _____

    _____

12. ✓**Assessment** Match the pair of ten-frames with the correct
    pair of equations that show how to solve by making 10.

    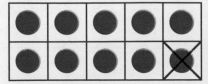   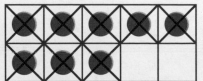

    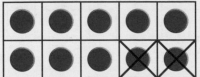   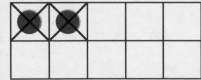

    $12 - 2 = 10, \ 10 - 2 = 8$

    $12 - 3 = 9, \ 9 - 1 = 8$

    $18 - 8 = 10, \ 10 - 1 = 9$

    $18 - 8 = 10, \ 10 - 2 = 8$

© Pearson Education, Inc. 1

Name _____

Another Look! Breaking numbers apart to make 10 can make it easier to subtract.

$13 - 4 = ?$

First, take away 3 to make 10.

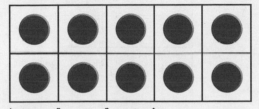

$13 - 3 = \underline{10}$

Then, take away 1 more because you need to subtract 4 in all.

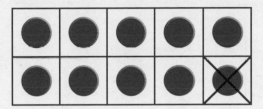

$10 - 1 = \underline{9}$

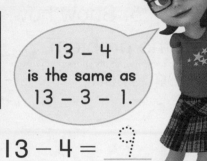
13 − 4 is the same as 13 − 3 − 1.

$13 - 4 = \underline{9}$

HOME ACTIVITY Write $12 - 7 = ?$ on a piece of paper. Have your child use small objects to find the difference. Tell your child to make a 10 to subtract: by adding on to get 10 or by subtracting to get 10. Have your child explain each step of the process as he or she solves the problem.

Make 10 to subtract.
Complete each subtraction fact.

1.

$14 - 5 = \underline{\quad}$

2.
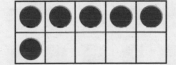

$16 - 7 = \underline{\quad}$

3.
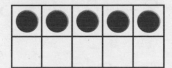

$15 - 8 = \underline{\quad}$

Topic 4 | Lesson 2   Digital Resources at PearsonRealize.com   two hundred forty-one **241**

Make 10 to help you find the missing number in each problem.

4. Algebra

$5 = 12 - \underline{\quad}$

5. Algebra

$\underline{\quad} - 6 = 8$

6. Algebra

$15 - \underline{\quad} = 7$

---

7. Higher Order Thinking Write a story problem for $15 - 6$. Show how to make 10 to solve the problem. Then complete the equation.

$15 - 6 = \underline{\quad}$

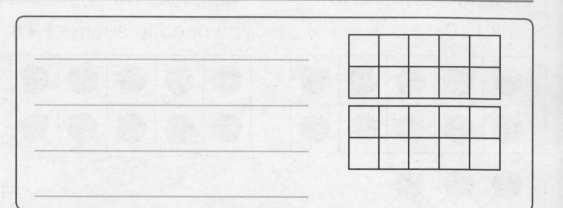

---

8. ✅**Assessment** Match the pair of ten-frames with the correct pair of equations that show how to solve by making 10.

$17 - 7 = 10,\ 10 - 2 = 8$

$12 - 2 = 10,\ 10 - 4 = 6$

$12 - 2 = 10,\ 10 - 5 = 5$

$17 - 8 = 9,\ 9 - 1 = 8$

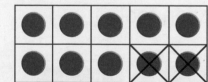

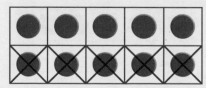

© Pearson Education, Inc. 1

Topic 4 | Lesson 2

Name _____

Solve & Share

Emily counts on to find 11 − 7. She makes 10 while counting. Use counters and the ten-frames to explain what Emily could have done.

I can …
count on to subtract using 10 as a landmark.

I can also make math arguments.

11 − 7 = _____

Digital Resources at PearsonRealize.com

Counting on to make 10 can help you subtract.

$14 - 6 = \underline{?}$

Start with 6.

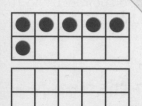

Add 4 to make 10.

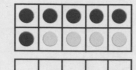

$6 + \underline{4} = 10$

I add 4 to 6 to make 10.

Add 4 more to make 14.

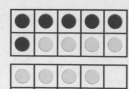

$10 + \underline{4} = 14$

How many did you count on?

$6 + \underline{4} + \underline{4} = 14$

$6 + \underline{8} = 14$

I added 8 to 6 to make 14. So, $14 - 6 = 8$.

Do You Understand?

Show Me! How can counting on to make 10 help you find $15 - 8$?

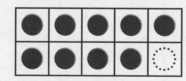
Guided Practice Subtract. Count on to make 10. Complete the facts.

1. $13 - 9 = ?$

$9 + \underline{1} = 10$

$10 + \underline{3} = 13$

$9 + \underline{} = 13$, so

$13 - 9 = \underline{}$.

© Pearson Education, Inc. 1

Name _____

Independent Practice Subtract. Count on to make 10. Show your work.

2.

$8 + \underline{\hphantom{00}} = 10$

$10 + \underline{\hphantom{00}} = 12$

$8 + \underline{\hphantom{00}} = 12$, so $12 - 8 = \underline{\hphantom{00}}$.

3.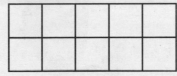

$7 + \underline{\hphantom{00}} = 10$

$10 + \underline{\hphantom{00}} = 15$

$7 + \underline{\hphantom{00}} = 15$, so $15 - 7 = \underline{\hphantom{00}}$.

4.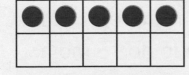

$5 + \underline{\hphantom{00}} = 10$

$10 + \underline{\hphantom{00}} = 14$

$5 + \underline{\hphantom{00}} = 14$, so $14 - 5 = \underline{\hphantom{00}}$.

5.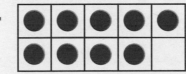

$9 + \underline{\hphantom{00}} = 10$

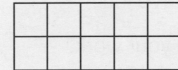

$10 + \underline{\hphantom{00}} = 16$

$9 + \underline{\hphantom{00}} = 16$, so $16 - 9 = \underline{\hphantom{00}}$.

6. **Math and Science** Hoshi watches either the sunrise or sunset for 13 days. She watches sunsets for 5 of the days. How many of the days did Hoshi watch sunrises? Make 10 to help you solve.

$5 + \underline{\hphantom{00}} = 10$

$10 + \underline{\hphantom{00}} = 13$

$5 + \underline{\hphantom{00}} = 13$, so $13 - 5 = \underline{\hphantom{00}}$.

7. Make Sense Sage has 13 stickers.

She gives 7 to her brother.

How many stickers does Sage have left?

What's my plan for solving the problem?

Sage has _____ stickers left.

---

8. Higher Order Thinking Colin has 12 toys. He gives 9 toys away. How many toys does Colin have left?

Make 10 to solve. Show your work.

_____ ◯ _____ = _____

Colin has _____ toys left.

9. ✅ **Assessment** Shay does 7 math problems. She has to do 16 math problems in all. How many problems does Shay have left to do?

Which equations show how to make 10 to solve the problem?

Ⓐ $16 - 7 = 9$

Ⓑ $7 + 3 = 10, 10 + 6 = 16$

Ⓒ $7 + 3 = 10, 10 + 7 = 17$

Ⓓ $9 + 7 = 16$

Name _____

Another Look! Counting on to make 10 can help you subtract.

$16 - 7 = ?$

You added 3 and then 6 more.
$3 + 6 = 9$. You added 9 in all.
So, $16 - 7 = \underline{9}$.

HOME ACTIVITY Give your child a subtraction fact, such as $14 - 5$. Ask how many you need to add to 5 to make 10. Then ask your child how many you need to add to 10 to get to 14. Ask your child to tell you how many he or she counted on in all. Repeat with different subtraction facts.

Start with 7.

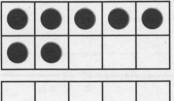

Add 3 to make 10.

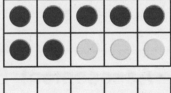

Then add 6 more to make 16.

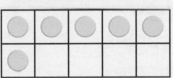
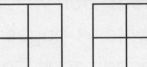

Subtract. Count on to make 10. Show your work.

1. $17 - 8 = ?$

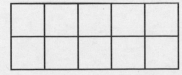
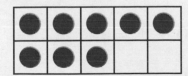

$8 + \underline{} = 10$

$10 + \underline{} = 17$

$8 + \underline{} = 17$, so

$17 - 8 = \underline{}$.

Subtract. Count on to make 10. Show your work.

2.
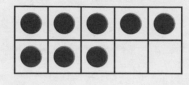

$8 + \underline{\quad} = 10$

$10 + \underline{\quad} = 13$

$8 + \underline{\quad} = 13$, so $13 - 8 = \underline{\quad}$.

3.
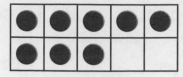

$8 + \underline{\quad} = 10$

$10 + \underline{\quad} = 15$

$8 + \underline{\quad} = 15$, so $15 - 8 = \underline{\quad}$.

4. Higher Order Thinking Andrew makes 11 saves in 2 soccer games. He made 8 saves in the first game. How many saves did Andrew make in the second game?

Make 10 to solve. Show your work.

$\underline{\quad} \bigcirc \underline{\quad} = \underline{\quad}$

Andrew made $\underline{\quad}$ saves.

5. ✅ **Assessment** Dori writes 5 pages. She has to write 11 pages in all. How many pages does Dori have left to write?

Which equations show how to make 10 to solve the problem?

ⓐ $5 + 5 = 10$, $10 + 2 = 12$

ⓑ $11 + 5 = 16$

ⓒ $5 + 5 = 10$, $10 + 1 = 11$

ⓓ $10 + 5 = 15$

Lesson 4-4
Fact Families

Solve & Share

Can you write 2 addition and 2 subtraction facts that use the numbers 8, 9, and 17? Use cubes to help you.

I can ...
make addition and subtraction facts using the same three numbers.

I can also look for patterns.

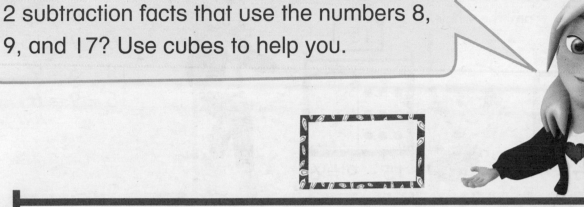

___ + ___ = ___   ___ − ___ = ___

___ + ___ = ___   ___ − ___ = ___

Write 2 addition facts for this model.

$9 + 6 = 15$

15

Add the parts in any order.

$6 + 9 = 15$

You can also write 2 subtraction facts.

15

Subtract 1 part from the whole.

$15 - 6 = 9$

Subtract the other part from the whole.

15

$15 - 9 = 6$

These are **related facts**. They are a **fact family**.

$9 + 6 = 15$
$6 + 9 = 15$
$15 - 6 = 9$
$15 - 9 = 6$

Do You Understand?

Show Me! How are $15 - 6 = 9$ and $15 - 9 = 6$ related?

Guided Practice   Write the fact family for each model.

1.   14

$14 = 6 + 8$
$14 = 8 + 6$
$8 = 14 - 6$
$6 = 14 - 8$

2.   16

____ + ____ = ____
____ + ____ = ____
____ − ____ = ____
____ − ____ = ____

© Pearson Education, Inc. 1

Name _____

Tools Assessment

Independent Practice   Write the fact family for each model.

3.

17

9 | 8

___ + ___ = ___

___ + ___ = ___

___ − ___ = ___

___ − ___ = ___

4.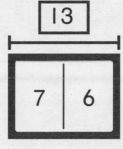

13

7 | 6

___ = ___ + ___

___ = ___ + ___

___ = ___ − ___

___ = ___ − ___

5.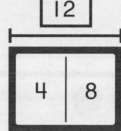

12

4 | 8

___ + ___ = ___

___ + ___ = ___

___ − ___ = ___

___ − ___ = ___

6. **Number Sense** Are the following equations a fact family? Explain your answer.

$9 + 5 = 14$

$15 - 5 = 10$

$4 + 4 = 8$

$15 = 6 + 9$

What is the whole? What are the parts?

_____

_____

_____

_____

Topic 4 | Lesson 4

two hundred fifty-one **251**

7. **Look for Patterns** Pat arranged the counters below. Write the fact family for the set of counters.

_____ = _____ + _____

_____ = _____ + _____

_____ = _____ − _____

_____ = _____ − _____

8. **Higher Order Thinking** Write an equation to solve the problem below. Then write 3 related facts to complete a fact family.

Tanya has 8 stickers. Miguel gave her 5 more. How many stickers does Tanya have in all? _____ stickers

_____ ◯ _____ = _____

_____ ◯ _____ = _____

_____ ◯ _____ = _____

_____ ◯ _____ = _____

9. ✅ **Assessment** Write a fact family to match the picture of the yellow robots and green robots.

_____ + _____ = _____

_____ + _____ = _____

_____ − _____ = _____

_____ − _____ = _____

© Pearson Education, Inc. 1

Name _____

Help   Tools   Games

Homework & Practice 4-4
Fact Families

Another Look! You can use models to make a fact family.

17

| 7 | 10 |

$7 + 10 = 17$
$10 + 7 = 17$
$17 - 10 = 7$
$17 - 7 = 10$

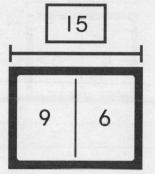

15

| 9 | 6 |

$9 + 6 = 15$
$6 + 9 = 15$
$15 - 6 = 9$
$15 - 9 = 6$

Fact families use the same numbers.

HOME ACTIVITY Write an addition problem, such as $9 + 4 = ?$ Have your child find the sum and write the related addition fact. $(4 + 9 = 13)$ Then ask your child to write the 2 related subtraction equations to complete the fact family. $(13 - 9 = 4$ and $13 - 4 = 9)$ Continue with several other fact families.

Write the fact family for each model.

1.

18

| 10 | 8 |

___ + ___ = ___
___ + ___ = ___
___ − ___ = ___
___ − ___ = ___

2.

14

| 9 | 5 |

___ + ___ = ___
___ + ___ = ___
___ − ___ = ___
___ − ___ = ___

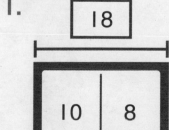

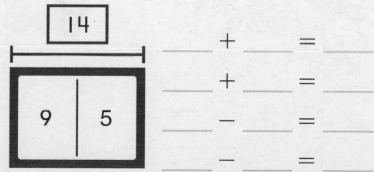

Write the fact family for each model.

Write the fact family for each model.

3.

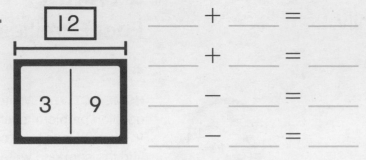

12

3 | 9

____ + ____ = ____

____ + ____ = ____

____ − ____ = ____

____ − ____ = ____

4.

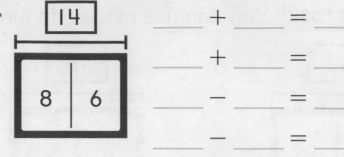

14

8 | 6

____ + ____ = ____

____ + ____ = ____

____ − ____ = ____

____ − ____ = ____

5. Higher Order Thinking Circle the 3 numbers that make up a fact family. Write the fact family.

5   7   8   4   13

____ + ____ = ____

____ + ____ = ____

____ − ____ = ____

____ − ____ = ____

6. ✓**Assessment** Write a fact family to match the picture.

How does the solution to one problem help you solve another problem?

____ + ____ = ____   ____ − ____ = ____

____ + ____ = ____   ____ − ____ = ____

© Pearson Education, Inc. 1

Topic 4 | Lesson 4

Name _____

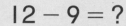

$12 - 9 = ?$

How can you use a related fact to help you find the difference? Write the related addition and subtraction facts. Use counters to help you.

I can ...
use addition facts to find subtraction facts.

I can also model with math.

____ + ____ = ____   ____ − ____ = ____

$13 - 8 = ?$

Use addition to help you subtract.

13

$8 + ? = 13$

What can I add to 8 to make 13?

Model the addition fact.

13

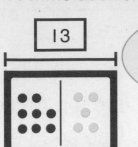

The missing part is 5. $8 + 5 = 13$, so $13 - 8 = 5$.

Do You Understand?

Show Me! How could you use addition to solve $16 - 9$?

☆ **Guided Practice** ☆ Complete each model. Then complete the equations.

1. $14 - 8 = ?$

14

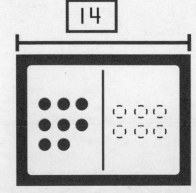

$8 + \underline{6} = 14$

$14 - 8 = \underline{6}$

2. $17 - 9 = ?$

17

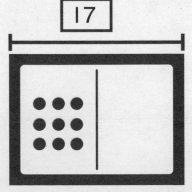

$9 + \underline{} = 17$

$17 - 9 = \underline{}$

© Pearson Education, Inc. 1

Name _____

Independent Practice   Complete each model. Then complete the equations.

3. 13 − 9 = ?

┌──────┐
│ 13 │
└──────┘

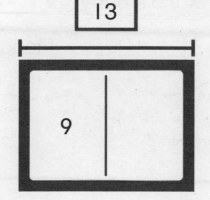

9

9 + _____ = 13

13 − 9 = _____

4. 20 − 10 = ?

┌──────┐
│ 20 │
└──────┘

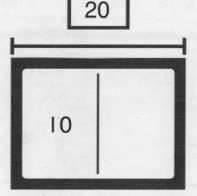

10

10 + _____ = 20

20 − 10 = _____

5. 15 − 7 = ?

┌──────┐
│ 15 │
└──────┘

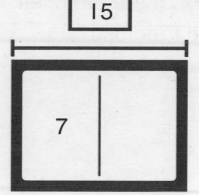

7

7 + _____ = 15

15 − 7 = _____

Draw the missing shape for each problem.

6. Algebra

If ● + ■ = ▲ ,

then ▲ − ■ = _____ .

7. Algebra

If ▬ − ■ = ▮ ,

then _____ + ■ = ▬ .

8. **Generalize** There are 17 robot parts in a box. Fred uses some of the parts. Now there are 8 left. How many parts did Fred use?

_____ parts

____ + ____ = ____

____ − ____ = ____

9. **Generalize** Maria invites 10 friends to her party. 3 cannot come. How many friends will be at Maria's party?

_____ friends

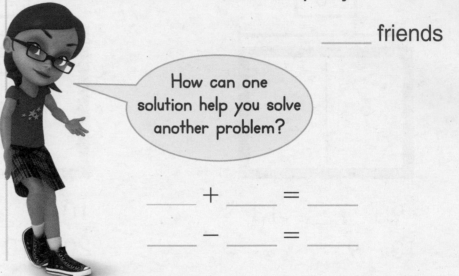

How can one solution help you solve another problem?

____ + ____ = ____

____ − ____ = ____

10. **Higher Order Thinking** Complete the subtraction equation with 11. Then write a related addition fact you could use to solve it.

____ + ____ = ____

11 − ____ = ____

11. ✓**Assessment** Write an addition fact that will help you solve this subtraction fact.

13 − 7 = ?

____ + ____ = ____

Help   Tools   Games

Another Look! You can use an addition fact to help you solve a related subtraction fact.

$18 - 8 = ?$

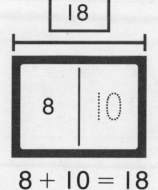

18

8 | 10

$8 + 10 = 18$

$18 - 8 = 10$

$15 - 6 = ?$

15

6 |

$6 + \underline{9} = 15$

$15 - 6 = \underline{9}$

HOME ACTIVITY Write a subtraction problem for your child to solve. Have him or her say a related addition fact to help solve the subtraction problem. Provide pennies or other small objects to be used as counters, if necessary. Repeat using different subtraction problems.

Complete each model.
Then complete the equations.

1. $11 - 6 = ?$

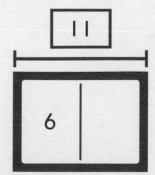

11

6 |

$6 + \underline{} = 11$

$11 - 6 = \underline{}$

2. $12 - 9 = ?$

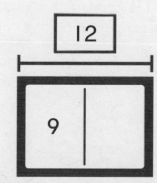

12

9 |

$9 + \underline{} = 12$

$12 - 9 = \underline{}$

Complete each model. Then complete the equations.

3. What addition fact can Amy use to find 10 − 6?

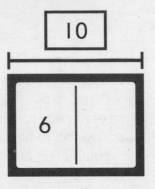

6 + ____ = 10

10 − 6 = ____

4. What addition fact can Dan use to find 16 − 8?

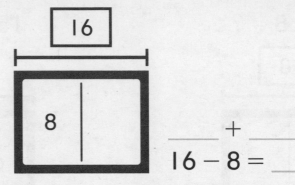

____ + ____ = ____

16 − 8 = ____

5. Higher Order Thinking Draw the missing shape. Then explain how you know your answer is correct.

If ⬜ + ◯ = △ ,

then △ − ⬜ = ____ .

_____

_____

_____

6. ✓Assessment Write an addition fact that will help you solve 14 − 9.

____ + ____ = ____

7. ✓Assessment Which addition fact will help you solve 18 − 10?

____ + ____ = ____

© Pearson Education, Inc. 1

Solve & Share

Complete the subtraction facts.
Use the addition facts on the right to help you.

How are the subtraction facts and the completed addition facts the same? What parts are alike?

Solve

Lesson 4-6
Continue to Use Addition to Subtract

I can …
use addition facts to find subtraction facts.

I can also look for things that repeat.

$18 - 9 =$ _____

$17 - 9 =$ _____

$16 - 9 =$ _____

$9 + 9 = 18$

$9 + 8 = 17$

$9 + 7 = 16$

For every subtraction fact there is a related addition fact.

$$15 - 7 = \boxed{?}$$

You can think addition to help you subtract.

$$15 - 7 = \boxed{?}$$

$$7 + \boxed{?} = 15$$

I add 8 to 7 to make 15.

$$7 + \boxed{8} = 15$$

If 7 + 8 = 15, then 15 – 7 = 8.

$$15 - 7 = \boxed{8}$$

Do You Understand?

Show Me! How does the fact 6 + 9 = 15 help you solve 15 – 6?

☆ Guided Practice ☆ Complete the addition fact. Then solve the related subtraction fact.

1.

$$9 + \boxed{5} = 14$$

$$14 - 9 = \boxed{5}$$

2.

$$10 + \boxed{} = 20$$

$$20 - 10 = \boxed{}$$

3.

$$7 + \boxed{} = 11$$

$$11 - 7 = \boxed{}$$

4.

$$8 + \boxed{} = 13$$

$$13 - 8 = \boxed{}$$

Topic 4 | Lesson 6

Name _____

Independent Practice ☆   Think addition to solve each subtraction fact.

5. 15
   − 8
   [ ]

6. 18
   − 9
   [ ]

7. 13
   − 9
   [ ]

8. 11
   − 2
   [ ]

9. 16
   − 7
   [ ]

10. 14
    − 8
    [ ]

11. 17
    − 7
    [ ]

12. 12
    − 4
    [ ]

Vocabulary Circle **True** or **False** to show whether or not the **related facts** are correct.

13. If 8 + 8 = 16,

then 16 − 8 = 8.

True   False

14. If 7 + 6 = 13,

then 16 − 7 = 3.

True   False

15. **Reasoning** Sam has some crayons. He finds 6 more. Now Sam has 13 crayons. How many crayons did Sam have before he found more?

How are the numbers in the problem related?

_____ + _____ = _____

_____ − _____ = _____

_____ crayons

---

16. **Higher Order Thinking** Solve 13 − 4 using any strategy you choose. Use pictures, numbers, or words to show how you solved it.

17. ✓ **Assessment** Susan solves a subtraction problem. She uses 8 + 6 = 14 to help her solve it.

Which related subtraction problem did she solve?

Ⓐ 16 − 8 = 8

Ⓑ 14 − 6 = 8

Ⓒ 13 − 8 = 5

Ⓓ 8 − 6 = 2

© Pearson Education, Inc. 1

Topic 4 | Lesson 6

Name _____

Another Look! You can use a related addition
fact to help you subtract.

$8 - 5 = ?$

Think: $5 + ? = 8$

You can use the cubes to add.

If $5 + 3 = 8$, then $8 - 5 = 3$.

$9 - 7 = ?$

If $\underline{7} + \underline{2} = \underline{9}$,

then $\underline{9} - \underline{7} = \underline{2}$.

HOME ACTIVITY Collect
15 pennies to use
as counters. Make a
subtraction problem for
your child to solve by
removing some of the
pennies. Have him or her
tell you the subtraction
equation. Then have
your child say the related
addition equation that
helped him or her subtract.

Complete each addition fact.
Then solve each subtraction fact.

1. $16 - 7 = ?$

   If $7 + \underline{\quad} = 16$,

   then $16 - 7 = \underline{\quad}$.

2. $14 - 6 = ?$

   If $6 + \underline{\quad} = 14$,

   then $14 - 6 = \underline{\quad}$.

3. $17 - 8 = ?$

   If $8 + \underline{\quad} = 17$,

   then $17 - 8 = \underline{\quad}$.

4. $13 - 7 = ?$

   If $7 + \underline{\quad} = 13$,

   then $13 - 7 = \underline{\quad}$.

Write a related subtraction and addition fact to help you solve each problem.

5. **Reasoning** Josh has 12 pencils. He gives some of them to his friends. Now he has 7 pencils left. How many pencils did Josh give to his friends?

How does the word problem help me understand what the numbers mean?

_____ + _____ = _____

_____ − _____ = _____   _____ pencils

6. **Higher Order Thinking** Your friend says he can use the related fact $4 + 7 = 11$ to help find $11 - 3$. Is your friend correct?

Explain your answer.

7. ✓**Assessment** Which related addition fact helps you solve $12 - 3 = $?

Ⓐ $10 + 3 = 13$

Ⓑ $3 + 6 = 9$

Ⓒ $2 + 10 = 12$

Ⓓ $3 + 9 = 12$

8. ✓**Assessment** Which related addition fact helps you solve $17 - 7 = $?

Ⓐ $6 + 7 = 13$

Ⓑ $7 + 8 = 15$

Ⓒ $10 + 7 = 17$

Ⓓ $10 + 4 = 14$

© Pearson Education, Inc. 1

Solve & Share

Choose a strategy to solve the problem.

Jeff has 12 apples. He gives away 6 apples. How many apples are left? Use words, objects, or pictures to explain your work.

I can ...
explain the strategies I use to solve subtraction problems.

I can also make math arguments.

_____ – _____ = _____

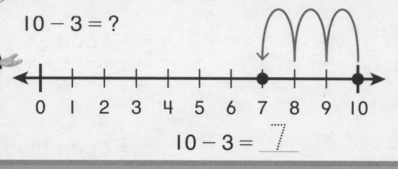

You can use different ways to solve subtraction facts.

You can count on or back to solve subtraction facts.

$10 - 3 = ?$

$10 - 3 = \underline{7}$

You can make a 10 to subtract $12 - 8$.

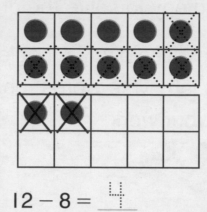

$12 - 8 = \underline{4}$

You can think addition to subtract $14 - 6$.

| 14 |

| 6 | ? |

$6 + \underline{8} = 14$

$14 - 6 = \underline{8}$

Do You Understand?

Show Me! What is one strategy you can use to solve $13 - 4$?

☆ **Guided Practice** ☆ Find each difference. Circle the strategy that you used.

1. $\begin{array}{r} 15 \\ -\ 9 \\ \hline \end{array}$ $\boxed{6}$ Count   (Make 10)   Think Addition   My Way

2. $\begin{array}{r} 9 \\ -\ 7 \\ \hline \end{array}$ $\square$ Count   Make 10   Think Addition   My Way

3. $\begin{array}{r} 13 \\ -\ 3 \\ \hline \end{array}$ $\square$ Count   Make 10   Think Addition   My Way

4. $\begin{array}{r} 17 \\ -\ 8 \\ \hline \end{array}$ $\square$ Count   Make 10   Think Addition   My Way

Topic 4 | Lesson 7

Independent Practice Choose a strategy to find each difference.

5. 15
    − 5
    ☐

6.   8
    − 4
    ☐

7.   9
    − 3
    ☐

8. 18
    −10
    ☐

9. 14
    − 9
    ☐

10. 11
    − 2
    ☐

11. 12
    − 4
    ☐

12. 16
    − 8
    ☐

13.   7
    − 7
    ☐

14. 20
    −10
    ☐

15. 13
    − 5
    ☐

16. 10
    − 7
    ☐

Write a subtraction equation to solve the problem.
Explain which strategy you used.

17. **Higher Order Thinking** Maya has a box
of 16 crayons. 7 crayons are broken. The
rest are **NOT** broken. How many crayons
are **NOT** broken?

____ − ____ = ____

____ crayons

_____

_____

_____

_____

18. **Make Sense** Holly has 11 books. She has 4 more books than Jack. How many books does Jack have?

Jack has ____ books.

Circle the strategy you used to find the difference.

Count   Think Addition

Make 10   My Way

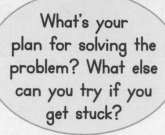

What's your plan for solving the problem? What else can you try if you get stuck?

19. **Higher Order Thinking** What strategy would you use to solve $10 - 6$?

20. ✅**Assessment** Which addition facts will help you solve $16 - 9 = ?$ Choose all that apply.

- ☐ $9 + 7 = 16$
- ☐ $7 + 10 = 17$
- ☐ $7 + 9 = 16$
- ☐ $10 + 7 = 17$

Another Look! You can use different strategies to solve problems.

Use an addition fact to solve a related subtraction problem.

$18 - 9 = ?$

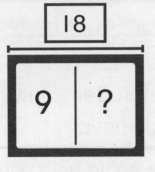

18

9 | ?

$9 + 9 = 18$

$18 - 9 = 9$

Count on to make 10.

$14 - 6 = ?$

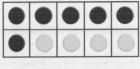

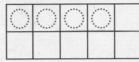

Choose the strategy that works best.

$6 + \underline{4} = 10$

$10 + \underline{4} = 14$

$14 - 6 = \underline{8}$

HOME ACTIVITY Write a subtraction equation like $19 - 9 = ?$ Ask your child to solve the problem. Ask what strategy he or she used to solve the problem, for example, making 10, using a related addition fact, counting, or another strategy.

Find each difference. Circle the strategy that you used.

1.   11
   − 5
   ☐

Think: 11 is close to 10.

Count   Think Addition
Make 10   My Way

2.   15
   − 9
   ☐

Think: Can an addition fact I know help me?

Count   Think Addition
Make 10   My Way

Find each difference. Circle the strategy that you used.

3.
$$15$$
$$-\ 7$$
[ ]

Count
Make 10
Think Addition
My Way

4.
$$14$$
$$-\ 5$$
[ ]

Count
Make 10
Think Addition
My Way

5.
$$14$$
$$-\ 9$$
[ ]

Count
Make 10
Think Addition
My Way

---

6. **Higher Order Thinking** Use pictures, numbers, or words to solve the problem.

Beth finds 13 dolls in her room.
4 of the dolls have curly hair.
How many dolls do **NOT** have curly hair?

_____ − _____ = _____ dolls

7. ✓**Assessment** Ben has 10 baseballs. Andy has 2 fewer than Ben. How many baseballs does Andy have?

Which addition facts could help you solve the problem? Choose all that apply.

☐ $10 + 0 = 10$

☐ $8 + 2 = 10$

☐ $9 + 1 = 10$

☐ $2 + 8 = 10$

© Pearson Education, Inc. 1

Topic 4 | Lesson 7

Solve & Share

Some books are on a shelf. Aiden puts 4 more books on the shelf. Now there are 12 books. How many books were on the shelf to start? Use objects, drawings, or equations to show your thinking.

I can ...
solve different kinds of addition and subtraction problems.

I can also make sense of problems.

There were ____ books to start.

Hunter has some pencils.

He gives 6 of them to Margo.

Now Hunter has 5 pencils.

How many pencils did Hunter start with?

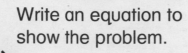

Write an equation to show the problem.

Hunter gives 6 pencils away. He has 5 left.

$\underline{\ ?\ } - 6 = 5$

You can think addition to subtract.

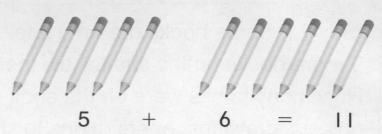

$$5 \quad + \quad 6 \quad = \quad 11$$

So, $\underline{11} - 6 = 5$.
Hunter starts with 11 pencils.

Do You Understand?

Show Me! Sue has 8 crayons. She gets 8 more crayons. How many crayons does she have now? Would you add or subtract to solve the problem? Explain.

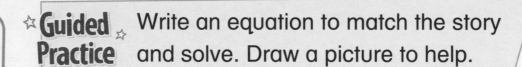
☆ **Guided Practice** ☆ Write an equation to match the story and solve. Draw a picture to help.

1. Cal rides his bike on Monday. He rides 8 miles on Tuesday. He rides 14 miles in all. How many miles did Cal ride on Monday?

$$\underline{\quad\quad} \ \oplus \ \underline{8} \ = \ \underline{14}$$

miles on Monday   miles on Tuesday   miles in all

© Pearson Education, Inc. 1

Tools   Assessment

Independent Practice

Write an equation to match the story. Then solve. Draw a picture to help.

2. Maggie wrote 9 pages of a story yesterday. She writes some more pages today. She writes 12 pages in all. How many pages did Maggie write today?

_____ ◯ _____ = _____

_____ pages

3. Gemma has 6 games. Chris has 13 games. How many fewer games does Gemma have than Chris?

_____ ◯ _____ = _____

_____ fewer games

4. Lily has 4 fewer ribbons than Dora. Lily has 7 ribbons. How many ribbons does Dora have?

_____ ◯ _____ = _____

_____ ribbons

5. **Reasoning** Will has 11 toy cars. How many can he put in his red case and how many in his blue case? Draw a picture and write an equation to solve.

$$11 = \underline{\hspace{1cm}} \bigcirc \underline{\hspace{1cm}}$$

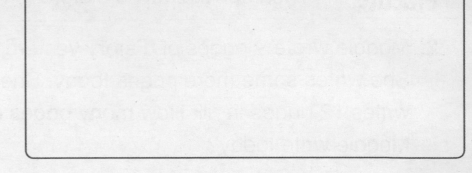

6. **Higher Order Thinking** Write an addition and subtraction equation to match the problem. Then solve.

Jon has 5 oranges. Tiana has 12 oranges. How many more oranges does Tiana have than Jon?

$$\underline{\hspace{1cm}} \bigcirc \underline{\hspace{1cm}} = \underline{\hspace{1cm}}$$

$$\underline{\hspace{1cm}} \bigcirc \underline{\hspace{1cm}} = \underline{\hspace{1cm}}$$

Tiana has ____ more oranges than Jon.

7. ✔**Assessment** Mackenzie picks some apples. She eats 3 apples. Now she has 9 apples. How many apples did Mackenzie pick to start?

3	6	9	12
Ⓐ	Ⓑ	Ⓒ	Ⓓ

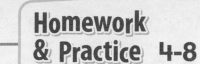

Another Look! You can solve word problems even when you do not know the starting number.

Carrie works on Monday and Tuesday.
She works 10 hours on Tuesday.
She works 20 hours in all.
How many hours did Carrie work on Monday?

Write an equation to show the problem.

I start with 10 and count on until I get to 20.

HOME ACTIVITY Give your child the following problem: I have some pennies in my hand. I put 3 in a piggy bank. Now I have 8 pennies in my hand. How many pennies did I have to start with? Think of other word problems or ask your child to come up with a problem that involves adding to or subtracting from an unknown amount.

$$ \underline{10} \quad + \quad 10 \quad = \quad 20 $$

Hours on Monday   Hours on Tuesday   Hours in All

Carrie worked __10__ hours on Monday.

Write an equation to match the story. Then solve. Draw a picture to help.

1. Jim picks some red flowers. He also picks 7 yellow flowers. He picks 15 flowers in all. How many red flowers did Jim pick?

_____ ◯ _____ = _____

_____ red flowers

Add or subtract to solve each problem.

2. **Reasoning** Sloane has 13 dollars. She spends 5 dollars at the store. How many dollars did Sloane have left? Draw a picture and write an equation to solve.

_____ ◯ _____ = _____

_____ dollars

3. **Higher Order Thinking** Write an addition and a subtraction equation to match the problem. Then solve.

Li has 14 crackers. Joe has 8 crackers. How many more crackers does Li have than Joe?

_____ ◯ _____ = _____

_____ ◯ _____ = _____

Li has _____ more crackers than Joe.

4. ✓**Assessment** Charlie makes some muffins for a bake sale. Then he makes 8 more muffins. Now he has 11 muffins. How many muffins did Charlie make at first?

19   11   8   3

Ⓐ   Ⓑ   Ⓒ   Ⓓ

© Pearson Education, Inc. 1

Name _____

Solve & Share

Write a number story for $14 - 8$. Then write an equation to match your story.

I can ...
use reasoning to write and solve number stories.

I can also add and subtract within 20.

_____

_____

_____

_____

_____

Thinking Habits

What do the numbers stand for?

How can I use a word problem to show what an equation means?

_____ − _____ = _____

Write a number story for 5 + 7. Then write an equation to match your story.

How can I show what the numbers and symbols mean?

I think about what 5, 7, and the + sign mean in the problem. I can use that to write a story.

Lee sees 5 bugs in her garden.
Then 7 more bugs fly in.
How many bugs does Lee see in all?
12 bugs in all

There were 5 bugs and 7 more bugs came. So, you add.

5 + 7 = 12.
Lee sees 12 bugs.

Do You Understand?

Show Me! How would a story about 12 − 7 be alike and different than a story about 5 + 7?

Guided Practice Complete the number story. Then complete the equation to match the story. Draw a picture to help, if needed.

1. 17 − 9 = _____

Carlos has _17_ dog treats.
Tom has _9_ dog treats.
How many more treats does Carlos have?

_____ dog treats

© Pearson Education, Inc. I

Tools Assessment

Independent Practice

Write a number story to show the problem.
Complete the equation to match your story.

2. $9 + 4 =$ _____

_____

_____

_____

3. $12 - 4 =$ _____

_____

_____

_____

4. $19 - 10 =$ _____

_____

_____

_____

Think about how your stories match the equations and how the equations match your stories!

Problem Solving

School Books Jon takes 2 books home.
He leaves 4 books at school. How can Jon write
an addition story about his school books?

5. **Reasoning** Write an addition question
about Jon's books.

6. **Model** Draw a picture and write an
equation to solve your addition question.

$$\underline{\hspace{2cm}} + \underline{\hspace{1.5cm}} = \underline{\hspace{1.5cm}}$$

7. **Explain** Is $6 - 4 = 2$ in the same
fact family as your addition equation?
Circle **Yes** or **No.** Use words, pictures,
or equations to explain.

Yes   No

Name _____

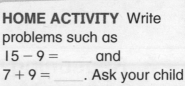
Another Look! You can write a number story for each problem.
Then you can complete the equation to match.

$$12 - 5 = \underline{7}$$

Cindy picks 12 lemons.
She gives 5 away.
How many lemons does Cindy have now?
Now Cindy has 7 lemons.

$$9 + 5 = \underline{14}$$

Sarah picks __9__ flowers.

Then she picks __5__ more.

How many flowers does Sarah pick in all?

Sarah picks __14__ flowers in all.

Write a number story to show the problem.
Complete the equation to match your story.

1. $14 - 8 = $ ____

_____

_____

_____

2. $8 + 8 = $ ____

_____

_____

_____

Socks Melissa finds 5 blue socks. Then she finds 3 purple socks. She writes addition and subtraction stories about the socks.

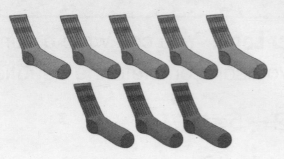

3. **Reasoning** Melissa writes this question about the socks:
How many socks did I find in all?

Write an equation to solve Melissa's question.

____ ◯ ____ = ____   ____ socks

4. **Reasoning** Melissa writes another question about the socks:
How many more blue socks than purple socks did I find?

Write an equation to solve Melissa's question.

____ ◯ ____ = ____   ____ more blue socks

5. **Explain** Melissa says the addition and subtraction equations for her problems are related facts. Is Melissa correct?
Circle **Yes** or **No.** Use words, pictures, or equations to explain.

Yes   No

© Pearson Education, Inc. I

Color these sums and differences. Leave the rest white.

| 6 | 7 | 4 |

9 − 5	8 − 4	1 + 3	10 − 3	4 + 3	1 + 6	7 − 1	9 − 3	5 + 1
2 + 1	6 − 2	7 − 4	5 + 2	9 − 7	7 − 0	6 − 0	6 + 2	2 + 4
8 + 2	10 − 6	2 + 6	7 + 0	6 + 3	10 − 3	4 + 2	6 + 0	10 − 4
4 + 4	3 + 1	4 − 3	8 − 1	4 + 5	6 + 1	8 − 2	2 + 1	9 + 1
8 − 7	4 + 0	6 + 4	9 − 2	3 + 4	2 + 5	3 + 3	6 − 1	6 + 3

The word is

_____ _____ _____

A-Z Glossary

Word List
- difference
- doubles fact
- fact family
- related facts

Understand Vocabulary

1. Cross out the numbers below that do **NOT** show the difference for $18 - 8$.

16   14

11   10

2. Cross out the problems below that do **NOT** show a doubles fact.

$4 + 5$ $6 + 4$

$4 + 4$ $5 + 4$

---

3. Write the related fact.

$12 - 7 = 5$

____ ◯ ____ ◯ ____

4. Write the related fact.

$10 + 9 = 19$

____ ◯ ____ ◯ ____

5. Write the related fact.

$6 = 14 - 8$

____ ◯ ____ ◯ ____

Use Vocabulary in Writing

6. Write equations using the numbers shown in the model. Then explain what the equations are called using a word from the Word List.

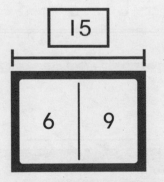

15

| 6 | 9 |

____ + ____ = ____

____ + ____ = ____

____ − ____ = ____

____ − ____ = ____

Name _____

Set A _____

You can count back on a number line to subtract.

Find 10 − 6.

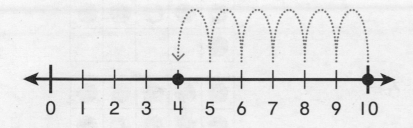

Start at 10 and count back 6 to get to 4.

10 − 6 = __4__

You can also count on to subtract.

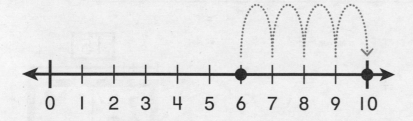

Start at 6 and count on 4 to get to 10.

6 + 4 = 10, so 10 − 6 = 4.

10 − 6 = __4__

Use the number line to count back or count on and find the difference.

1. Find 9 − 6.

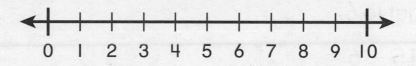

9 − 6 = ____

2. Find 10 − 5.

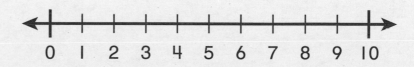

10 − 5 = ____

You can make 10 to subtract.

$15 - 6 = ?$

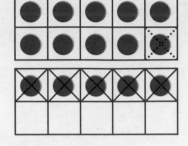

First subtract 5 from 15 to get to 10.

$15 - 5 = 10$

Then take away 1 more to get to 6.

$15 - 6 = \underline{9}$

Make 10 to subtract. Then complete the subtraction fact.

3. $16 - 7 = \underline{\quad}$

$16 - \underline{\quad} = 10$

$10 - \underline{\quad} = \underline{\quad}$

4. $13 - 6 = \underline{\quad}$

$13 - \underline{\quad} = 10$

$10 - \underline{\quad} = \underline{\quad}$

You can write a fact family to match the model.

14

$14 = 6 + 8$

$\underline{14} = \underline{8} + \underline{6}$

$6 = 14 - 8$

$\underline{8} = \underline{14} - \underline{6}$

Write a fact family to match the model.

5. $\underline{\quad} + \underline{\quad} = \underline{\quad}$

$\underline{\quad} + \underline{\quad} = \underline{\quad}$

$\underline{\quad} - \underline{\quad} = \underline{\quad}$

$\underline{\quad} - \underline{\quad} = \underline{\quad}$

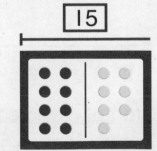

15

© Pearson Education, Inc. 1

Name _____

Set D

You can use addition to help you subtract.

$15 - 7 = ?$

Think:

$7 + \underline{8} = 15$

The missing part is 8.

So, $15 - 7 = 8$.

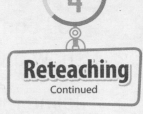

15

?

Use addition to subtract. Complete the equations.

6. $13 - 8 = ?$

Think:

$8 + \underline{} = 13$

So, $13 - 8 = \underline{}$.

13

?

Set E

You can use different strategies to subtract $14 - 6$.

14

6 | ?

Think
Addition

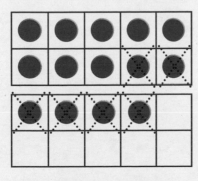

Make 10

Find each difference. Circle the strategy that you used.

7.   12
    − 4
   ▢

Count

Think Addition

Make 10

My Way

8.   17
    − 8
   ▢

Count

Think Addition

Make 10

My Way

You can write an equation to show a word problem.

Jaime mows some lawns on Saturday and Sunday. He mows 8 lawns on Sunday. He mows 13 lawns in all. How many lawns did Jaime mow on Saturday?

$$5 \oplus 8 = 13$$

__5__ lawns

9. Davis has some pens. He gives 4 to Glenn. Now he has 7 pens. How many pens did Davis start with? Write an equation to solve. Draw a picture to help.

___ ◯ ___ = ___

___ pens

Thinking Habits

Reasoning

What do the numbers stand for?

How can I use a word problem to show what an equation means?

Write a number story for the problem. Then complete the equation.

10. $9 + 4 =$ ___

_____

_____

_____

_____

© Pearson Education, Inc. 1

Name _____

1. Frank has 15 books to read.
   He reads 9 of them.
   How many books does Frank
   have left to read?

_____ books

2. Mark has some red marbles.
   He has 8 blue marbles.
   Mark has 13 marbles in all.
   How many red marbles does
   he have?

   Ⓐ 4   Ⓑ 5

   Ⓒ 6   Ⓓ 7

---

3. Which fact family matches the picture of the big ducks and small ducks?

8 + 0 = 8	5 + 9 = 14	5 + 8 = 13	8 + 9 = 17
0 + 8 = 8	9 + 5 = 14	8 + 5 = 13	9 + 8 = 17
8 − 0 = 8	14 − 5 = 9	13 − 5 = 8	17 − 9 = 8
8 − 8 = 0	14 − 9 = 5	13 − 8 = 5	17 − 8 = 9
Ⓐ	Ⓑ	Ⓒ	Ⓓ

4. Which related subtraction fact can be solved using $7 + 8 = 15$?

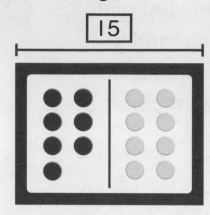

15

Ⓐ $15 - 8 = 7$

Ⓑ $14 - 7 = 7$

Ⓒ $8 - 7 = 1$

Ⓓ $8 - 8 = 0$

5. There are 13 birds in a tree.
Then 6 birds fly away.
How many birds are still in the tree?

Make 10 to solve. Use the counters and ten-frame.

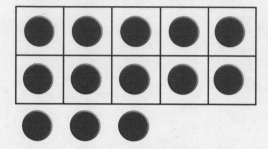

$13 - \underline{\quad} = 10$

$10 - \underline{\quad} = \underline{\quad}$

$13 - 6 = \underline{\quad}$

6. Gloria has 7 yellow pencils. She has 9 red pencils. Which strategy would **NOT** help you find $9 - 7$?

Ⓐ Make 10

Ⓑ Think Addition

Ⓒ Count to Subtract

Ⓓ My Way

© Pearson Education, Inc. 1

Name _____

7. Nina bakes 14 corn muffins.
She gives away 8 corn muffins.
There are 6 left.

Which equation matches the story?

Ⓐ $15 - 8 = 7$

Ⓑ $7 + 8 = 15$

Ⓒ $14 - 8 = 6$

Ⓓ $8 + 6 = 14$

8. Which related addition fact can help you solve the subtraction fact? Choose all that apply.

$16 - 7 = ?$

☐ $7 + 9 = 16$

☐ $7 + 8 = 15$

☐ $6 + 7 = 13$

☐ $9 + 7 = 16$

9. Use the number line to count on or count back to find the difference.
Show your work.

$12 - 4 =$ _____

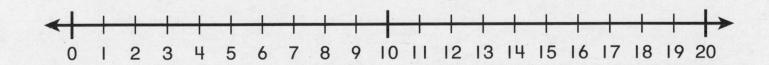

10. Ming has 14 books. She sells 8 books. How many books does she have left?

Make 10 to solve. Use counters and the ten-frame.

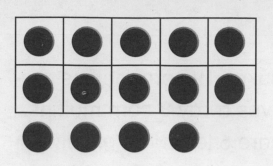

_____ books

11. A box has 16 skateboard parts. Maria used some of the parts. Now there are 7 parts left. Write a subtraction equation to show how many parts Maria used.

_____ − _____ = _____   Maria used _____ parts.

12. Write a number story for 19 − 10.

Then write an equation to match your story and solve the problem.

_____

_____

_____

_____

Name _____

Maria's Stickers

Maria collects stickers.
The chart shows the different stickers
she has.

Maria's Stickers	
Type of Sticker	**Number of Stickers**
🌙	15
☁️	7
☀️	9
🌈	8
⭐	12

1. How many more moon
   stickers than sun stickers
   does Maria have?

   Count, make 10, or think
   addition to solve.

   _____ more moon stickers

2. Maria gives some cloud stickers to Tom.
   Now she has 5 cloud stickers. How many
   cloud stickers did Maria give away?

   Write an equation to solve the
   problem.

   _____ ◯ _____ = _____

   _____ cloud stickers

3. Complete the fact family using the number of cloud and rainbow stickers.

7 + 8 = 15

___ + ___ = ___

___ − ___ = ___

___ − ___ = ___

4. Wendy gives Maria 3 more rainbow stickers. How many rainbow stickers does Maria have now? Complete the equation to solve.

8 ◯ ___ = ___

___ rainbow stickers

5. Write a story to show and solve 12 − 8. Make your problem about star stickers. Draw a picture and write an equation to match your story.

_____

_____

_____

_____

_____

___ ◯ ___ = ___

© Pearson Education, Inc. 1

Topic 4 | Performance Assessment

Work with Addition and Subtraction Equations

Essential Question: How can adding and subtracting help you solve or complete equations?

Digital Resources

Solve   Learn   Glossary

Tools   Assessment   Help   Games

Animals cannot speak like we do. They communicate in other ways.

Some animals that live underwater communicate using sonar.

Wow! Let's do this project and learn more.

Math and Science Project: Underwater Communication

Find Out Talk to friends and relatives about how animals such as dolphins use sonar. Ask them to help you learn more about sonar in a book or on a computer.

Journal: Make a Book Show what you found out. In your book, also:

- Draw a picture of one way that sonar is used.
- Make up and solve addition and subtraction problems about the animals that use sonar to communicate.

Name _____

Review What You Know

A-Z Vocabulary

1. Circle the **addends** in the equation.

$$4 + 5 = 9$$

2. Circle the equation that is a **related fact** for $10 - 8 = 2$.

$$8 - 6 = 2$$

$$8 + 2 = 10$$

3. Circle the number that will complete the **fact family**.

$$3 + \underline{\ ?\ } = 10$$

$$\underline{\ ?\ } + 3 = 10$$

$$10 - 3 = \underline{\ ?\ }$$

$$10 - \underline{\ ?\ } = 3$$

8 14 7 5

Subtraction Stories

Use cubes to solve. Write the subtraction equation.

4. 8 squirrels are on the ground. 5 are eating acorns. How many squirrels are **NOT** eating acorns?

_____ − _____ = _____

5. Brett has 5 markers. Pablo has 3 markers. How many more markers does Brett have than Pablo?

_____ − _____ = _____

Related Facts

6. Write the related subtraction facts.

$$9 = 4 + 5$$

_____ = _____ − _____

_____ = _____ − _____

Name _____

Solve & Share

Find the missing number in this equation:

$$7 + \underline{\quad} = 13$$

Explain how you found the missing number.

I can ...
find the unknown number in an equation.

I can also make math arguments.

Look at this problem:

$$12 - \underline{} = 3$$

This means that 12 take away some number is the same as 3.

You can use counters to find the missing number.

$$12 - \underline{9} = 3$$

You can also use addition to find the missing number.

$$3 + \underline{9} = 12,$$

so $12 - \underline{9} = 3$.

9 is the missing number. 9 makes the equation true.

Do You Understand?

Show Me! What is the missing number in the equation $\underline{} + 4 = 9$? How do you know?

☆ **Guided Practice** ☆ Write the missing numbers. Then draw or cross out counters to show your work.

1. $14 - \underline{7} = 7$

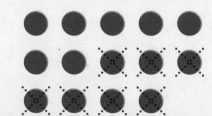

2. $4 + \underline{} = 12$

● ● ● ●

© Pearson Education, Inc. 1

Independent Practice

Write the missing numbers. Draw counters to show your work.

3. ____ − 9 = 8

4. ____ = 8 + 3

5. ____ + 6 = 12

6. 8 + ____ = 15

7. 14 − ____ = 6

8. ____ = 11 − 8

9. **Number Sense** Write the missing number to make each equation true.

9 + ____ = 19

20 = ____ + 10

____ − 10 = 9

____ − 10 = 10

How does solving one problem help you with the next?

Solve each number story. Write the missing numbers. Use counters if needed.

10. **Reasoning** Adam wants to visit 13 states on a road trip. He has visited 7 states so far.
How many states does Adam have left to visit?

13 $\bigcirc$ ____ = ____

____ states

11. **Reasoning** Chelsea makes costumes for her dance class. She needs to make 11 costumes in all. She has 4 costumes left to make. How many costumes did Chelsea already make?

11 = ____ $\bigcirc$ ____

____ costumes

12. **Higher Order Thinking** Find the missing number in the equation
$5 + \underline{\quad} = 14$. Then write a story that matches the problem.

13. **Assessment** Match each number with the equation it is missing from.

$17 - \underline{\quad} = 7$ 6

$\underline{\quad} + 6 = 12$ 3

$4 + \underline{\quad} = 13$ 10

$\underline{\quad} - 1 = 2$ 9

Name _____

Help   Tools   Games

Another Look! You can find the missing number in an addition or subtraction equation. Add counters to the empty side of the mat until there are 17 in all.

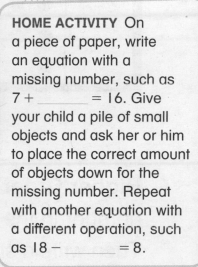

You need 8 more counters to have 17 in all.

17

$\underset{8}{} + 9 = 17$ $17 - \underset{8}{} = 9$

HOME ACTIVITY On a piece of paper, write an equation with a missing number, such as $7 + \underline{} = 16$. Give your child a pile of small objects and ask her or him to place the correct amount of objects down for the missing number. Repeat with another equation with a different operation, such as $18 - \underline{} = 8$.

Draw the missing counters. Then complete the equation.

1.   14

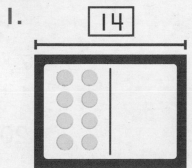

$8 + \underline{} = 14$

2.   20

$20 - 10 = \underline{}$

Topic 5 | Lesson 1

Digital Resources at PearsonRealize.com

three hundred three **303**

Complete the mat to help you find the missing numbers.

3. ____ = 8 + 5

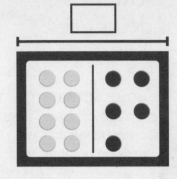

4. 16 − ____ = 9

16

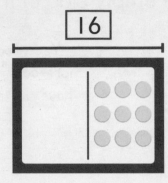

5. 9 + ____ = 18

18

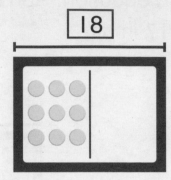

6. **Higher Order Thinking** Find the missing number in the equation 18 = 10 + ____. Then write a story that matches the problem.

7. ✓**Assessment** Match each number with the equation it is missing from.

17 − ____ = 10   8

____ + 6 = 14   5

4 + ____ = 9   7

____ − 10 = 10   20

© Pearson Education, Inc. 1

Topic 5 | Lesson 1

Lesson 5-2
True or False Equations

Solve & Share

This equation looks different to me. Do you think it's a true equation?

Explain how you know.

I can ...
understand that the equal sign means "has the same value as."

I can also reason about math.

$$5 = 11 - 6$$

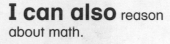

Is this equation true?

$$3 + 6 = 4 + 5$$

To find out, solve each side of the equation.

$$3 + 6$$

$$4 + 5$$

This equation is true. Both sides equal 9.

$$3 + 6 = 4 + 5$$

$$9 = 9$$

Even equations with no operation symbols can be true.

8 = 8 is a true statement.

Do You Understand?

Show Me! Is the equation $4 = 11 - 6$ true? Explain.

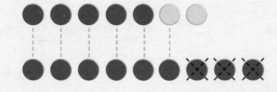

Guided Practice Tell if each equation is **True** or **False**. Use the counters to help you.

1. $5 + 2 = 9 - 3$

True   (False)

2. $7 = 8 - 1$

True   False

© Pearson Education, Inc. 1

Topic 5 | Lesson 2

Name _____

Tools   Assessment

Independent Practice   Tell if each equation is **True** or **False**. You can draw counters to help.

3. $5 + 5 = 6 + 4$

True   False

4. $9 = 9 - 1$

True   False

5. $3 + 3 = 11 - 8$

True   False

6. $13 - 4 = 15 - 6$

True   False

7. $7 + 7 = 12 - 5$

True   False

8. $10 + 8 = 9 + 9$

True   False

9. $7 + 3 = 10 + 2$

True   False

10. $6 + 8 = 8 + 6$

True   False

11. $4 + 2 = 6 + 1$

True   False

12. **Be Precise** Shawna has 8 paper airplanes. She gives away 1 plane. Frank has 5 paper airplanes and gets 2 more.

Make sure you use numbers, units, and symbols correctly. Does the equation match the story?

_____ − _____ = _____ + _____

True   False

Shawna has _____ planes. Frank has _____ planes.

13. **Higher Order Thinking** Can you prove that $4 + 2 = 5 + 1$ is true without solving both sides of the equation? Explain.

_____

_____

_____

_____

14. ✅ **Assessment** Which equations shown below are **false**? Choose all that apply.

☐ $10 − 3 = 14 − 7$

☐ $4 + 3 = 7 + 1$

☐ $6 + 6 = 8 + 3$

☐ $17 − 8 = 9$

Name _____

Another Look! Use connecting cubes to model true or false equations of different types.

Draw lines to match the cubes.

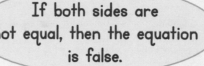
If both sides are not equal, then the equation is false.

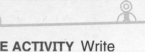

$4 = 4$

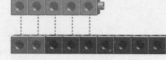

This equation is **true**.

$5 = 2 + 7$

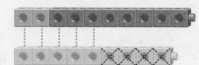

This equation is **false**.

$2 + 8 = 9 - 4$

This equation is **false**.

HOME ACTIVITY Write a plus sign, minus sign, and equal sign, each on three notecards or pieces of paper. Gather 20 small objects, such as buttons or pennies. Set up the notecards and objects to show true or false equations, such as $3 + 5 = 9 - 1$ or $6 - 2 = 3 + 3$. Ask your child to tell if each equation is **true** or **false**.

Draw lines to match the cubes. Tell if each equation is **True** or **False**.

1. $9 = 7 + 2$

True   False

2. $7 + 3 = 9 - 3$

True   False

3. $10 - 2 = 1 + 7$

True   False

Model Draw pictures to show each equation. Then circle **True** or **False**.

4. $10 - 2 = 7 + 4$

True False

5. $6 = 9 - 5$

True False

6. $8 + 5 = 10 + 3$

True False

7. **Higher Order Thinking** Jamie says that $19 - 10$ is equal to $20 - 10$ because both sides use subtraction. Is Jamie correct? Explain why or why not.

8. **Assessment** Which equations below are **true**? Choose all that apply.

- ☐ $8 - 7 = 11 - 10$
- ☐ $12 - 4 = 6 + 3$
- ☐ $10 - 1 = 9 + 2$
- ☐ $9 + 2 = 10 + 1$

Solve & Share

What number goes in the blank to make the equation true? How do you know?

I can …
fill in the missing number in equations to make them true.

I can also reason about math.

$$2 + 5 = \underline{\quad} + 6$$

Fill in the missing number to make this equation true.

$$10 - \underline{\quad} = 3 + 4$$

I can solve one side of the equation first. I know that $3 + 4 = 7$.

You can use counters to find the missing number.

$$10 - \underline{\quad} = 7$$

The equal sign means "the same value as," so I need to subtract something from 10 to get 7.

I took away 3 counters to get to 7, so the missing number is 3.

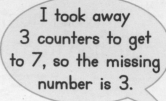

$$10 - \underline{3} = 3 + 4$$

Do You Understand?

Show Me! What number can you write in the blank to make this equation true? Use pictures or words to show how you know.

$$8 + \underline{\quad} = 6 + 6$$

 **Guided Practice** Write the missing numbers to make the equations true. Draw counters to help.

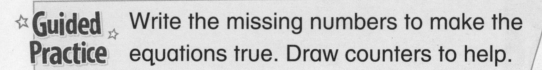

1. $10 + \underline{\ ?\ } = 5 + 7$

$10 + \underline{\ ?\ } = \underline{12}$

$10 + \underline{2} = \underline{12}$

2. $4 + 5 = 6 + \underline{\ ?\ }$

$\underline{\quad} = 6 + \underline{\ ?\ }$

$\underline{\quad} = 6 + \underline{\quad}$

Name _____

Independent Practice ☆ Write the missing number that makes each equation true.

3. ____ + 6 = 4 + 9

4. 14 − 7 = ____ − 3

5. 8 + ____ = 9 + 4

6. 10 − ____ = 7 − 3

7. 15 − 10 = 10 − ____

8. 7 + 4 = 8 + ____

9. 10 + 2 = ____ + 4

10. 13 − 10 = ____ − 7

11. ____ + 7 = 9 + 1

12. **Math and Science** Kari and Chris make "telephones" with paper cups and string. They take a piece of string that is 13 feet long and cut it into two pieces. One piece is 8 feet long. How long is the other piece of string? Write the missing number in the addition and subtraction equations.

You can think about subtraction as a missing addend problem.

____ = 13 − 8

13 = ____ + 8   ____ feet

13. Reasoning Kim has 14 tennis balls. Danny has 4 tennis balls. How many more tennis balls does Kim have than Danny?

$14 -$ ____ $=$ ____   ____ more

14. Reasoning Ron finds 10 rocks but drops 1 rock. Anson finds 3 rocks. How many more rocks would Anson have to find to have the same number of rocks as Ron?

$10 - 1 = 3 +$ ____   ____ rocks

15. Higher Order Thinking Jose has 5 red crayons and 8 blue crayons. Tasha has 10 red crayons and some blue crayons. If Tasha has the same number of crayons as Jose, how many blue crayons does she have? Tell how you know.

_____

_____

_____

16. ✓**Assessment** Draw an arrow to show which number will make the equation true.

1   2   3   4   5   6   7   8

$4 + 7 = 5 +$ ____

Name _____

Another Look! Solving one side of a true equation can help you determine the value of the other side.

$$9 + \underline{\quad} = 7 + 8$$

Both sides of a true equation must have the same value.

First, solve $7 + 8$.

Next, solve $9 + \underline{?} = 15$

So, $9 + \underline{6} = 7 + 8$.

$7 + 8 = 15$

$9 + \underline{6} = 15$

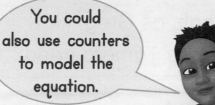

You could also use counters to model the equation.

HOME ACTIVITY Write down a number between 0 and 20. Ask your child to write down an addition or subtraction fact that would equal the number. Repeat with other numbers. Have your child give you a number and then you give an addition or subtraction fact. Ask him or her to tell you if you made a true or false equation.

Write the missing numbers to make the equations true. Draw counters to help.

1.

$7 + \underline{\quad} = 8 + 6$

$8 + 6 = \underline{\quad}$

$7 + \underline{\quad} = \underline{\quad}$

2.

$2 + 4 = 16 - \underline{\quad}$

$2 + 4 = \underline{\quad}$

$\underline{\quad} = 16 - \underline{\quad}$

Solve each problem below.

3. **Reasoning** Greg has 15 hats. Tamara has 10 hats. She wants to have the same number of hats as Greg. How many more hats does Tamara need?

$$15 = 10 + \underline{\quad}$$

_____ more

4. **Reasoning** Laila uses the same number of counters as Frank. What number would make this equation true?

$$8 + 1 = 16 - \underline{\quad}$$

5. **Higher Order Thinking** Write the missing number that makes the equation true. Use pictures or words to explain how you know.

$$3 + 4 = 8 - \underline{\quad}$$

6. ✓**Assessment** Draw an arrow to show which number will make the equation true.

1   2   3   4   5   6   7   8

$$4 + \underline{\quad} = 1 + 8$$

© Pearson Education, Inc. 1

Name _____

Solve & Share

I have 6 oranges, Alex has 2 pears, and Jada has 4 apples. How many pieces of fruit do we have in all?

Write 2 different addition equations to solve the problem.

I can ...
use different strategies to solve word problems with 3 addends.

I can also model with math.

___ + ___ + ___ = ___

___ + ___ + ___ = ___

Vince collects red rocks. He separates them into 3 baskets. How many red rocks does he have in all?

 5    4    6

I can add 5 + 4 first and then add 6.

$5 + 4 = 9$
$9 + 6 = 15$

I can add 4 + 6 to make 10 and then add 5.

$4 + 6 = 10$
$10 + 5 = 15$

 5    4   6

I can group the numbers either way. The sum is the same.

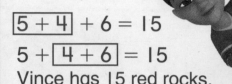

$\boxed{5 + 4} + 6 = 15$
$5 + \boxed{4 + 6} = 15$
Vince has 15 red rocks.

Do You Understand?

Show Me! How can grouping numbers in a different way help you to solve a problem?

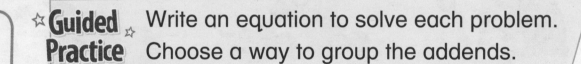

☆ **Guided Practice** ☆   Write an equation to solve each problem. Choose a way to group the addends.

1. Tess finds some shells at the beach. She finds 7 pink shells, 3 black shells, and 4 white shells. How many shells does Tess find in all?

   $\underline{7} + \underline{3} + \underline{4} = \underline{14}$ $\underline{14}$ shells

2. Tom sees some birds. He sees 4 red birds, 2 blue birds, and 6 black birds. How many birds does Tom see in all?

   ___ + ___ + ___ = ___   ___ birds

Topic 5 | Lesson 4

Tools   Assessment

Independent Practice   Write an equation to solve each problem. Choose a way to group the addends.

3. Pat has cards of his favorite athletes. He has 8 baseball cards, 2 football cards, and 3 basketball cards. How many cards does Pat have in all?

____ + ____ + ____ = ____

____ cards

4. Bob plants seeds. He plants 2 brown seeds, 6 white seeds, and 8 black seeds. How many seeds does Bob plant in all?

____ + ____ + ____ = ____

____ seeds

Write the missing numbers for each problem.

5. **Algebra** $16 = 7 + \underline{} + 6$

6. **Algebra** $11 = 2 + 2 + \underline{}$

7. **A-Z Vocabulary** Julio finds 3 ladybugs and some ants. Then he finds 5 beetles. Julio finds 14 bugs in all. How many ants did Julio find? Write the missing **addend**.

$14 = 3 + \underline{} + 5$

Julio finds ____ ants.

8. **Higher Order Thinking** Rosa picks 12 flowers from her garden. She picks some purple flowers. Then she picks 4 pink flowers and 3 yellow flowers. How many purple flowers did Rosa pick?

$12 = ? + 4 + 3$

She picks ____ purple flowers.

9. **Generalize** Dan throws 3 beanbags at the target. The numbers on the target show the score for each beanbag.

Write an addition equation to find Dan's score.

Does something repeat in the problem?

____ + ____ + ____ = ____

10. **Higher Order Thinking** Write a story problem about toys. The story should match the addition equation below.

$4 + 1 + 9 = 14$

11. ✅ **Assessment** Joy throws 3 beanbags at the target. She scores 17 points. Which picture shows her target?

Ⓐ

Ⓑ

Ⓒ

Ⓓ

Name _____

Help   Tools   Games

Another Look! You can group addends in different ways.
Then you can write an equation.

 +  +

Sally has some fruit.
She has 3 apples,
5 bananas, and 5 pears.
How many pieces of fruit
does she have in all?

First, add the bananas and pears.

$5 + 5 = \underline{10}$

Then add the apples.

$\underline{10} + \underline{3} = \underline{13}$

Sally has $\underline{13}$ pieces of fruit in all.

HOME ACTIVITY Gather several different kinds of small objects, such as buttons, paper clips, and pennies. Tell your child a word problem using the objects. Have your child add the objects together, telling you how many in all.

 Find each sum. Choose a way to group the addends.

1.

___ + ___ + ___ = ___

2.

___ + ___ + ___ = ___

Write an equation to solve each problem.

3. Todd plays with some blocks. He has 3 red blocks, 3 yellow blocks, and 6 blue blocks. How many blocks is Todd playing with in all?

____ + ____ + ____ = ____

____ blocks

4. Emma has 7 green beads, some purple beads, and 6 yellow beads. She has 17 beads in all. How many purple beads does Emma have?

____ + ____ + ____ = ____

____ purple beads

5. Rita plants 3 rows of carrots, 4 rows of onions, and 7 rows of lettuce. How many rows of vegetables did Rita plant in all?

____ + ____ + ____ = ____

____ rows

6. Julien builds 8 tables, 3 chairs, and 4 desks. How many pieces of furniture did Julien build?

____ + ____ + ____ = ____

____ pieces

7. Higher Order Thinking Write a story problem about the lunchroom that matches the equation $5 + 8 + 2 = 15$.

_____

_____

_____

8. ✔**Assessment** At the animal shelter, Kim feeds 2 rabbits, 6 dogs, and 4 cats. How many animals does Kim feed in all?

| 18 | 16 | 15 | 12 |
| Ⓐ | Ⓑ | Ⓒ | Ⓓ |

© Pearson Education, Inc. I

Solve

Solve & Share

Carlos made stacks of 6 books, 4 books, and 6 books. How can you use addition to find the number of books in all three stacks?

Write two different equations to show how many books in all.

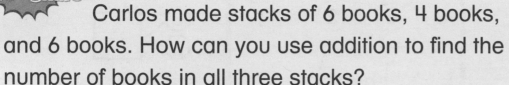

I can ...
find different strategies to add three numbers.

I can also model with math.

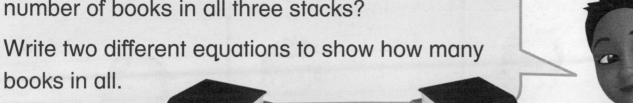

$$\underline{\hspace{1.5em}} + \underline{\hspace{1.5em}} + \underline{\hspace{1.5em}} = \underline{\hspace{1.5em}}$$

$$\underline{\hspace{1.5em}} + \underline{\hspace{1.5em}} + \underline{\hspace{1.5em}} = \underline{\hspace{1.5em}}$$

You can add three numbers.

$$8 + 6 + 2$$

Pick 2 numbers to add first.

You can make 10.

$⑧ + 6 + ② = 16$

10

$8 + 2 = 10$
$10 + 6 = 16$

You can make a double.

$8 + ⑥ + ② = 16$

8

$6 + 2 = 8$
$8 + 8 = 16$

You can add any two numbers first.

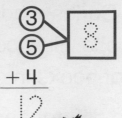

$$\begin{array}{c} ③ \\ ⑤ \\ +4 \hline 12 \end{array} \quad \boxed{8} \qquad \begin{array}{c} 3 \\ ⑤ \\ +④ \hline 12 \end{array} \quad \boxed{9}$$

The sums are the same.

Do You Understand?

Show Me! Why can you pick any two numbers to add first when you add three numbers?

☆ **Guided Practice** ☆ Add the circled numbers first. Write their sum in the box. Then write the sum of all three numbers.

1. $② + ⑨ + 1 = 12$

11

$2 + ⑨ + ① = 12$

10

2. $⑥ + ③ + 2 = \underline{\hspace{1cm}}$

$\boxed{}$

$6 + ③ + ② = \underline{\hspace{1cm}}$

$\boxed{}$

© Pearson Education, Inc. 1

Topic 5 | Lesson 5

Independent Practice

Circle two numbers to add first. Write their sum in the box at the right. Then write the sum of all three numbers.

3.
```
  6
  6
+ 1
```
☐

☐

4.
```
  3
  7
+ 8
```
☐

☐

5.
```
  2
  8
+ 3
```
☐

☐

6.
```
  7
  3
+ 3
```
☐

☐

7.
```
  2
  2
+ 8
```
☐

☐

8.
```
  5
  0
+ 9
```
☐

☐

9. Number Sense Find the missing numbers.
The numbers on each branch add up to 15.

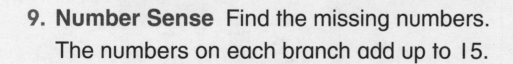

Remember, you can add in any order.

10. **Look for Patterns** Maya puts 7 books on a shelf and 3 books on another shelf. Then she puts 5 books on the last shelf. How many books did Maya put on all three shelves?

Can you break the problem into simpler parts?

_____ + _____ + _____ = _____

_____ books

11. **Higher Order Thinking** Explain how to add 7 + 2 + 3. Use pictures, numbers, or words.

12. ✅ **Assessment** Ken buys 4 pencils, 6 markers, and 7 pens. He wants to know how many items he bought in all. He added 4 + 6 first. What should Ken add next? Explain.

4 PENCILS   6 MARKERS   7 PENS

Another Look! When you add three numbers, look for facts you know. Then add the third number.

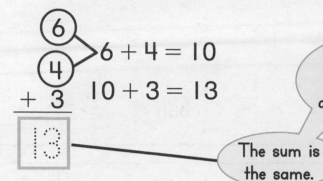

$$\begin{array}{r} ⑥ \\ ④ \\ + 3 \\ \hline \boxed{13} \end{array}$$

$6 + 4 = 10$

$10 + 3 = 13$

I can add the numbers in a different order.

The sum is the same.

$$\begin{array}{r} ⑥ \\ 4 \\ + ③ \\ \hline \boxed{13} \end{array}$$

$3 + 6 = \underline{9}$

$9 + 4 = \underline{13}$

HOME ACTIVITY Tell your child three numbers that have a sum less than or equal to 20. Have him or her add the three numbers to find the sum. Ask your child to think aloud as he or she adds the first two numbers, and then the third number to that sum. Repeat with several sets of numbers.

Find each sum using different ways. Add the circled numbers first. Then add the third number.

1.
$$\begin{array}{r} ⑤ \\ 2 \\ + ⑤ \\ \hline \boxed{} \end{array}$$

$5 + 5 = \underline{}$

$\underline{} + 2 = \underline{}$

$$\begin{array}{r} 5 \\ ② \\ + ⑤ \\ \hline \boxed{} \end{array}$$

$2 + 5 = \underline{}$

$\underline{} + 5 = \underline{}$

Add the numbers shown. Circle the numbers you add first.

2.

□
□
+ □
_____
□ turtles

3.

□
□
+ □
_____
□ fish

4. **Higher Order Thinking** Explain how to add $3 + 3 + 4$. Use pictures, numbers, or words.

5. **✓Assessment** Matt buys pieces to make a model car. He buys 1 block of wood, 4 tires, and 2 cans of paint. Matt wants to know how many items he bought in all. If he adds $1 + 2$ first, what should Matt add next? Explain.

© Pearson Education, Inc. 1

Solve & Share

Jose has 5 more erasers than Lois. Jose has 7 erasers. How many erasers does Lois have? Write your answers below.

Solve

Lesson 5-6
Solve Addition and Subtraction Word Problems

I can ...
solve word problems involving comparisons.

I can also make sense of problems.

Jose's erasers

Lois' erasers

Steve has 13 books. Claire has 4 fewer books than Steve. How many books does Claire have?

You can use a bar model to show the problem.

Steve's books

13

?	4

Claire's   **4 fewer**
books   **books**

You can write an addition or subtraction equation to see how many books Claire has.

$13 - 4 = \underline{9}$

$4 + \underline{9} = 13$

13

9	4

So, Claire has 9 books.

Do You Understand?

Show Me! Tom made 8 fewer sandcastles than Tina. Tina made 10 sandcastles. How many sandcastles did Tom make?

☆ Guided ☆ Practice
Use the models to solve the problems.

1. Sal has 8 more magazines than Gemma. Sal has 15 magazines. How many magazines does Gemma have?

Sal's magazines

15

7	8

Gemma's   **8 more**
magazines   **magazines**

$\underline{8} + \underline{7} = \underline{15}$

Gemma has ____ magazines.

Independent Practice   Use the models to complete the problems.

2. Alan picks up 3 toys. Then he picks up 8 more. How many toys did Alan pick up in all?

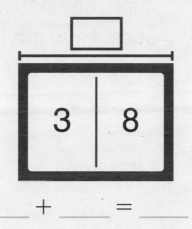

____ + ____ = ____

Alan picked up ____ toys in all.

3. Jack makes 5 fewer fruit cups than Sandi. Sandi makes 11 fruit cups. How many fruit cups did Jack make?

11

5

____ – ____ = ____

Jack makes ____ fruit cups.

 Fill in the missing number for the model or the equation. Choose addition or subtraction to solve.

4. Harry has 5 fewer buttons than Tina. Harry has 7 buttons. How many buttons does Tina have?

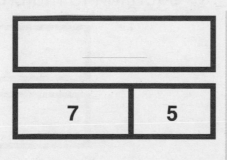

7   5

____ ◯ ____ = ____ buttons

5. Mark calls some people. Jane calls 8 people. They called 17 people in all. How many people did Mark call?

17

8

____ ◯ ____ = ____ people

6. Make Sense Ashlyn had some stuffed animals. She gives 5 to Anna. Now Ashlyn has 7 stuffed animals. How many stuffed animals did Ashlyn have before?

_____ ◯ _____ = _____

Ashlyn had _____ stuffed animals before.

7. Make Sense Lucy and Tim find 15 bottle caps together. Tim finds 7 of the bottle caps. How many of the bottle caps does Lucy find?

_____ ◯ _____ = _____

Lucy finds _____ bottle caps.

8. Higher Order Thinking Draw a model to show the equation. Then write and solve the equation.

$$16 - 10 = \underline{\quad ? \quad}$$

_____ − _____ = _____

9. ✓**Assessment** Tanner's family has 3 more pets than Ava's family. Tanner's family has 7 pets. How many pets does Ava's family have?

Complete the bar diagram and write an equation to match the story.

7

_____	3

_____ ◯ _____ = _____

Name _____

Another Look! You can use addition or subtraction to solve word problems.

Bill has 10 more berries than Ken.

Bill has 14 berries.

How many berries does Ken have?

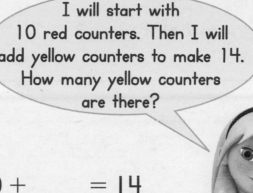
I will start with 10 red counters. Then I will add yellow counters to make 14. How many yellow counters are there?

Bill has 10 more than Ken. I will subtract.

$14 - 10 = $ _____

$10 + $ _____ $= 14$

$14 - 10 = \underline{4}$

$10 + \underline{4} = 14$

Ken has 4 berries.

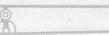

HOME ACTIVITY Model a comparison situation, such as, Tom has 3 more cards than Julie. Tom has 10 cards. How many cards does Julie have? Have your child use small objects to model the story. Then ask him or her to write an equation that matches the story. Repeat with other similar comparison problems.

Draw counters to show the problem. Then solve.

1. Shelly has 10 pumpkins. She gives some to Nola. Now Shelly has 6 pumpkins. How many pumpkins did Shelly give Nola?

_____ ◯ _____ = _____

Shelly gives Nola _____ pumpkins.

Draw counters to solve.

2. Victor writes 10 more poems than Ann. Ann writes 10 poems. How many poems does Victor write?

___ ◯ ___ = ___

Victor writes ___ poems.

3. Barb has 13 crayons. She gives 6 crayons to Javier. How many crayons does Barb have left?

___ ◯ ___ = ___

Barb has ___ crayons left.

4. Higher Order Thinking Write a story that uses the word **more**. Then solve.

___ ◯ ___ = ___

5.  **Assessment** Sam draws 6 fewer pictures than Tina. Tina draws 15 pictures. How many pictures does Sam draw? Draw or cross out counters and write an equation to match the story.

___ ◯ ___ = ___

Sam draws ___ pictures.

Name _____

Solve & Share

Discuss the equation below with a partner.
Decide whether it is true or false. Explain your thinking.

$$9 = 5 + 2 + 2$$

I can ...
understand that the equal sign means "the same value as" and I will use precise language when talking about it.

I can also add and subtract within 20.

Thinking Habits

Am I using numbers and symbols correctly?

Is my answer clear?

What missing number can you write to make the equation true?

$14 = 5 + \underline{\quad} + 8$

How can I be precise as I solve this problem?

I can use words, numbers, and symbols correctly.

The equal sign means "the same value as." 14 has the same value as 5 plus some number plus 8.

$5 + 8 = 13$, so $14 = 13 + \underline{\quad}$.

$13 + 1 = 14$, so 1 is the missing number.

$14 = 5 + \underline{1} + 8$.

Do You Understand?

Show Me! Is the equation below true or false? How do you know?

$10 + 5 = 9 + 3 + 3$

Guided Practice Write the symbol ($+$, $-$, or $=$) or number to make the equation true. Then tell how you know you found the correct symbol or number.

1. $3 + 8 = 4 + \boxed{7}$

_____

_____

_____

_____

2. $4 + 3 + \boxed{} = 13$

_____

_____

_____

_____

Independent Practice Write the symbol (+, −, or =) or number to make the equation true. Then tell how you know you found the correct symbol or number.

3. 19 ◯ 10 = 9

_____

_____

_____

4. 20 = ☐ + 5 + 5

_____

_____

_____

5. 10 + 1 ◯ 6 + 5

_____

_____

_____

6. 9 − 2 = 10 ◯ 3

_____

_____

_____

7. **Algebra** Write the missing number in the equation below. Explain how you know.

42 + 55 = 55 + ☐

_____

_____

Think about the meanings of the symbols.

Problem Solving

Balloon Party Dani has 7 green and 4 yellow balloons. Gene has 15 blue balloons.

8. **Explain** If Gene gives 4 of his balloons away, then he and Dani will have the same number. Fill in the blanks to make the equation true. Use $+$, $-$, or $=$.

7 ◯ 4 ◯ 15 ◯ 4

Explain how you chose the symbols.

_____

_____

_____

How do you know the equation is true?

_____

_____

_____

9. **Be Precise** If Gene keeps all 15 blue balloons, how many balloons would Dani need to buy to have the same number as Gene? Complete the equation to find the answer.

7 ◯ 4 ◯ ____ ◯ 15

Did you use numbers and symbols correctly? Explain how you know.

_____

_____

_____

_____

© Pearson Education, Inc. 1

Topic 5 | Lesson 7

Help   Tools   Games

Another Look! You can write a missing number to make an equation true.

$$3 + 9 = \underline{\quad} + 6$$

First, solve the side you know.

$$3 + 9 = \underline{12}$$

I know the meaning of the = symbol is "the same as".

Then, use what you know to solve the other side.

$$12 = \underline{6} + 6$$

12 is a double: 6 + 6. The missing number is 6!

$3 + 9 = 6 + 6$ is the same as $12 = 12$.

Write the missing number to make the equation true. Then, write the number that makes both sides equal.

1. $\boxed{} - 0 = 7 + 8$

   $\underline{\quad} = \underline{\quad}$

2. $6 + 4 = \boxed{} + 9$

   $\underline{\quad} = \underline{\quad}$

3. $8 - 5 = 13 - \boxed{}$

   $\underline{\quad} = \underline{\quad}$

Checkers James and Amy played 12 games of checkers last week. This week they played 7 games on Monday and 2 games on Wednesday.

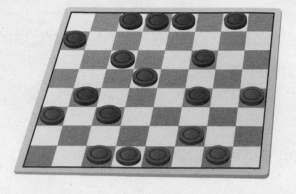

4. **Explain** James and Amy play 3 more games. They have played the same number of games as last week. Fill in the blanks to make the equation true. Use +, −, or =.

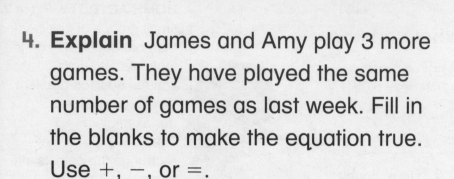

Explain how you chose the symbols.

_____

_____

_____

_____

How do you know the equation is true?

_____

5. **Be Precise** Amy lost 4 of the games she played last week. How many games did she win?

Write an equation to find your answer.

____ ◯ ____ ◯ ____

Amy won _____ games.

Use precise math language to explain how you know your equation and answer are correct.

_____

_____

_____

_____

© Pearson Education, Inc. 1

Point & Tally

Find a partner. Get paper and a pencil.

Each partner chooses a different color: light blue or dark blue.

Partner 1 and Partner 2 each point to a black number at the same time. Subtract Partner 1's number from Partner 2's number.

If the answer is on your color, you get a tally mark.

Work until one partner gets twelve tally marks.

I can ...
add and subtract within 10.

Partner 1

5
0
3
1
4
2

| 6 | 4 | 1 | 8 | 9 | 5 |
| 2 | 10 | 0 | 3 | 1 | 7 |

Partner 2

8
6
5
10
7
9

| Tally Marks for Partner 1 | Tally Marks for Partner 2 |

A-Z Glossary

Word List
- add
- equation
- more
- subtract

Understand Vocabulary

1. Circle **True** or **False** for the addition equation below.

$$4 + 6 = 5 + 2 + 3$$

True   False

2. Circle **True** or **False** for the subtraction equation below.

$$10 = 11 - 2$$

True   False

3. Write the number you need to add to make the equation true.

$$7 - 3 = 2 + \underline{\quad}$$

4. Write the number you need to add to make the equation true.

$$\underline{\quad} + 4 + 2 = 10$$

5. Write the number you need to subtract to make the equation true.

$$9 = 10 - \underline{\quad}$$

Use Vocabulary in Writing

6. Write a story problem with a true equation using at least two words from the Word List.

Name _____

Set A

Solve to find out if the equation is **True** or **False**.

$$6 + 5 = 3 + 8$$

Solve one side first. $6 + 5 = 11$
Solve the other side. $3 + 8 = 11$

$$11 = 11$$

This equation is **True**.

Tell whether each equation is **True** or **False**.

1. $8 - 5 = 4 + 1$

   True   **False**

2. $3 + 1 = 12 - 8$

   True   **False**

Set B

Write the missing numbers to make the equations true.

$4 + 7 = 6 + $ _____

Both sides should be equal.

$4 + 7 = 11$

So, $6 + \underline{5} = 11$.

The missing number is 5.

$4 + 7 = 6 + \underline{5}$

Find and write the missing numbers to make the equations true.

3. $11 = $ _____ $+ 4$

4. _____ $- 4 = 5$

5. $10 + 5 = 6 + $ _____

6. $9 - $ _____ $= 13 - 10$

7. $14 - $ _____ $= 2 + 2$

You can add three numbers in any order. $2 + 8 + 2 =$ ___?___

Make a 10. Then add 2.

$(2) + (8) + 2 =$ _12_

Make a double. Then add 8.

$(2) + 8 + (2) =$ _12_

Find the sum. Solve in any order.

8. $5 + 5 + 4 =$ ___

9. $9 + 5 + 1 =$ ___

10. $6 + 4 + 4 =$ ___

11. $3 + 3 + 5 =$ ___

Thinking Habits

Precision

Am I using numbers and symbols correctly?

Am I adding and subtracting accurately?

Write the symbol ($+$, $-$, or $=$) or number to make the equation true. Then tell how you know you chose the correct symbol or number.

12. $10 - 5 = 2 \bigcirc 3$

_____

_____

_____

13. $4 + 5 = 10 \bigcirc 1$

_____

_____

_____

© Pearson Education, Inc. 1

Name _____

1. Complete the model. Then write the missing number in the equation.

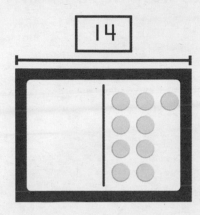

14 = ____ + 9

2. Tell if the equation is **True** or **False**.

$$4 + 7 = 13 - 3$$

True   False

3. Which number is missing?

$$16 - \underline{\ ?\ } = 2 + 6$$

Ⓐ 10

Ⓑ 9

Ⓒ 8

Ⓓ 7

4. Tasha has 2 dogs and 3 cats.
She also has 7 goldfish.
How many pets does Tasha have in all?

$$2 + 3 + 7 = \underline{\ \ \ \ }$$

5. Bill has 10 apples. He uses 8 of them to make muffins. Josh has 6 apples. How many should he use so he has the same number as Bill?

$$10 - 8 = 6 - \underline{\hspace{1cm}}$$

_____ apples

6. Kerry, Tom, and Nicole want to play tennis. Kerry has 5 tennis balls. Tom has 5 tennis balls. Nicole has 3 tennis balls. How many tennis balls do they have in all?

Ⓐ 13

Ⓑ 14

Ⓒ 15

Ⓓ 16

7. In a soccer game, Andrew scores 3 fewer goals than Elsie. Elsie scores 9 goals. How many goals did Andrew score? Complete the bar diagram and write an equation to match the story.

9

_____	3

_____ ◯ _____ = _____

_____ goals

8. Write the missing symbol (+, −, or =) to make the equation true. Use precise math language to explain how you chose the symbol.

$$16 = 4 + 8 \bigcirc 4$$

_____

_____

_____

© Pearson Education, Inc. I

A Vase of Flowers

Terry and his brother, Dave, put flowers in a vase for their mother.

5 Roses

5 Daisies

2 Carnations

8 Lilies

1. Complete the equation below to show the number of lilies and roses. Use numbers and symbols (+, −, =).

_____ + 5 ◯ _____

2. How many roses, daisies, and carnations are in the vase?

Write an equation to solve.

____ + ____ + ____ = ____

Explain how you added. Use pictures, numbers, or words.

3. Terry puts the roses and the daisies in the vase. Dave puts the carnations and the lilies in the vase. Did they put an equal number of flowers in the vase?

Complete the equation.

_____ + _____ = _____ + _____

Fill in the missing numbers.

Terry puts _____ flowers in the vase.

Dave puts _____ flowers in the vase.

Did Terry and Dave each put an equal number of flowers in the vase? Circle **Yes** or **No**.

Yes   No

4. Dave says there are 3 more daisies than carnations. What equation can he use to find out if he is right?

5 ◯ _____ ◯ _____

5. Terry says that if there were 2 fewer lilies, then the number of lilies would be equal to the number of daisies. He writes the equation below. Is this equation true or false? Explain how you know.

$8 - 2 = 5$

_____

_____

6. Terry and Dave buy more carnations. Now they have 10 in all. How many carnations did they buy? Complete the equation using $+$, $-$, or $=$.

10 ◯ 2 ◯ 8 _____ more carnations

Use precise math language to explain how you chose the symbols.

_____

_____

_____

© Pearson Education, Inc. 1

Represent and Interpret Data

Essential Question: What are some ways you can collect, show, and understand data?

Digital Resources

Solve Learn Glossary

Tools Assessment Help Games

There are many different types of telephones.

The first telephone was invented over 100 years ago.

Wow! Let's do this project and learn more.

Math and Science Project: Different Types of Phones

Find Out Talk to friends and relatives about the types of phones they use. Ask how phones have changed in their lifetimes.

Journal: Make a Book Show what you found out. In your book, also:

- Draw pictures of more than one type of phone. Which phone do you think is better for making calls?
- Collect data about the types of phones people use.

Name _____

Review What You Know

A-Z Vocabulary

1. Circle the cubes that make the **equation** true.

$5 + 3 = 4 + ?$

2. Write the numbers that tell how many pieces of fruit. Then circle the group with **fewer**.

____ ____

$- - - -$ $- - - -$

____ ____

3. Write the numbers that tell how many balls. Then circle the group with **more**.

____ ____

$- - - -$ $- - - -$

____ ____

Find the Missing Part

4. Write the number that will make the equation true.

$15 - 8 = \underline{\hphantom{00}} + 1$

5. Write each missing number.

$5 + 3 + 2 = \underline{\hphantom{00}}$

$9 + \underline{\hphantom{00}} + 7 = 17$

Near Doubles Facts

6. Write the missing number to solve this near doubles fact.

$7 + \underline{\hphantom{00}} = 15$

© Pearson Education, Inc. 1

My Word Cards Study the words on the front of the card.
Complete the activity on the back.

A-Z
Glossary

tally marks

marks that are used to record data

Cats	III
Dogs	II

data

information you collect

Favorite Pets
cat
dog
cat
cat
dog

tally chart

a chart that uses tally marks to show data

Broccoli	Carrots
⊪ I	⊪ IIII

survey

to gather information

Cats III
Dogs II

Do you like cats or dogs better?

picture graph

a graph that uses pictures to show data

Favorite Pets

Cat	🐱	🐱	🐱
Dog	🐶	🐶	

Use what you know to complete the sentences.
Extend learning by writing your own sentence using each word.

A chart that uses tally marks to show data is a

_____

_____.

_____ are information that you collect.

You can use

_____

_____

to show data.

A _____

_____

is a graph that uses pictures to show data.

You can ask

_____

questions to collect information.

© Pearson Education, Inc. 1

Solve

Solve & Share

Judy wants to show a friend how many crayons she has of each color. How can she show this? Show one way.

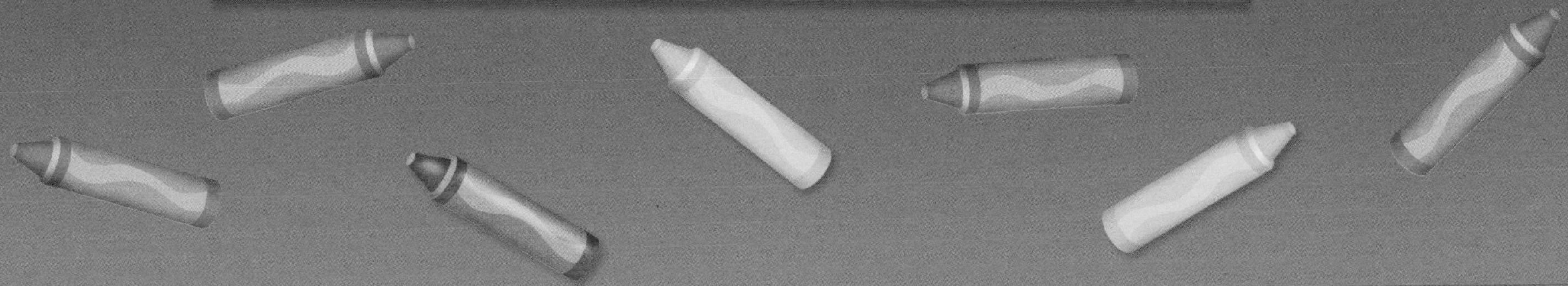

I can …
organize data into categories.

I can also model with math.

These are **tally marks**.

There are 3 tally marks.

Each tally mark stands for 1 piece of information.

Count the tally marks by 5s.

There are 20. Each ⟋⟋⟋⟍ stands for 5 pieces of information.

m a t h e m a t i c s
Make tally marks to show how many letters are black.

There are 6 black letters.

You can put the **data** in a **tally chart**.

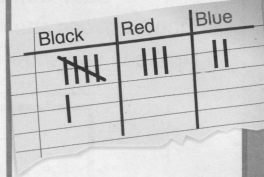

Black	Red	Blue

Do You Understand?

Show Me! How can a tally chart help you with data you collect?

☆ **Guided Practice** ☆ In the chart, make tally marks to show how many socks there are for each color.

1.

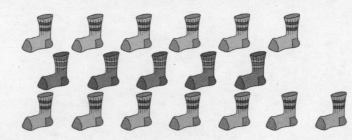

Green	Orange	Blue
⟋⟋⟋⟍ ⟋		

Name _____

Independent Practice   Use the tally chart from Guided Practice to answer each question.

2. Which color sock has the most tally marks?

_____

3. How many blue socks are there?

_____

4. How many socks are there in all?

_____

Use the tally chart below to answer each question.

Saul's Closet

Shirts	Shorts	Shoes
IIII II	IIII	II

5. How many shorts does Saul have?

_____

6. Which item in his closet does Saul have the most of?

_____

7. Math and Science Rita recorded data about different types of shoes. She made a tally mark each month for each shoe until that type of shoe wore out. Which type of shoe lasted the longest? How many months before it wore out?

Rita's Shoes

Sneakers	Sandals	Loafers
IIII	II	IIII

8. Model Draw tally marks to show how many hats there are of each color.

Blue	Green	Purple

9. Be Precise How do you know that purple caps are shown the least?

_____

_____

_____

Think about the definition of *least*.

10. Higher Order Thinking Write and answer your own question about the tally chart used in Items 8 and 9.

_____

_____

11. ✓ Assessment Which sentences are true? Choose all that apply.

☐ There are 12 blue caps.

☐ There are 7 green caps.

☐ There are 3 purple caps.

☐ There are 12 caps in all.

Name _____

Homework & Practice 6-1
Organize Data into Three Categories

Another Look! You can make tally marks to show information.
The tally chart shows the ways students get to school.

Getting to School

Walk	School Bus
卌 II	卌 卌

I equals 1 and 卌 equals 5.

To count the students that walk, count 5, 6, 7.
7 students walk to school.

_7_ students walk.

To count the students that ride the bus, count 5, 10.
10 students ride the bus.

_10_ students ride the bus.

_17_ students in all go to school.

Use the tally chart to answer each question.

Balloons

Red	Blue
卌	卌 II

1. Which color balloon has the most tally marks?

_____

2. How many balloons are there in all?

_____

A first grade class voted on their favorite colors. Answer each question about the tally chart.

Favorite Colors

Blue	Red	Green
卌 II	III	卌 I

3. How many students like red?

_____

4. How many students like green?

_____

5. How many students voted in all?

_____

6. Higher Order Thinking Write and answer another question about the tally chart shown above.

_____
_____
_____
_____
_____

7. ✓**Assessment** Which sentences are true? Choose all that apply.

☐ 3 students like green.

☐ 7 students like blue.

☐ The colors blue and green have the same number of votes.

☐ Red has the least votes.

Solve

Solve & Share

What is your favorite activity to do outside?

Ask several classmates to choose Jump Rope, Basketball, or Ride a Bike. Complete the tally chart to show your data. Then answer the questions.

I can ...
collect information and organize it using a picture graph.

I can also reason about math.

Favorite Outside Activity	
Jump Rope	
Basketball	
Ride a Bike	

1. Which activity has the least votes? _____

2. Which activity has the most votes? _____

Joey asks 9 friends a survey question.

Which is your favorite sport to play? Basketball, soccer, or baseball?

Joey makes I tally mark to show what each friend says.

Favorite Sport		
🏀 Basketball	III
⚽ Soccer	THL
⚾ Baseball	I

Joey uses the data in the tally chart to make a **picture graph**.

Favorite Sport						
🏀 Basketball	🏀	🏀	🏀			
⚽ Soccer	⚽	⚽	⚽	⚽	⚽	
⚾ Baseball	⚾					

Look at the pictures! Students like Soccer the most.

Do You Understand?

Show Me! Look at the **Favorite Sport** picture graph above. What sport do Joey's friends like least? How do you know?

☆ Guided Practice ☆ Kurt asks his friends a survey question. Use the data he collected to make a picture graph.

I.

Favorite Fruit		
Pear 🍐	Banana 🍌	Apple 🍎
THL III	III	THL

Favorite Fruit								
🍐 Pear	🍐	🍐	🍐	🍐	🍐	🍐	🍐	🍐
🍌 Banana								
🍎 Apple								

© Pearson Education, Inc. I

Tools Assessment

★ **Independent** ☆
☆ **Practice** ✕ Use the data in the tally chart to make a picture graph.
Then answer each question.

2. **Favorite Rainy Day Activity**

Games	Paint	Read
◇	🖌️	📘
⊮⊮⊮ II	III	⊮⊮⊮ I

Favorite Rainy Day Activity

◇ Games							
🖌️ Paint							
📘 Read							

3. Which activity is the favorite?

_____

4. How many students chose Read?

_____

5. **Higher Order Thinking** Look at the picture graph you made for
Item 2. Write two sentences that are true about the data.

_____

_____

_____

6. **Model** Gina asks her friends a survey question. Then she makes a tally chart to show their favorite music instrument. Use her data to make a picture graph.

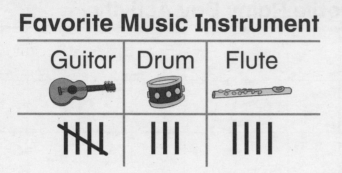

Favorite Music Instrument

Guitar	Drum	Flute
𝍷𝍷𝍷𝍷𝍷	|||	||||

Favorite Music Instrument						
Guitar						
Drum						
Flute						

7. **Higher Order Thinking** How many students voted in all? _____

Write an equation to show your answer.

_____ = _____ + _____ + _____

8. ✓**Assessment** Which musical instrument has the most votes?

Ⓐ Guitar

Ⓑ Piano

Ⓒ Flute

Ⓓ Drum

9. ✓**Assessment** How many students like the flute?

5	4	3	2
Ⓐ	Ⓑ	Ⓒ	Ⓓ

Name _____

Another Look! The data in a tally chart can be used to complete the picture graph.

Draw pictures to show how many students like to collect shells, stamps, and coins.

HOME ACTIVITY Make a tally chart titled Favorite Fruit. Show 4 tally marks next to Apples, 6 tally marks next to Bananas, and 3 tally marks next to Cherries. Have your child make a picture graph to illustrate the data. Then ask him or her questions about the information in the picture graph such as, "Which fruit is the least favorite?"

Favorite Items to Collect

Shells	Stamps	Coins

Favorite Items to Collect

	Shells					
🐚 Shells	🐚	🐚	🐚			
🏷 Stamps	☐	☐	☐	☐	☐	☐
🪙 Coins	○	○	○	○		

The graph shows that most students like to collect stamps.

How many students like to collect coins? __4__

Use the data in the picture graph to solve each problem.

1. Write the items in order from the favorite item to the least favorite item.

_____ _____
favorite

_____
least
favorite

2. The graph shows that ____ students in all like to collect shells, stamps, or coins.

Use the picture graph to solve each problem below.

Favorite School Subject							
📖 Reading	📖	📖	📖	📖	📖		
🔍 Science	🔍	🔍	🔍	🔍	🔍	🔍	
👟 Gym	👟	👟	👟	👟	👟	👟	👟

3. How many students voted for reading as their favorite subject? _____

4. Which is the favorite school subject? _____

5. **Higher Order Thinking** Write a question that can be answered by the picture graph. Then write an equation to match your question.

_____ ◯ _____ = _____

6. ✓**Assessment** How many students voted for Science?

5   6   7   13
Ⓐ   Ⓑ   Ⓒ   Ⓓ

7. ✓**Assessment** How many students voted in all?

18   17   12   11
Ⓐ   Ⓑ   Ⓒ   Ⓓ

Name _____

Solve & Share

12 students were asked, "Which vegetable do you like most at lunch, corn or peas?" This list shows their answers.

Complete the tally chart and picture graph to show the data. What do these data tell you about what students like?

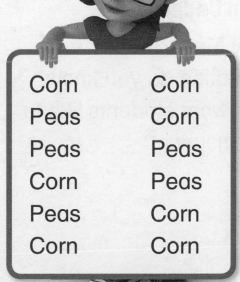

Corn	Corn
Peas	Corn
Peas	Peas
Corn	Peas
Peas	Corn
Corn	Corn

Favorite Lunchtime Vegetable

Corn	
Peas	

Favorite Lunchtime Vegetable

Corn								
Peas								

The picture graph shows how many students like milk, water, or juice with lunch.

What does the graph tell you about what students like to drink at lunch?

Lunch Drinks

Milk	🥛	🥛	🥛	🥛	🥛	🥛
Water	💧					
Juice	🧃	🧃	🧃			

6 students like milk.
3 students like juice.
Only I student likes water.

I can count and compare what drinks students like.

So, the graph tells me that students like milk better than juice or water with lunch.

Do You Understand?

Show Me! What other information do you know about what students like to drink at lunch?

⭐ Guided Practice ⭐ Use the picture graph above to answer the questions.

I. How many more students like milk than juice?

_3_ more students

2. How many fewer students like water than milk?

_____ fewer students

3. How many more students like juice than water?

_____ more students

Name _____

Independent Practice   Use the data in the tally chart to answer each question.

4. Use the data in the tally to make a picture graph.

Our Favorite Colors

Red ◄—	Blue ◄—	Purple ◄—
IIII	III̶II II	III̶II III

5. How many more students like purple than red?

_____ more students

6. Which color is the favorite?

_____

Our Favorite Colors

🖍											
🖍											
🖍											

7. Algebra Use this equation to determine how many fewer students like blue than purple.

_____ $+ 7 = 8$

_____ fewer

8. Higher Order Thinking Write and answer a question about the data in the picture graph.

_____

_____

9. Look at the tally chart.

Our Pets

Dogs	Cats	Fish
𝕀𝕀𝕀𝕀 𝕀	𝕀𝕀𝕀	𝕀𝕀

How many friends have dogs for pets? _____

How many friends have fish for pets? _____

10. **Be Precise** Look at the picture graph.

How many more friends have dogs than fish? _____

How many fewer friends have cats than dogs? _____

Our Pets

Dogs	Cats	Fish

Think about the meaning of *more* and *fewer*.

11. **Higher Order Thinking** Look at the tally chart in Item 9. How many friends have pets? Write an equation to show your work.

_____

_____

12. ✓**Assessment** Which question **CANNOT** be answered by looking at the graph in Item 10?

Ⓐ How many friends have cats?

Ⓑ How many friends have hamsters?

Ⓒ How many fewer friends have fish than dogs?

Ⓓ How many more friends have dogs than cats?

© Pearson Education, Inc. 1   **Topic 6 | Lesson 3**

Name _____

Help   Tools   Games

Another Look! Ms. Olson asked her students a survey question. She put tally marks in the tally chart to show the data.

Use the data in the tally chart to complete the picture graph.

Stickers We Like

Moon	Flower	Star
☾	✿	★
II	卌 II	卌 I

HOME ACTIVITY Draw a 2-column picture graph. Label one column "Heads" and the other column "Tails." Then have your child flip a penny. Have him or her record 10 flips in the picture graph. Talk about the results.

Stickers We Like

Moon	Flower	Star
	⚙	
	⚙	☆
	⚙	☆
	⚙	☆
	⚙	☆
☾	⚙	☆
☾	⚙	☆
Moon ☾	**Flower** ✿	**Star** ★

Picture graphs can show the data in a different way.

Use the data in the picture graph to answer each question.

1. Which sticker is the least favorite?

   _____

2. Write the stickers in order from favorite to least favorite.

   _____
   favorite

   _____
   least
   favorite

3. How many more students like the star than the moon?

   _____

Use the picture graph to answer each question.

What We Like to Do on a Trip

〰		
〰		🚲
〰	👢	🚲
〰	👢	🚲
Swim	Hike	Bike
〰	👢	🚲

4. Model How many fewer people like to ride a bike than swim? Show how you added or subtracted to find the answer.

____ ◯ ____ = ____

5. Model How many more people like to swim than hike? Show how you added or subtracted to find the answer.

____ ◯ ____ = ____

6. Higher Order Thinking Use the picture graph above to make a tally chart. Show the tally marks.

What We Like to Do on a Trip

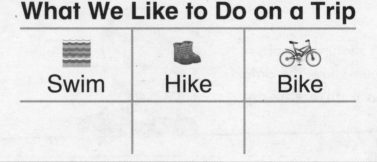

Swim	Hike	Bike

7. ✓**Assessment** Which question **CANNOT** be answered by looking at the picture graph from Items 4 and 5?

Ⓐ How many more people like to swim than ride a bike?

Ⓑ How many people like to dance?

Ⓒ How many fewer people like to hike than ride a bike?

Ⓓ How many people voted?

© Pearson Education, Inc. I

Solve & Share

At the park, Susan sees 13 animals in all. 9 are birds. The rest are rabbits. How can Susan complete the table to show this? Show your work.

Solve

Lesson 6-4

Continue to Interpret Data

I can ...
use a picture graph to interpret data.

I can also break apart problems.

Birds	Rabbits

Abby asks 15 students if they like broccoli or carrots better. 6 choose broccoli. The rest choose carrots. How many chose carrots?

Use a tally chart to find the missing data.

Broccoli	Carrots
IIII	NII
I	IIII

6 choose broccoli. I can count up to 15 to find how many chose carrots.

You can also write an equation to show the problem.

$15 - 6 = \underline{9}$

How many more students chose carrots than broccoli? Write an equation to compare.

$9 - 6 = \underline{3}$

3 more classmates like carrots than like broccoli.

Do You Understand?

Show Me! How did Abby know to count up from 6 to 15 in the problem above?

☆ **Guided Practice** ☆ Draw the missing symbols in the picture graph. Then use the graph to solve the problem.

1.

Favorite Fruit

Apple	🍎	🍎	🍎			
Orange	🍊	🍊	🍊	🍊	🍊	🍊

Jim asks 9 members of his family for their favorite fruit.

6 people say they like oranges. The rest say they like apples.

How many people say they like apples? _____ people

Tools Assessment

Independent Practice Use the graphs to answer the questions. Fill in the missing data.

2. A shelf at a store holds 11 stuffed animals. There are 5 stuffed bears and the rest are stuffed penguins.

How many stuffed penguins are on the shelf?

Sylvie's Stuffed Animals

Bears	🧸	🧸	🧸	🧸	🧸			
Penguins								

_____ stuffed penguins

3. Zach plays 17 games in a season. 9 of the games are soccer games and the rest are baseball.

How many baseball games does Zach play in one season?

Zach's Games

Baseball									
Soccer	⚽	⚽	⚽	⚽	⚽	⚽	⚽	⚽	⚽

_____ baseball games

4. **Number Sense** Jen's class makes a graph about two of their favorite kinds of movies.

How many students took the survey?

_____ students

Favorite Kind of Movie

Funny	Scary

5. **Reasoning** Jaime makes a weather graph. He records the weather each day. How many days has Jaime recorded the weather?

_____ days

Weather							
Sunny	◯	◯	◯	◯			
Cloudy	☁	☁	☁	☁	☁	☁	

6. **Higher Order Thinking** Ryan asks 20 students which subject is their favorite. He forgot to record responses for the students that chose Science.

Draw the missing tally marks. Explain how you know you drew the right number.

Reading	Math	Science	Social Studies
ЖЖ	ЖЖ III		III

_____

_____

7. ✔**Assessment** Daisi asks 9 students if they like cats or dogs better. 4 choose cats. The rest choose dogs.

How many chose dogs? Help Daisi finish her graph.

_____ students

Favorite Animal						
Cat	🐱	🐱	🐱	🐱			
Dog	🐶	🐶	🐶				

Name _____

Another Look! You can use a picture graph to solve problems.

Adam asks 13 friends whether they like butter or jelly on their toast.

How many students' responses does he have left to record?

How Do You Like Your Toast?							
Butter	🧈	🧈	🧈				
Jelly	🫙	🫙	🫙	🫙	🫙		

There are 8 pictures on the graph.

If I start at 8, I need to count up 5 more to get to 13.

$13 - 8 = \underline{5}$ responses

Fill in the missing tally marks. Then use the chart to solve the problem.

1. Maggie asks 12 members of her family for their favorite kind of cereal. 4 people say they like Corny Cones. The rest say they like Great Granola.

   How many people said they liked Great Granola?

   _____ people

Corny Cones	Great Granola
IIII	

Use the data to solve the problems.

2. Lindsay asks her friends whether they like Recess or Gym more.

How many friends took the survey? _____ friends

Recess	Gym
~~卌~~ ~~卌~~	~~卌~~ II

---

3. Higher Order Thinking Write a problem that can be solved using this picture graph.

_____

_____

_____

Flowers in the Garden							
Roses	🌹	🌹	🌹	🌹	🌹		
Daisies	🌼	🌼	🌼	🌼	🌼	🌼	🌼

---

4. ✓**Assessment** Miguel asks 16 friends to come to his birthday party. He makes a graph to show who is coming and who is not.

How many of Miguel's friends have not responded yet? Write an equation to solve.

 _____ friends

Birthday Party											
Coming	🙂	🙂	🙂	🙂	🙂	🙂					
Not Coming	🙁	🙁	🙁								

© Pearson Education, Inc. 1

Name _____

Solve & Share

Kelly asks 12 students if they like using pens, markers, or pencils best. The tally chart shows their responses.

How many students would need to change their vote from markers to pencils to make pencils the favorite? Complete the new chart to explain.

I can ...
persevere to solve problems about sets of data.

I can also add and subtract using data.

Pens	Markers	Pencils
✎	▬	✏
III	ℍℍ II	II

Pens	Markers	Pencils
✎	▬	✏

_____ students need to change to pencils.

Thinking Habits

What do I need to find?

What do I know?

Sarah asks 15 people if they like football or baseball. 1 more person chose football than chose baseball.

How many people chose each sport? What would the tally chart look like?

What's my plan for solving this problem?

I can...
• think about what I know.
• think about what I need to find.

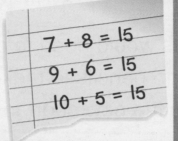

Think of all the addition facts you know that add to 15.

$7 + 8 = 15$
$9 + 6 = 15$
$10 + 5 = 15$

7 and 8 add to 15 and 8 is 1 more than 7.

So, 8 people chose football and 7 people chose baseball.

Favorite Sport

Baseball	Football
𝍷𝍷𝍷𝍷 𝍷𝍷	𝍷𝍷𝍷𝍷 𝍷𝍷𝍷

Do You Understand?

Show Me! For the survey above, why couldn't 9 choose football and 6 choose baseball?

☆Guided Practice☆

Use the tally chart to answer the questions.

1. 3 more students take the survey. Now, football and baseball have the same number of votes.

How many votes does each have? Use pictures, words, or equations to explain.

Favorite Sport

Baseball	Football
卌 IIII	卌 IIII

_____

_____

© Pearson Education, Inc. 1   **Topic 6 | Lesson 5**

Independent Practice ☆ Use the chart and graph to solve the problems below.

Linzie asks 18 students if they like milk, water, or juice with lunch. 7 students like milk. 3 students like water. The rest of the students like juice.

Lunch Drinks

Milk	Water	Juice
🥛	💧	🧃
𝍷𝍷𝍷𝍷𝍷 𝍷𝍷	𝍷𝍷𝍷	

2. How many students like juice? Complete Linzie's tally chart to solve.

_____ students like juice.

_____

3. What is the favorite drink?

_____

4. The next day Linzie asks the same question again. 3 students change their response from juice to water. What is the favorite drink now?

_____

5. 🅰🆉 **Vocabulary** Linzie records her new **survey** results in the picture graph below.

Complete the graph to show how many students like juice.

Draw pictures to show the data!

Lunch Drinks								
🥛 Milk	🥛	🥛	🥛	🥛	🥛	🥛	🥛	
🧴 Water	🧴	🧴	🧴	🧴	🧴	🧴		
🧃 Juice								

Going to School

Ebony asks 14 classmates if they take the bus, walk, or ride in a car to school.

4 students ride in a car. The remaining students vote equally for taking the bus or walking to school.

Going to School

Bus	Walk	Ride
		IIII

6. **Make Sense** How can you find out how many students take the bus or walk to school?

_____

_____

_____

7. **Model** Complete the tally chart to show how Ebony's classmates voted. Write an equation to show how many walk and take the bus.

____ ◯ ____ ◯ ____

8. **Explain** How do you know your answers are correct? Use pictures, words, or equations to explain.

_____

_____

© Pearson Education, Inc. 1

Name _____

Another Look! 9 students answer a survey about their favorite pet.

4 students vote for dog. 3 students vote for fish.

The rest of the students vote for cat.

How many students vote for cat? Complete the picture graph to show the results of the survey.

2 students chose cat as their favorite pet.

What strategies can you use to solve the problem?

HOME ACTIVITY Along with your child, think of a survey question to ask friends or family members. For instance, "Do you prefer grapes, bananas, or pineapples?" Record the results of your survey in a tally chart. Think of some questions about the data, such as, "How many more people chose bananas than grapes?" Have your child write an equation to solve the problem.

Favorite Pet

Dog						
Fish						
Cat						

$9 = 4 + 3 + \underline{\ ?\ }$

$9 = 7 + \underline{2}$

Use the picture graph above to answer the question.

1. 4 more students take the survey. Now cat has the most votes and fish has the fewest votes. Use pictures, words, or equations to explain how the 4 students voted.

_____

Snack Time

Phil asks friends to choose their favorite snack.

The tally chart at the right shows the results.

Favorite Snack

Pretzels	Yogurt
IIII	⊬⊬⊬ IIII

2. **Reasoning** Which snack is the favorite? How many more friends chose that snack?

_____

_____

3. **Model** How many of Phil's friends answered the survey? Write an equation to show your thinking.

_____

_____

4. **Make Sense** Phil adds grapes as a third choice in his survey. He asks the same friends to answer the survey again. The new survey results are shown in the tally chart at the right. How did the votes change? Use pictures, words, or equations to explain.

Favorite Snack

Pretzels	Yogurt	Grapes
III	⊬⊬⊬ I	IIII

_____

_____

Name _____

Find a Match

Find a partner. Point to a clue. Read the clue. Look below the clues to find a match. Write the clue letter in the box next to the match. Find a match for every clue.

I can …
add and subtract within 10.

Clues

A $4 + 6$

B $8 - 2$

C $3 - 1$

D $10 - 5$

E $8 + 1$

F $3 + 4$

G $8 - 7$

H $1 + 3$

☐ $1 + 0$	☐ $7 + 3$	☐ $8 - 1$	☐ $1 + 1$
☐ $5 + 4$	☐ $2 + 3$	☐ $3 + 3$	☐ $4 - 0$

Understand Vocabulary

Circle the correct answer for each question using the image at the left.

Blue	Red	Green
IIII	III	ᚤᚤᚤ

Word List
- data
- picture graph
- survey
- tally chart
- tally marks

1. Green shows ____ tally marks.

     3   4   5   6

2. The picture is called a _____.

   picture graph   tally chart   survey   tally mark

Fill in the blanks using words from the Word List.

Favorite Drinks

Milk	🥛	🥛	
Juice	🧃	🧃	🧃

3. This graph is called a

   _____.

4. "What is your favorite drink?" could be the

   _____

   question for this graph.

5. You can use the

   _____

   to answer questions about the graph.

Use Vocabulary in Writing

6. Write a story problem using at least two words from the Word List. Draw and write to solve.

   _____

   _____

   _____

   _____

   _____

Name _____

You can collect and sort data into a table.

Jimmy asks 10 friends what meal takes the longest to eat.

Longest Meal

Breakfast	Lunch	Dinner
III	I	~~IIII~~ I

Each I is one friend's answer.

....

The graph shows Jimmy's data using objects.

Longest Meal						
🔲 Breakfast	🔲	🔲	🔲			
🔲 Lunch	🔲					
🔲 Dinner	🔲	🔲	🔲	🔲	🔲	🔲

Each 🔲 is one friend's answer.

_6_ friends said dinner was their longest meal.

Use the data from Jimmy's survey to solve each problem.

Reteaching

1. How many friends said dinner was their longest meal?

_____ friends

2. How many friends said breakfast or dinner was their longest meal?

_____ friends

Write an equation to answer each question.

3. How many more friends chose breakfast than lunch?

____ − ____ = ____   _____ more

4. How many more chose dinner than breakfast?

____ − ____ = ____   _____ more

You can use data in a picture graph to ask and answer questions.

Mari asks 16 of her friends for their favorite activity. She records their answers in a graph.

Favorite Activity

Soccer	⚽	⚽	⚽	⚽			
Tennis	🎾	🎾	🎾	🎾	🎾	🎾	🎾
Running	👟	👟	👟	👟	👟		

Thinking Habits

Make Sense and Persevere

What are the amounts?

What am I trying to find?

Use Mari's picture graph to answer each question.

5. How many people chose soccer or running?

_____ − _____ = _____ OR _____ + _____ = _____

6. Mari asks some more friends and they all chose tennis as their favorite activity.

Now the number of students who like tennis is the same as the number of students who like soccer or running.

How many more friends did Mari ask?

_____ more

Explain how you know.

_____

_____

_____

© Pearson Education, Inc. 1

Name _____

1. Which set of tally marks shows the number of hats in the picture graph?

 Hat				
Mitt				

Ⅱ
Ⓐ

ⅠⅠⅠⅠ
Ⓑ

卌
Ⓒ

卌Ⅰ
Ⓓ

2. Look at the picture graph in Item 1. How many fewer mitts than hats are there?

4
Ⓐ

3
Ⓑ

2
Ⓒ

1
Ⓓ

3. Use the picture graph to answer the question.

Which of the following statements are true?
Choose all that apply.

Zoo Animals

☐ There are 2 more penguins than bears.

☐ There are 2 fewer bears than penguins.

☐ There are more bears than penguins.

☐ There are 8 bears and penguins.

Use the tally chart to solve each problem below.

4.

Favorite Winter Activity

🥾 Skating		卌
🎿 Skiing		|||
🛷 Sledding		卌 ||

Kyla asks her friends a survey question. Which is their favorite winter activity?

_____

5. Use the tally chart from Item 4 to complete the picture graph below.

Favorite Winter Activity							
🥾 Skating	🥾	🥾	🥾	🥾	🥾		
🎿 Skiing							
🛷 Sledding							

6. How many students took the survey? Write an equation to show your work.

_____ students

7. More students take the survey. Skiing is now the favorite activity. What is the fewest number of votes needed for this to happen? Explain.

_____

_____

_____

Name _____

Dinosaur Project Mrs. Johnson's class is doing a dinosaur
project. The tally chart shows which dinosaurs the students
chose.

1. How many more students chose
   T-Rex than Triceratops?
   Explain how you know. Use pictures,
   numbers, or words.

Dinosaur Project

Triceratops	T-Rex	Apatosaurus
𝍦𝍦 IIII	𝍦𝍦 𝍦𝍦 II	𝍦𝍦 II

2. Two students were absent when the class
   made the tally chart. They chose their
   dinosaur the next day. Mrs. Johnson said
   that now two dinosaurs had the same
   number. Which dinosaur did the 2 students
   choose? How do you know?

_____ more students

3. Mrs. Bee's class is also doing a dinosaur project. The tally chart shows which dinosaurs the students chose.

The students will draw their dinosaurs on the picture graph below when they finish their reports.

Fill in the picture graph to show what it will look like when all the reports are finished.

Dinosaur Project

Triceratops	T-Rex	Apatosaurus
卌 |||	卌 ||||	卌	

4. How many students still need to finish a report on the T-Rex? How many need to finish a report on the Apatosaurus? Use pictures, words, or equations to explain.

© Pearson Education, Inc. 1

Topic 6 | Performance Assessment

Extend the Counting Sequence

Essential Question: How can you use what you already know about counting to count past 100?

Digital Resources

Solve Learn Glossary

Tools Assessment Help Games

All babies do different things to help themselves survive.

They might cry or make noise to let their parents know that they need something.

Wow! Let's do this project and learn more.

Math and Science Project: Parents and Babies

Find Out Talk to friends and relatives about different types of animal parents and babies. Ask for help finding information about how babies communicate with their parents.

Journal: Make a Book Show what you found out. In your book, also:

- Draw how animal parents protect babies and how animal babies communicate with parents.

- Go outside or to the zoo and count animal parents and babies. How high can you count?

Review What You Know

A-Z Vocabulary

1. Circle the number that is the **sum** in the equation.

$$17 = 9 + 8$$

2. Write the **parts** shown in the model.

8

_____ + _____

3. Circle the word that tells which part is missing.

$$7 + \underline{\ ?\ } = 17$$

sum

equals

addend

Find the Sum

4. Margie finds 7 rocks. Kara finds 6 rocks. How many rocks did they find in all?

_____ rocks

5. Tom has 6 toy cars. Jane has some toy cars. They have 11 toy cars in all. How many toy cars does Jane have?

_____ toy cars

The Missing Number

6. Find the missing number to solve this addition fact.

$$\underline{\quad\quad} = 10 + 5$$

© Pearson Education, Inc. 1

My Word Cards

Study the words on the front of the card. Complete the activity on the back.

hundred chart

1	2	3	4	5	6	7	8	9	10
11	12	13	14	15	16	17	18	19	20
21	22	23	24	25	26	27	28	29	30
31	32	33	34	35	36	37	38	39	40
41	42	43	44	45	46	47	48	49	50
51	52	53	54	55	56	57	58	59	60
61	62	63	64	65	66	67	68	69	70
71	72	73	74	75	76	77	78	79	80
81	82	83	84	85	86	87	88	89	90
91	92	93	94	95	96	97	98	99	100

tens digit

The **tens digit** in 25 is 2.

tens digit

row

1	2	3	4	5
11	12	13	14	15
21	22	23	24	25
31	32	33	34	35

row ⟶

ones digit

The **ones digit** in 43 is 3.

ones digit

column

1	2	3	4	5
11	12	13	14	15
21	22	23	24	25
31	32	33	34	35

column

My Word Cards

Use what you know to complete the sentences.
Extend learning by writing your own sentence using each word.

A straight line of numbers or objects going from left to right is called a

______________________.

A number that tells how many tens is called a

____

______________________.

A ______________________

____

shows all of the numbers from 1 to 100.

A straight line of numbers or objects going from top to bottom is called a

______________________.

A number that tells how many ones is called a

____

______________________.

Solve & Share

Alex put counters in some ten-frames. How can you find out how many counters there are without counting each one?

Write the number.

I can ...
count by 10s to 120.

I can also look for patterns.

_____ counters in all.

How can you count to 50 by tens?

I can use ten-frames to count by 10s!

1 ten	2 tens	3 tens	4 tens	5 tens
10 ten	20 twenty	30 thirty	40 forty	50 fifty

You can also follow the pattern to count by 10s.

6 tens is 60 sixty   10 tens is 100 one hundred

7 tens is 70 seventy   11 tens is 110 one hundred ten

8 tens is 80 eighty   12 tens is 120 one hundred twenty

9 tens is 90 ninety

Do You Understand?

Show Me! When might it be better to count by 10s instead of by 1s?

☆ Guided Practice ☆

Count by 10s. Then write the numbers and the number word.

1.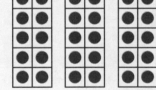

   4 tens is 40
   forty

2. _____ tens is _____

   _____

Independent Practice ⭐ Count by 10s. Write the numbers and the number word.

3.

_____ tens is _____

_____

4.

_____ tens is _____

_____

5.

_____ tens is _____

_____

Write the missing numbers.

6. **Number Sense** Jake wrote a pattern.

He forgot to write some numbers.

What numbers did Jake forget to write?

10, 20, 30, 40, _____, 60, _____, _____, 90, 100, _____, 120

Problem Solving

Draw counters in the ten-frames to solve each problem below. Then write the numbers and the number word.

7. **Model** José has 3 boxes. 10 books are in each box. How many books does José have in all?

_____ tens

_____

_____

8. **Model** Juan has 4 boxes. There are 10 books in each box. How many books does Juan have in all?

_____ tens

_____

9. **Higher Order Thinking** Dan counts by 5s to 50. Ed counts by 10s to 50. Write the numbers Dan says.

5, _____, _____, _____, _____,

_____, _____, _____, _____, 50

Write the numbers Ed says.

10, _____, _____, _____, 50

What numbers do both boys say?

_____, _____, _____, _____, _____

10. ✓ **Assessment** Mary has some books. She puts them in piles of 10 without any left over. Which number does **NOT** show how many books Mary could have?

Ⓐ 50

Ⓑ 60

Ⓒ 65

Ⓓ 70

© Pearson Education, Inc. 1

Help   Tools   Games

Another Look! You can use ten-frames to count groups of 10.

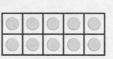

The ten-frame shows 1 group of 10.

You can count the ten-frames by 10s.

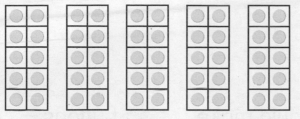

10   20   30   40   50

50 is 5 groups of 10.

50 is fifty.

HOME ACTIVITY Have your child practice counting by 10s to 120. Then ask questions such as, "How many 10s make 50? What number does 3 groups of 10 make?"

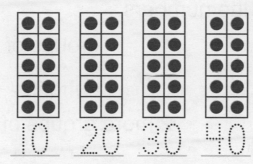

10   20   30   40

40 is __4__ groups of 10.

40 is forty .

Count by 10s. Write the numbers and the number word.

1.

____ ____ ____ ____ ____ ____ ____

____ is ____ groups of 10.   ____ is _____ .

Count by 10s. Write each missing number.

2. _____, 20, _____, _____, 50, _____ | 3. 70, _____, 90, _____, _____, _____

4. 50, _____, _____, _____, 90, _____ | 5. _____, _____, 50, _____, _____, 80

6. **Higher Order Thinking** Circle groups of 10.
   Then count by 10s and write the numbers.

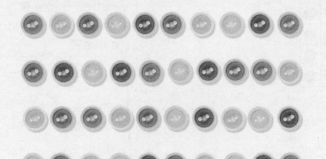

_____ groups of 10

_____ buttons

2 more groups of 10 would make _____ buttons.

7. ✓**Assessment** Jen buys 2 bags of
marbles. Each bag has 10 marbles.
How many marbles does Jen buy?

2   12   20   22
Ⓐ   Ⓑ   Ⓒ   Ⓓ

8. ✓**Assessment** Mike has 4 boxes of
crayons. Each box has 10 crayons.
How many crayons does Mike have?

4   10   14   40
Ⓐ   Ⓑ   Ⓒ   Ⓓ

© Pearson Education, Inc. 1

Solve

Solve & Share

Jada and Alex take turns counting by 1s. Jada counts on from 98 to 100. Now, it is Alex's turn to keep counting. Write the next three numbers Alex should count. Tell how you know you are right.

I can ...
count by 1s to 120.

I can also look for patterns.

98, 99, 100

_____ , _____ , _____

This block shows 100. You say one hundred for this number.

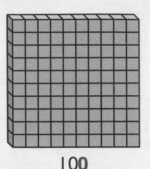

100

The next number you say is one hundred one because you have 1 hundred and 1 one.

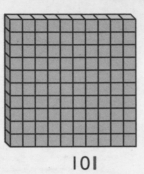

101

When you count forward, you keep counting by 1s.

101, 102, 103, 104, 105

105 means 1 hundred and 5 ones. You say one hundred five.

When you count higher, you start with the words one hundred.

116, 117, 118, 119, 120

116 is one hundred sixteen.

Do You Understand?

Show Me! How would you say and show 110 when you count? What number comes next?

☆ Guided Practice ☆

Count forward by 1s. Write the numbers.

1. 116, 117, 118, 119, 120

_____

2. _____, 110, _____, _____, 113

_____

3. 104, _____, _____, 107, _____

Independent Practice   Count forward by 1s. Write the numbers.

4. 110, _____, _____, _____, 114

5. 52, _____, _____, 55, _____

6. _____, 94, _____, 96, _____

7. _____, 102, 103, _____, _____

8. _____, _____, 115, _____, 117

9. 67, _____, _____, _____, 71

 Use the clues to find each mystery number.

10. **Number Sense** Clue 1: The number comes after 116. Clue 2: The number comes before 120.
The mystery number might be:

_____, _____, _____

Clue 3: The number has 8 ones.
Circle the mystery number.

11. **Number Sense** Clue 1: The number comes before 108. Clue 2: The number comes after 102.
The mystery number might be:

_____, _____, _____, _____, _____

Clue 3: The number has 5 ones.
Circle the mystery number.

12.  🅰🅩 **Vocabulary** Marta is counting to 120. She says the number that is one **more** than 113. What number does she say?

13. In this chart, Tom writes the numbers 102 to 108 in order. Then he spills water on it. Some numbers rub off. Help Tom fill in the missing numbers.

102		104	105			108

14. Reasoning Shelly counts 109 bottle caps. Then she counts 4 more. How many bottle caps has Shelley counted?

_____ bottle caps

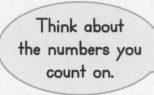 Think about the numbers you count on.

15. Higher Order Thinking Pick a number greater than 99 and less than 112. Write the number in the box.

Then write the three numbers that come before it and the number that comes after it.

_____ , _____ , _____ , ☐ , _____

16. ✅ **Assessment** Which shows the correct order for counting forward by 1s? Choose all that apply.

☐ 103, 104, 105, 102

☐ 117, 118, 119, 120

☐ 101, 102, 103, 104

☐ 114, 112, 110, 108

Name _____

Another Look! You can use place-value blocks to count forward by 1s.

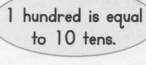
1 hundred is equal to 10 tens.

 **=**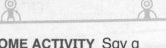

HOME ACTIVITY Say a number between 100 and 105. Have your child count forward by 1s to 120. Repeat with other numbers.

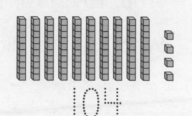   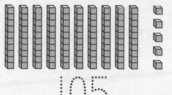   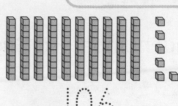

103   104   105   106

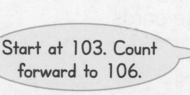
Start at 103. Count forward to 106.

Count forward by 1s. Write the numbers.

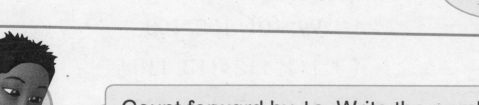

1.       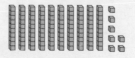

105   _____   _____

2.    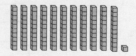

_____   110   _____

Write the numbers to solve each problem.

3. Start at 118. Count forward. What are the next 2 numbers you will say?

_____ and _____

4. Start at 111. Count forward. What are the next 2 numbers you will say?

_____ and _____

5. **Look for Patterns** Sage starts counting at 99. She says, "101, 102, 103, 104..."

What number did Sage forget to say?

_____

6. **Look for Patterns** Cairo starts counting at 107. He says, "108, 109, 110, 112..."

What number did Cairo forget to say?

_____

7. **Higher Order Thinking** Write the missing numbers in the cards.

Try counting backward to find the number before 103.

| | | 103 | | 105 |
| 108 | | 110 |

8. ✓**Assessment** Which shows the correct order for counting forward by 1s? Choose all that apply.

☐ 99, 101, 102, 103

☐ 111, 112, 113, 114

☐ 116, 117, 119, 120

☐ 108, 109, 110, 111

© Pearson Education, Inc. 1

Name _____

Solve & Share

Pick a number. Write the number in the box. How can you find the number that is 1 more? Write that number. Then write the next 3 numbers.

1	2	3	4	5	6	7	8	9	10
11	12	13	14	15	16	17	18	19	20
21	22	23	24	25	26	27	28	29	30
31	32	33	34	35	36	37	38	39	40
41	42	43	44	45	46	47	48	49	50
51	52	53	54	55	56	57	58	59	60
61	62	63	64	65	66	67	68	69	70
71	72	73	74	75	76	77	78	79	80
81	82	83	84	85	86	87	88	89	90
91	92	93	94	95	96	97	98	99	100

☐ _____, _____, _____, _____

You can find patterns when you count forward on a **hundred chart**.

1	2	3	4	5	6	7	8	9	10
11	12	13	14	15	16	17	18	19	20
21	22	23	24	25	26	27	28	29	30
31	32	33	34	35	36	37	38	39	40
41	42	43	44	45	46	47	48	49	50
51	52	53	54	55	56	57	58	59	60
61	62	63	64	65	66	67	68	69	70
71	72	73	74	75	76	77	78	79	80
81	82	83	84	85	86	87	88	89	90
91	92	93	94	95	96	97	98	99	100

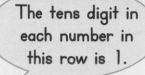
The tens digit in each number in this row is 1.

1	2	3	4
11	12	13	14
21	22	23	24
31	32	33	34

The ones digit in each number in this column is 4.

1	2	3	4
11	12	13	14
21	22	23	24
31	32	33	34

A number chart can extend past 100 to greater numbers.

81	82	83	84	85	86	87	88	89	90
91	92	93	94	95	96	97	98	99	100
101	102	103	104	105	106	107	108	109	110
111	112	113	114	115	116	117	118	119	120

The numbers past 100 follow the same pattern.

Do You Understand?

Show Me! How do the numbers in a number chart change?

Guided Practice Count by 1s. Write the numbers. Use a number chart to help you.

1. 14, 15 , 16 , 17 , 18

2. 21, _____, _____, _____, _____

3. 103, _____, _____, _____, _____

4. _____, _____, 49, _____, _____

© Pearson Education, Inc. 1

Topic 7 | Lesson 3

Name _____

Independent Practice   Count by 1s. Write the numbers. Use a number chart to help you.

5. _____, 65, _____, _____, _____

6. _____, 52, _____, _____, _____

7. _____, _____, 83, _____, _____

8. 110, _____, _____, _____, _____

9. _____, _____, _____, _____, 79

10. _____, _____, _____, _____, 98

11. _____, _____, _____, _____, 91

12. _____, _____, _____, 102, _____

Higher Order Thinking Look at each partial number chart.
Write the missing numbers.

13.

34		36	
	45		47

14.

	98		
107			110

1	2	3	4	5	6	7	8	9	10
11	12	13	14	15	16	17	18	19	20
21	22	23	24	25	26	27	28	29	30
31	32	33	34	35	36	37	38	39	40
41	42	43	44	45	46	47	48	49	50
51	52	53	54	55	56	57	58	59	60
61	62	63	64	65	66	67	68	69	70
71	72	73	74	75	76	77	78	79	80
81	82	83	84	85	86	87	88	89	90
91	92	93	94	95	96	97	98	99	100
101	102	103	104	105	106	107	108	109	110
111	112	113	114	115	116	117	118	119	120

15. **Use Tools** Billy counts forward to 50. What are the next 5 numbers he counts? Write the numbers.

50, _____, _____, _____, _____, _____

16. **Use Tools** Sasha counts forward to 115. What are the next 5 numbers she counts? Write the numbers.

115, _____, _____, _____, _____, _____

17. **Higher Order Thinking** Pick a number from the number chart. Count forward. Write the numbers.

_____, _____, _____, _____, _____,

_____, _____, _____, _____, _____,

18. ✓**Assessment** Draw an arrow to match the missing number to the number chart.

| 75 | | 100 | | 101 | | 114 |

| 112 | 113 | | 115 | 116 | 117 | 118 |

Name _____

Another Look! You can use a number chart to count forward.

1	2	3	4	5	6	7	8	9	10
11	12	13	14	15	16	17	18	19	20
21	22	23	24	25	26	27	28	29	30
31	32	33	34	35	36	37	38	39	40
41	42	43	44	45	46	47	48	49	50
51	52	53	54	55	56	57	58	59	60
61	62	63	64	65	66	67	68	69	70
71	72	73	74	75	76	77	78	79	80
81	82	83	84	85	86	87	88	89	90
91	92	93	94	95	96	97	98	99	100
101	102	103	104	105	106	107	108	109	110
111	112	113	114	115	116	117	118	119	120

What number comes after 33? __34__

What number comes after 34? __35__

What number comes after 35? __36__

33, __34__, __35__, __36__

HOME ACTIVITY Write the following series of numbers: 15, 16, ____, 18, ____, 20. Have your child write the missing numbers. If necessary, create a portion of a hundred chart on a sheet of paper for your child to use while filling in the missing numbers. Repeat with other numbers.

Count by 1s. Write the numbers. Use a number chart to help you.

1. 71, _____, _____, _____, _____

2. _____, _____, _____, 101, _____

3. _____, _____, _____, _____, 111

4. _____, _____, 65, _____, _____

Count by 1s. Write the numbers. Use a number chart to help you.

5. 40, _____, _____, _____, _____

6. _____, _____, _____, 32, _____

Higher Order Thinking Write the missing numbers. Look for patterns.

7.

			85			88		90
92		94		96			99	

8.

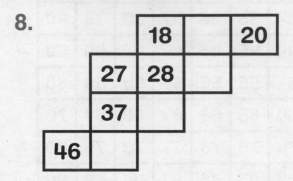

9. ✅**Assessment** Draw an arrow to match the missing number to the number chart.

92	70	55	31

54		56	57	58	59	60

10. ✅**Assessment** Draw an arrow to match the missing number to the number chart.

46	33	84	17

81	82	83		85	86	87

© Pearson Education, Inc. 1

Topic 7 | Lesson 3

Name _____

Solve & Share

Count by 10s, starting at 10. Color the numbers you count yellow. What pattern do you see? Count by 1s, starting at 102. Draw a red square around the numbers. Count by 10s, starting at 34. Draw a blue circle around the numbers. Describe the patterns for each.

1	2	3	4	5	6	7	8	9	10
11	12	13	14	15	16	17	18	19	20
21	22	23	24	25	26	27	28	29	30
31	32	33	34	35	36	37	38	39	40
41	42	43	44	45	46	47	48	49	50
51	52	53	54	55	56	57	58	59	60
61	62	63	64	65	66	67	68	69	70
71	72	73	74	75	76	77	78	79	80
81	82	83	84	85	86	87	88	89	90
91	92	93	94	95	96	97	98	99	100
101	102	103	104	105	106	107	108	109	110
111	112	113	114	115	116	117	118	119	120

You can count on a number chart to find a pattern.

1	2	3	4	5	6	7	8	9	10
11	12	13	14	15	16	17	18	19	20
21	22	23	24	25	26	27	28	29	30
31	32	33	34	35	36	37	38	39	40
41	42	43	44	45	46	47	48	49	50
51	52	53	54	55	56	57	58	59	60
61	62	63	64	65	66	67	68	69	70
71	72	73	74	75	76	77	78	79	80
81	82	83	84	85	86	87	88	89	90
91	92	93	94	95	96	97	98	99	100
101	102	103	104	105	106	107	108	109	110
111	112	113	114	115	116	117	118	119	120

Count by 10s.

10, 20, 30, 40

1	2	3	4	5	6	7	8	9	10
11	12	13	14	15	16	17	18	19	20
21	22	23	24	25	26	27	28	29	30
31	32	33	34	35	36	37	38	39	40

Count by 1s from 58 to 61.

58, 59, 60, 61

41	42	43	44	45	46	47	48	49	50
51	52	53	54	55	56	57	58	59	60
61	62	63	64	65	66	67	68	69	70
71	72	73	74	75	76	77	78	79	80

Count by 10s, starting at 84.

84, 94, 104, 114

81	82	83	84	85	86	87	88	89	90
91	92	93	94	95	96	97	98	99	100
101	102	103	104	105	106	107	108	109	110
111	112	113	114	115	116	117	118	119	120

Do You Understand?

Show Me! Compare counting by 1s and by 10s. How are the patterns alike? How are the patterns different?

☆Guided Practice☆

Write the numbers to continue each pattern. Use a number chart to help you.

1. Count by 1s.

12, 13, 14, __15__ , __16__ , __17__ , __18__ , __19__ , __20__

2. Count by 10s.

22, 32, 42, ____ , ____ , ____ , ____ , ____ , ____

3. Count by 1s.

90, 91, 92, ____ , ____ , ____ , ____ , ____ , ____

© Pearson Education, Inc. 1

Independent Practice

Write the numbers to continue each pattern.
Use a number chart to help you.

4. Count by 10s.

10, 20, 30, _____, _____, _____, _____, _____, _____, _____, _____, _____

5. Count by 10s.

35, 45, 55, _____, _____, _____, _____, _____, _____

6. Count by 1s.

102, 103, 104, _____, _____, _____, _____, _____, _____, _____, _____, _____

Number Sense Write the missing numbers on the number chart below.
Then write the next three numbers in the pattern you started.

7.

62	63	64	65	66	67	68	69	70
72	73	74	75	76	77	78	79	80
82	83	84	85	86	87	88	89	90

_____, _____, _____

8. **Look for Patterns** Anita walks her neighbor's dog to earn money. She starts on Day 13 and walks the dog once a day through Day 19. How many times does Anita walk the dog?

Use the chart to count.
Write the number.

1	2	3	4	5	6	7	8	9	10
11	12	13	14	15	16	17	18	19	20

_____ times

9. **Look for Patterns** Matt starts swimming lessons on Day 5. He goes every 10 days. How many lessons will Matt go to in 30 days?

Use the chart to count.
Write the number.

1	2	3	4	5	6	7	8	9	10
11	12	13	14	15	16	17	18	19	20
21	22	23	24	25	26	27	28	29	30

_____ lessons

10. **Higher Order Thinking** Anna counts to 30. She only counts 3 numbers. Did Anna count by 1s or 10s? Use pictures, numbers, or words to explain.

11. ✓ **Assessment** Tim counts by 10s, starting at 54.

54, 74, 84, 94, 114

What numbers did Tim forget to count?

_____

Name _____

Another Look! You can count on a number chart. When you count by 10s, the number in the tens digit goes up by one, but the number in the ones digit stays the same.

21	22	23	24	25	26	27	28	29	30
31	32	33	34	35	36	37	38	39	40
41	42	43	44	45	46	47	48	49	50
51	52	53	54	55	56	57	58	59	60
61	62	63	64	65	66	67	68	69	70
71	72	73	74	75	76	77	78	79	80
81	82	83	84	85	86	87	88	89	90
91	92	93	94	95	96	97	98	99	100
101	102	103	104	105	106	107	108	109	110
111	112	113	114	115	116	117	118	119	120

What numbers will you say when you count by 10s, starting at 60?

60, 70, 80, __90__, __100__, __110__, __120__

What numbers will you say when you count by 10s, starting at 25?

25, 35, 45, __55__, __65__, __75__, __85__

HOME ACTIVITY Practice orally counting by 1s and 10s with your child. If necessary, have him or her use a number chart. Ask: "What patterns do you see when you count by 10s?"

Write the numbers to continue each pattern. Use a number chart to help you.

1. Count by 10s.

38, 48, _____, _____, _____, _____

2. Count by 1s.

66, 67, _____, _____, _____, _____

Write the numbers to continue each pattern. Use a number chart to help you.

3. Count by 10s.

17, 27, _____, _____, _____, _____

4. Count by 1s.

108, 109, _____, _____, _____, _____

5. Higher Order Thinking Vicky has baseball practice every 10 days. She starts on May 5. Will she have practice on May 19? Write **Yes** or **No**. _____

How do you know?

_____

_____

Write 2 more dates that Vicky will have practice.

_____

_____

Use this calendar to help you!

May

Sunday	Monday	Tuesday	Wednesday	Thursday	Friday	Saturday
	1	2	3	4	5	6
7	8	9	10	11	12	13
14	15	16	17	18	19	20
21	22	23	24	25	26	27
28	29	30	31			

6. ✓Assessment What are the missing numbers?

65, _?_ , _?_ , 95, _?_

7. ✓Assessment Jamie counts by 1s.
He counts: 54, 56, 57, 59.
Which numbers did Jamie forget to count?

_____

© Pearson Education, Inc. 1

Topic 7 | Lesson 4

Solve & Share

Use the open number line to show how to count from 78 to 84.

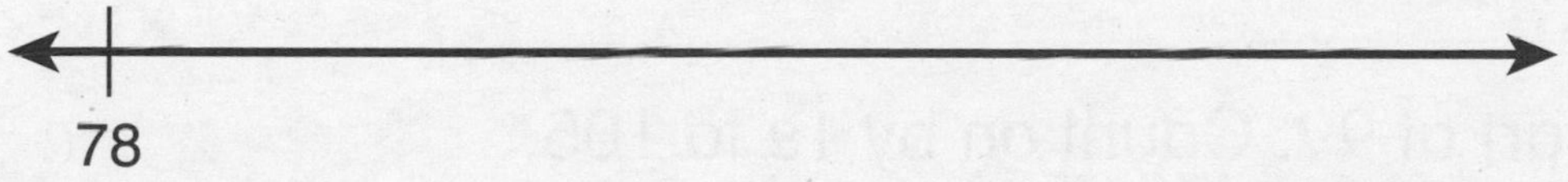

Lesson 7-5

Count on an Open Number Line

I can ...
count to 120 using an open number line.

I can also model with math.

78

You can use an open number line to count on by 1s.

Count on by 1s from 97 to 103.

97

+1 +1 +1 +1 +1 +1
97 98 99 100 101 102 103

I count the jumps by 1s until I get to 103!

You can use an open number line to count on by 10s.

Count on by 10s from 56 to 116.

56

+10 +10 +10 +10 +10 +10
56 66 76 86 96 106 116

I count the jumps by 10s until I get to 116!

Do You Understand?

Show Me! Use an open number line. What number comes after 109 when you count on by 1s?
What number comes after 109 when you count on by 10s?

☆Guided Practice☆ Show your counting on the open number line.

1. Start at 99. Count on by 1s to 105.

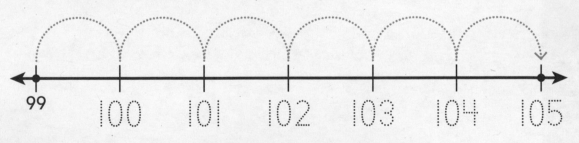
99   100   101   102   103   104   105

2. Start at 72. Count on by 10s to 112.

72

Name _____

Independent Practice ☆ Show your counting on the open number line.

3. Start at 89. Count on
by 10s to 119.

←――――――――――――――――――――→

4. Start at 111. Count
on by 1s to 118.

←――――――――――――――――――――→

5. **Number Sense** Teresa and Doug both draw a number line starting at 27. Teresa counts on by 1s five times. Doug counts on by 10s five times.

Will they stop counting at the same number? Use the number lines. Explain.

←―――|―――――――――→   ←―――|―――――――――→
   27   27

       Teresa   Doug

_____

_____

Fill in the number lines to help you find the answer.

6. **Model** Dennis counts 41 marbles. Then he counts 8 more marbles. How many marbles did he count in all?

41

_____ marbles

7. **Algebra** Serena used the number line to count on from 12 to 15. Complete the addition equation to show what she did.

$12 +$ _____ $=$ _____

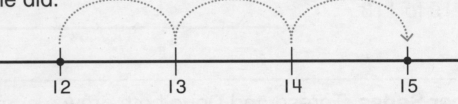

12   13   14   15

8. **Higher Order Thinking** On Monday, Kate puts 12 pennies in her piggy bank. On Tuesday, she puts some more pennies in her bank. She puts 19 pennies in all in her bank. How many pennies did she put in her bank on Tuesday?

12

_____ pennies

9. ✓**Assessment** Tim showed his counting on this number line. Complete the sentence to show how he counted.

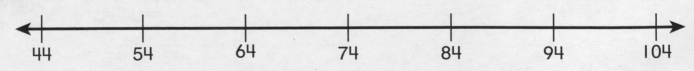

44   54   64   74   84   94   104

Tim counted by _____ from _____ to _____ .

Name _____

Another Look! Counting on is like adding.

Start at 87. Count on by 1s to 92.

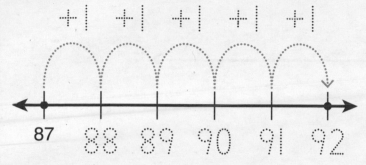

87 88 89 90 91 92

Start at 62. Count on by 10s to 112.

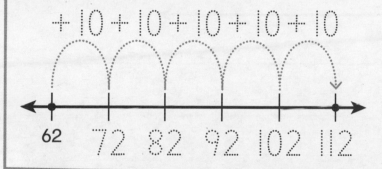

62 72 82 92 102 112

You add 1 each time you count!

You add 10 each time you count!

HOME ACTIVITY Draw two simple number lines with no labels. Ask your child to use the first number line to count by 1s from 53 to 58. Ask your child to use the second number line to count by 10s from 67 to 107.

Show your counting on the open number line. You can use addition to help.

1. Start at 115. Count on by 1s to 120.

115

2. **Math and Science** There are 16 baby chicks sleeping in a hen house. Outside the hen house, there are 6 more baby chicks chirping for their mothers. How many baby chicks in all?

3. Start at 18. Count on by 10s to 78.

4. **Higher Order Thinking** Lorna starts counting at 48.
   She counts on by 10s four times.
   Then she counts on by 1s three times.
   What was the last number she said?
   Tell how you know.

_____

_____

_____

5. ✅**Assessment** Ben showed part of his counting on this number line. Fill in the missing numbers. Complete the sentence.

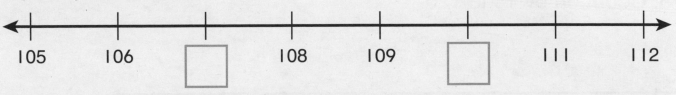

105   106   ☐   108   109   ☐   111   112

Ben counted by _____ from _____ to _____.

© Pearson Education, Inc. 1

Solve & Share

Look at the oranges below. Count to find out how many in all and then write the number. Explain how you counted the oranges.

Lesson 7-6
Count and Write Numerals

I can ...
write a numeral to show how many objects are in the group.

I can also make sense of problems.

There are _____ oranges.

How many stickers are shown?

What is the best way to count this many stickers?

You can count by 1s.

1	2	3	4	5	6	7	8	9	10
11	12	13	14	15	16	17	18	19	20
21	22	23	24	25	26	27	28	29	30
31	32	33	34	35	36	37	38	39	40
41									

There are 41 stickers!

You can also count by 10s.

10
20
30
40
41

I can count 10, 20, 30, 40. Then I add the 1 left to get 41 stickers.

Do You Understand?

Show Me! Start counting at 19 and count on 6 more. Then write the numeral that you ended on.

☆ **Guided** ☆
Practice

Count the objects any way you choose. Then write how many in all.

1.

46 balls

2.

_____ rabbits

© Pearson Education, Inc. 1

Tools Assessment

Independent Practice ☆ Count the objects. Then write how many in all.

3.

_____ socks

4.

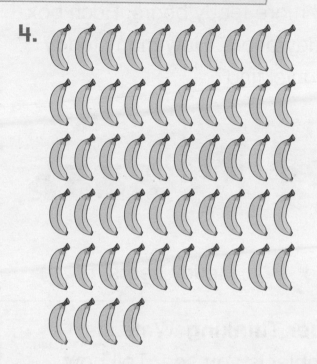

_____ bananas

Count the tens and ones. Then write how many in all.

5.

_____ tens _____ ones

_____ in all

6.

_____ tens _____ ones

_____ in all

7.

_____ tens _____ ones _____

_____ in all

8. **Reasoning** Daniel finds 3 boxes of teddy bears and 4 more teddy bears. Each box holds 10 teddy bears. How many teddy bears did Daniel find?

Daniel found _____ teddy bears.

9. **Reasoning** Kim throws a party. She has 8 boxes and 6 more party hats. There are 10 party hats in each box. How many party hats does Kim have?

Kim has _____ party hats.

10. **Higher Order Thinking** Write the number of objects you see. Tell how you counted them.

11. ✅ **Assessment** How many strawberries are in this set?

Ⓐ 18

Ⓑ 24

Ⓒ 26

Ⓓ 62

Name _____

Another Look! You can count groups of objects by 1s or 10s.

When you count by 1s, you count each object separately.

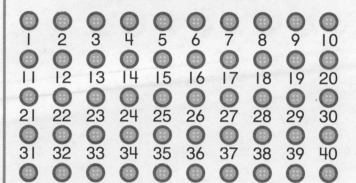

1 2 3 4 5 6 7 8 9 10
11 12 13 14 15 16 17 18 19 20
21 22 23 24 25 26 27 28 29 30
31 32 33 34 35 36 37 38 39 40
41 42 43 44 45 46 47 48 49 50
51 52 53

There are ___53___ buttons.

When you count by 10s, you count groups of 10, and then add the 1s.

10
20
30
40
50
51 52 53

There are ___53___ buttons.

HOME ACTIVITY Set up a pile of between 50 and 120 small objects. Ask your child to count them in the fastest way he or she can think of. Remind your child that sorting the objects into groups or counting more than one at a time will make it easier. Repeat with a different amount in between 50 and 120.

Count the tens and ones. Then write how many in all.

1. _____ tens _____ ones

Total _____

2. _____ tens _____ ones

Total _____

3. _____ tens _____ ones

Total _____

Count the objects. Show how you counted. Then write how many in all.

4.

_____

5.

_____

6. **Higher Order Thinking** Explain why counting by tens might be faster than counting by ones.

_____

_____

_____

7. ✓**Assessment** How many tens and ones are shown?

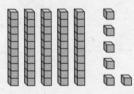

Ⓐ 4 tens and 5 ones

Ⓑ 4 tens and 6 ones

Ⓒ 5 tens and 5 ones

Ⓓ 5 tens and 6 ones

Solve

Solve & Share

How can you find the number of apples on the ground without counting them one at a time? Explain your shortcut.

I counted by _____.   _____ apples

I can ...
find better, faster ways to solve problems.

I can also count by tens and ones.

Thinking Habits

Is there a shortcut that makes sense?

What can I use from this problem to help with another problem?

Matt spills some puzzle pieces on the floor. 61 pieces are still in the box. How can Matt find the number of puzzle pieces in all?

61

How can you use what you know to solve the problem?

I can look for shortcuts and things that repeat.

Circle a group of 10 and count on. Repeat until there are no more groups of 10. Then count on by 1s.

61, 71, 81, 82, 83, 84, 85. There are 85 puzzle pieces in all.

61

71

81

82 83

84 85

Do You Understand?

Show Me! Why is counting by 10s and 1s better than counting 1 at a time?

☆ **Guided Practice** ☆   How many in all? Use a shortcut to count on. Tell what shortcut you used.

1.

30 shoes

58 shoes

I counted on by

10s and 1s .

2.

60 muffins

_____ muffins

I counted on by

_____ .

© Pearson Education, Inc. 1

Tools   Assessment

Independent Practice

How many in all? Use a shortcut to count on.
Tell what shortcut you used.

3.

25 watches

_____ watches

I counted on by _____.

4.

32 train cars

_____ train cars

I counted on by _____.

5.

45 books

_____ books

I counted on by _____.

6.

30 desks

_____ desks

I counted on by _____.

Problem Solving

Students and Snowmen

62 students stay inside at recess. The rest each build a snowman outside. How can you count to find the number of students in all?

62 students

7. **Make Sense** What do you know about the students? What do you need to find?

_____

_____

_____

8. **Reasoning** What does the number of snowmen tell me?

_____

_____

9. **Generalize** How many students in all? What shortcut can you use to find the answer?

_____

_____

_____

_____

_____

_____

_____

Another Look! Grouping objects makes it easier to count on.

Amy has some cars in a box and some on the floor.

How can she count to find how many in all?

I can count on from 100.

100 cars

_101_ , _102_, _103_, _104_

I will count by 1s with so few cars. Amy has 104 cars.

HOME ACTIVITY Talk to your child about counting on by 10s and 1s. How can it make things easier? Practice grouping and counting a number of objects, starting from zero and starting from other numbers between 1 and 100.

Generalize and count on by a number to help you find how many in all.

1.

82 dinosaurs

_____ dinosaurs

I counted on by _____.

2.

50 teddy bears

_____ teddy bears

I counted on by _____.

Baby Chicks

Kevin counts 75 chicks in the hen house. He also sees more chicks outside the hen house. How can Kevin count to find how many chicks in all?

75 chicks

3. **Make Sense** What do you know about the chicks? What do you need to find?

_____

_____

_____

4. **Reasoning** How do the pictures of the chicks help me?

_____

_____

5. **Generalize** How many chicks in all? What shortcut can you use to find the answer?

_____

_____

_____

_____

_____

_____

Name _____

Show the Word

Color these sums and differences. Leave the rest white.

I can ...
add and subtract within 10.

| 8 | 5 | 6 |

4 + 2	5 − 3	0 + 6	6 + 2	8 + 0	7 + 1	8 − 3	7 − 2	1 + 4
9 − 3	10 − 3	8 − 2	10 − 2	2 − 2	2 + 6	2 + 3	2 + 2	6 − 1
10 − 4	6 + 0	3 + 3	1 + 7	10 − 7	3 + 5	0 + 5	5 − 0	3 + 2
5 + 1	1 + 1	2 + 4	5 + 3	9 − 5	9 − 1	4 + 1	1 + 2	9 − 7
7 − 1	1 − 1	6 − 0	8 − 0	4 + 4	0 + 8	10 − 5	9 − 0	5 − 2

The word is

_____ _____ _____

Vocabulary Review

Glossary

Word List
- column
- hundred chart
- number chart
- ones digit
- row
- tens digit

Understand Vocabulary

1. Circle the number that shows the ones digit.

106

2. Circle the number that shows the tens digit.

106

---

3. Circle a column in the part of the hundred chart.

87	88	89	90
97	98	99	100

4. Circle a row in the part of the number chart.

107	108	109	110
117	118	119	120

5. Circle the number on the chart that is 1 more than 101.

97	98	99	100
101	102	103	104

Use Vocabulary in Writing

6. Fill in the number chart to count on from 96 to 105. Then explain the difference between a number chart and a hundred chart and label the chart using words from the Word List.

91	92	93	94	95					
					106	107	108	109	110

_____

_____

_____

Name _____

Set A

You can count by 10s when you have a lot of objects to count.

There are ___6___ tens.

6 tens = ___60___

The word name for 60 is _sixty_.

Count by 10s. Write the number 3 different ways.

1.

_____ tens

number: _____

word name: _____

Set B

You can use a number chart to count on by 1s or 10s.

81	82	83	84	85	86	87	88	89	90
91	92	93	94	95	96	97	98	99	100
101	102	103	104	105	106	107	108	109	110
111	112	113	114	115	116	117	118	119	120

Count on by 1s.

99, 100, _101_, _102_, _103_

Use a number chart to count on.

2. Count by 10s.

80, _____, _____, _____, _____

3. Count by 1s.

114, _____, _____, _____, _____

You can use an open number line to count on by 1s or 10s.

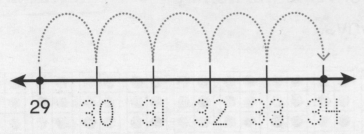

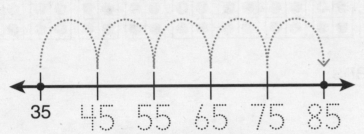

Count on using the open number line.

4. Start at 62. Count on by 10s to 102.

5. Start at 97. Count on by 1s to 101.

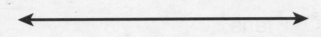

Thinking Habits

Repeated Reasoning

Does something repeat in the problem? How does that help?

Is there a shortcut that makes sense?

Count on by a number to find how many in all.

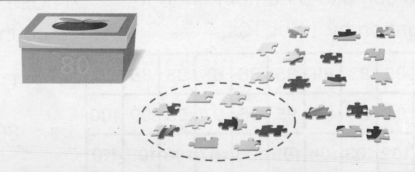

6. Sean spills some puzzle pieces. Eighty are still in the box. How many puzzle pieces are there in all?

_____ pieces

© Pearson Education, Inc. 1

Name _____

1. Count by 10s. What number is shown?
Write the number 3 different ways.

_____ tens

number: _____

word name: _____

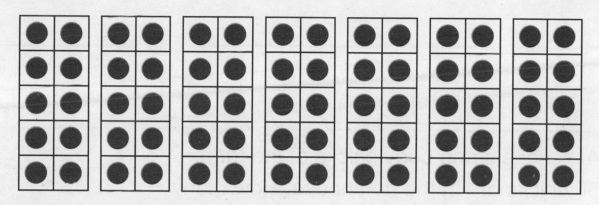

Use the partial number chart below to solve each problem.

91	92	93	94	95	96	97	98	99	100
101	102	103	104	105	106	107	108	109	110
111	112	113	114	115	116	117	118	119	120

2. Cathy counts pennies by 1s.
She counts to 98. Which number will
Cathy say next?

89	90	99	108
Ⓐ	Ⓑ	Ⓒ	Ⓓ

3. Sam counts by 10s. Which number did
he forget to count?

80, 90, 100, 120

89	105	110	115
Ⓐ	Ⓑ	Ⓒ	Ⓓ

4. Start at 58. Count on by 10s to 98.

5. Start at 114. Count on by 1s to 118.

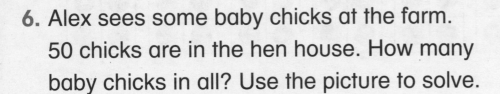

6. Alex sees some baby chicks at the farm. 50 chicks are in the hen house. How many baby chicks in all? Use the picture to solve.

Ⓐ 68

Ⓑ 72

Ⓒ 78

Ⓓ 80

7. The farm worker says there were 82 chicks this morning. How many chicks are hiding? Use the picture to solve. Then explain how you know.

Name _____

Mal's Marbles

Mal collects marbles and keeps them in jars.

1. How many blue marbles does Mal have?
Circle groups of 10. Then count by 10s.
Write the numbers and the number word.

●●●●●●●●●●●●
●●●●●●●●●●●●
●●●●●●●●●●●●
●●●●●●●●●●●●
●●●●●●●●●●●●

_____ groups of 10 marbles

_____ marbles

_____ marbles

2. Mal has some striped marbles. Use these clues to find out how many she has.

Clue 1: The number comes after 110.

Clue 2: The number comes before 120.

Clue 3: The number does **NOT** have 4 ones.

Clue 4: The number in the ones place is the same as the number in the tens place.

Mal has _____ striped marbles.

3. Mal has 105 small marbles in a jar. She puts 13 more small marbles in the jar. How many small marbles are in the jar now?

Solve using the number line or part of the number chart. Then explain how you solved.

81	82	83	84	85	86	87	88	89	90
91	92	93	94	95	96	97	98	99	100
101	102	103	104	105	106	107	108	109	110
111	112	113	114	115	116	117	118	119	120

_____

_____

_____

There are _____ small marbles in the jar.

4. Mal has 48 large marbles in a jar. There are more large marbles on the floor. How can you count to find how many large marbles Mal has in all?

 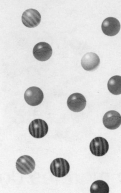

48 marbles

What do you know about the large marbles?

_____

_____

What shortcut did you use to count the marbles? Tell how you counted.

_____

_____

_____

Mal has _____ large marbles in all.

© Pearson Education, Inc. 1

Glossary

1 less

4 is 1 less than 5.

1 more

5 is 1 more than 4.

10 less

20 is 10 less than 30.

10 more

10 more than a number has 1 more ten or 10 more ones.

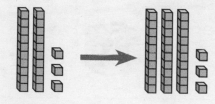

add

When you add, you find out how many there are in all.

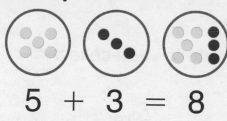

$$5 + 3 = 8$$

addend

the numbers you add together to find the whole

$$2 + 3 = 5$$

addition equation

$$3 + 4 = 7$$

addition fact

$$9 + 8 = 17$$

C

column

1	2	3	4	5
11	12	13	14	15
21	22	23	24	25
31	32	33	34	35

column

compare

to find out how things are alike or different

cone

corner

count on

You can count on by 1s or 10s.

15, 16, 17, 18

20, 30, 40, 50

cube

cylinder

D

data

information you collect

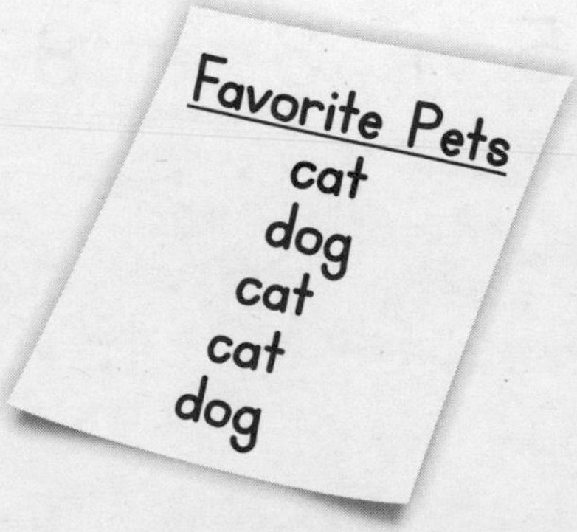
Favorite Pets
cat
dog
cat
cat
dog

difference

the amount that is left after you subtract

$$4 - 1 = 3$$

The difference is 3.

digits

Numbers have 1 or more digits.

43 has 2 digits.
The tens digit is 4.
The ones digit is 3.

43

doubles fact

an addition fact with the same addends

$$4 + 4 = 8$$

4 and 4 is a double.

doubles-plus-1 fact

The addends are 1 apart.

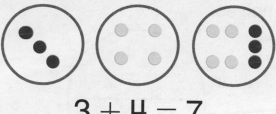

$$\underbrace{3 + 4}_{\text{addends}} = 7$$

doubles-plus-2 fact

The addends are 2 apart.

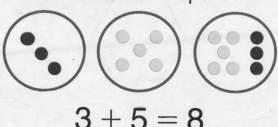

$$\underbrace{3 + 5}_{\text{addends}} = 8$$

E

edges

equal shares

4 equal parts

equal sign (=)

$$2 + 3 = 5$$

equal sign

equals

5 + 2 equals 7.

equation

$6 + 4 = 10$ $6 - 2 = 4$

$10 = 6 + 4$ $4 = 6 - 2$

F

faces

fact family

a group of related addition and subtraction facts

$3 + 5 = 8$
$5 + 3 = 8$
$8 - 3 = 5$
$8 - 5 = 3$

fewer

A group that has less than another group

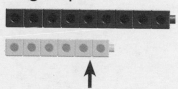

The yellow row has fewer.

flat surface

fourths

The square is divided into fourths.

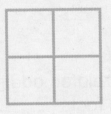

greater than (>)

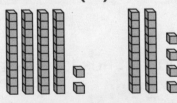

42 is greater than 24.

greatest

the number or group with the largest value

23 is the greatest number.

half hour

A half hour is 30 minutes.

1:30

halves

The circle is divided into halves.

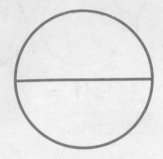

hexagon

hour

An hour is 60 minutes.

2:00

hour hand

The short hand on a clock is the hour hand.
The hour hand tells the hour.

It is 3:00.

hour hand

hundred chart

A hundred chart shows all of the numbers from 1 to 100.

1	2	3	4	5	6	7	8	9	10
11	12	13	14	15	16	17	18	19	20
21	22	23	24	25	26	27	28	29	30
31	32	33	34	35	36	37	38	39	40
41	42	43	44	45	46	47	48	49	50
51	52	53	54	55	56	57	58	59	60
61	62	63	64	65	66	67	68	69	70
71	72	73	74	75	76	77	78	79	80
81	82	83	84	85	86	87	88	89	90
91	92	93	94	95	96	97	98	99	100

 I

in all

There are 4 birds in all.

inside

The dogs are inside the dog house.

 J

join

to put together

3 and 3 is 6 in all.

 L

least

the number or group with the smallest value

7 is the least number.

length

the distance from one end of an object to the other end

less

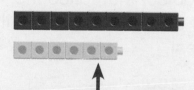

The yellow row has less.

less than (<)

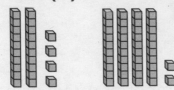

24 is less than 42.

longer

An object that is 7 cubes long is longer than an object that is 2 cubes long.

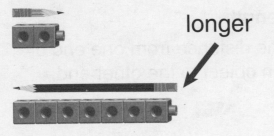

longer

longest

The object that takes the most units to measure is the longest.

longest

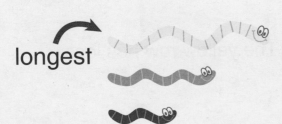

M

make 10

7 + 4 = ?

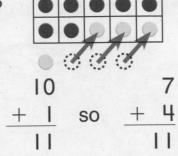

$$\begin{array}{r} 10 \\ + 1 \\ \hline 11 \end{array} \quad so \quad \begin{array}{r} 7 \\ + 4 \\ \hline 11 \end{array}$$

measure

You can measure the length of the shoe.

minus

$$5 \ - \ 3$$

5 minus 3

This means 3 is taken away from 5.

minus sign (−)

$$7 - 4 = 3$$

minute

60 minutes is 1 hour.

minute hand

The long hand on a clock is the minute hand.
The minute hand tells the minutes.

minute hand

It is 3:00.

missing part

the part that is not known

2 is the missing part.

more

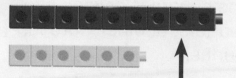

The red row has more.

near double

an addition fact that has an addend that is 1 or 2 more than the other addend

$$4 + 5 = 9$$

$4 + 4 = 8$. 8 and 1 more is 9.

number chart

A number chart can show numbers past 100.

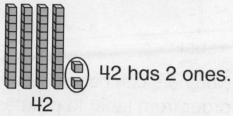

number line

A number line is a line that shows numbers in order from left to right.

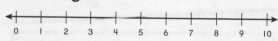

o'clock

8:00
8 o'clock

ones

The ones digit shows how many ones are in a number.

42 has 2 ones.

42

ones digit

The ones digit in 43 is 3.

43

ones digit

open number line

An open number line is a number line without marks in place.

order

60 61 62 63

↑ least   ↑ greatest

Numbers can be put in counting order from least to greatest or from greatest to least.

outside

5 dogs are playing outside of the dog house.

part

a piece of a whole

2 and 3 are parts of 5.

pattern

You can arrange 5 objects in any pattern, and there will still be 5 objects.

picture graph

a graph that uses pictures to show data

Favorite Pets			
🐱 Cat	🐱	🐱	🐱
🐶 Dog	🐶	🐶	

plus

5 + 4

5 plus 4

This means 4 is added to 5.

plus sign (+)

6 + 2 = 8

↑

Q

quarters

The square is divided into quarters, another word for fourths.

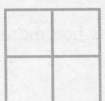

R

rectangle

rectangular prism

related facts

addition facts and subtraction facts that have the same numbers

$$2 + 3 = 5$$
$$5 - 2 = 3$$

These facts are related.

row

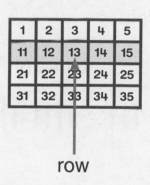

row

S

scale

A scale is used to measure how much things weigh.

shorter

An object that is 2 cubes long is shorter than one that is 7 cubes long.

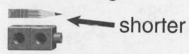 shorter

shortest

The shortest object is the one that takes the fewest units to measure.

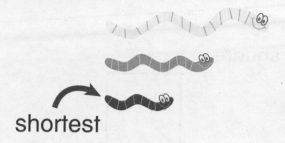

shortest

side

These shapes have straight sides.

sort

to group objects according to how they are similar

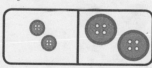

The buttons are sorted by size.

sphere

square

standard form

a number shown in digits

28

subtract

When you subtract, you find out how many are left.

$$5 - 3 = 2$$

subtraction equation

$$12 - 4 = 8$$

sum

$$2 + 3 = 5$$

↑
sum

survey

to gather information

Do you like cats or dogs better?

Cats |||
Dogs ||

take away

Start With	Take Away	Have Left
6	3	3

$$6 - 3 = 3$$

To take away is to remove or subtract.

tally chart

a chart that uses marks to show data

Walk	School Bus
卌 ||	卌 卌

© Pearson Education, Inc. 1

tally marks

marks that are used to record data

Cats	
Dogs	II

There are 5 cats and 2 dogs.

tens digit

The tens digit shows how many groups of 10 are in a number.

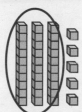 35 has 3 tens.

35

Three-dimensional (3-D) shapes

These are all 3-D shapes.

trapezoid

triangle

Two-dimensional (2-D) shapes

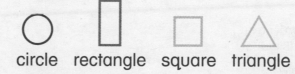

circle   rectangle   square   triangle

V

vertex (vertices)

a point where 3 or more edges meet

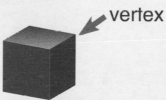 vertex

W

whole

You add parts to find the whole.

5

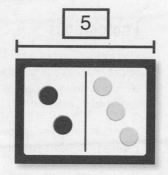

The whole is 5.

SCOTT FORESMAN · ADDISON WESLEY

Photographs

Every effort has been made to secure permission and provide appropriate credit for photographic material. The publisher deeply regrets any omission and pledges to correct errors called to its attention in subsequent editions.

Unless otherwise acknowledged, all photographs are the property of Pearson Education, Inc.

Photo locators denoted as follows: Top (T), Center (C), Bottom (B), Left (L), Right (R), Background (Bkgd)

001 MattiaATH/Shutterstock;**075** Karen Faljyan/ Shutterstock;**151L** fotografie4you/Shutterstock;**151R** Chris Sargent/Shutterstock;**227L** Galyna Andrushko/ Shutterstock;**227R** Alexey Stiop/Shutterstock;**297** Willyam Bradberry/Shutterstock;**349C** Umberto Shtanzman/ Shutterstock;**349L** Nick barounis/Fotolia;**349R** Gudellaphoto/ Fotolia;**391** John Foxx Collection/Imagestate;**445L** Chaoss/ Fotolia;**445R** Lipsett Photography Group/Shutterstock;**493** Anton Petrus/Shutterstock;**541L** Baldas1950/ Shutterstock;**541R** Shooarts/Shutterstock;**609** Barbara Helgason/Fotolia;**661** Studio 37/Shutterstock;**705** Vereshchagin Dmitry/Shuhtterstock;**741** Sergey Dzyuba/ Shutterstock;**813BL** Isuaneye/Fotolia;**813BR** Ftfoxfoto/ Fotolia;**813TL** Sumire8/Fotolia;**813TR** Janifest/Fotolia.